Experiences of the Sacred

Introductory Readings in Religion

FIRST EDITION

Experiences of the Sacred

Introductory Readings in Religion

EDITED BY Linh Hoang

cognella®

SAN DIEGO

Bassim Hamadeh, CEO and Publisher
John Remington, Executive Editor
Gem Rabanera, Senior Project Editor
Celeste Paed, Associate Production Editor
Emely Villavicencio, Senior Graphic Designer
Trey Soto, Licensing Associate
Natalie Piccotti, Director of Marketing
Kassie Graves, Vice President of Editorial
Jamie Giganti, Director of Academic Publishing

Cover image copyright © 2019 iStockphoto LP/valio84sl.

Printed in the United States of America.

3970 Sorrento Valley Blvd., Ste. 500, San Diego, CA 92121

CONTENTS

PREFACE

There are some experiences in life that cannot be fully expressed in words. Many of these experiences are explained through actions, rituals, and sounds. These experiences are usually ones that human beings have of the transcendent, the sacred, or deities. For human beings, sacred experiences are so overwhelming that the only possible utterances are stirred from the heart. As human beings, we need to communicate about these experiences. We do so because it gives us an understanding of who we are and also of how we perceive the world and the sacred.

Why are experiences of the sacred so difficult to fully articulate? The reason may be simply that the sacred is a mystery. Anything that is mysterious is hard to fully comprehend. The sacred is considered to be different from the human person. The sacred stands outside the realm of human beings. In religion, the sacred is also called "the holy," which means "the other." This distinction between the sacred and the human is usually described as the *sacred* and the *profane*. For example, the sacred is usually considered to be in a temple, church, or shrine, and that which is profane is outside of those places. Therefore, some people would say that the sacred experience is within a religious worship space, but that in itself can be limiting. The reason is that some religious traditions believe creation created by a deity is filled with the deity's spirit—naturally making the experience of creation an experience of the sacred. But this does not account for the difficulty in articulating the experience of the sacred, because the human experience does not exhaust the whole of the sacred, which continues to be a mystery. The search continues to explain the experience of the sacred.

The study of the experiences of the sacred is not about giving a definitive description of the sacred. Rather, it provides examples of ways human beings have experienced the sacred in their lives. More importantly, the study of the experiences of the sacred is an introduction to religious studies. The purpose of this study is to provide tools for you to learn about religions, their place within human society, and the impact of religion on human life.

The first step to studying religion is to come to an agreed-upon definition of *religion*. There is not a universally agreed-upon definition of religion; however, a definition of religion is necessary to study religion, because one needs to be able to identify religion before studying it. Many different definitions of religion have already been created. Thus, you will not be provided here with one definition, but several will be given to you. All the definitions have similar threads or essential elements in them. At the core of these definitions is humans' reaction to something or someone other than themselves. The human experience is important, because people are the essential element in the definition.

Definitions of Religion

Why is it difficult to have an agreed-upon definition? The difficulty lies in who has defined religion. It is a definition coined in the Western world, which has practiced mainly Christianity. The Christian tradition influenced the definition by providing the essential element: that of needing a deity. But as Christianity expanded and interacted with other cultures, Christians started to apply this definition of religion to newly discovered cultures and traditions as well. Can this idea be applied to other cultures and traditions, such as Confucianism, Buddhism, and Daoism? This added an interesting turn to the definition of religion, because these other religious traditions did not rely on deities. Rather, they were systems of belief that provided strong community and moral codes. The strong Christian influence on the definition of religion changed and was also challenged by other traditions that did not fully have the components of the Christian religion. The move toward a more neutral approach to defining religion referred to the whole system of belief and action practiced by a group of people. These systems tended not to be directed toward service of a personal God but rather encompassed how the human experience provided meaning.

What is, then, a definition of religion? What are essential points that underscore universal aspects of human behavior toward the other, the sacred? These points are varied and debated, but they somehow capture many of the definitions of religion. Moving away from trying to agree on a definition of religion, this introduction will highlight some of the definitions of religion already accepted and used by the academy. They all provide a perspective on a definition of religion but do not fully exhaust the meaning of religion, which again shows the inadequacies of a definition of religion.

These definitions capture various aspects of religion and provide some essential and salient points for understanding religion. These definitions try to be broad in order to capture the undefinable term *religion*. But some are limited because they still rely on a divine controller.

Definitions are one way to begin a study of religion. Since religion is such a complex system and touches all of humanity, it has also been taken up in various academic disciplines. Due to its complicated character, religion as an object of study needs broader approaches. These academic approaches try to not only define religion but also provide a particular method for studying religion. The following are some examples of approaches to studying religion that will be covered in this text.

The approaches to studying religion are discussed in the first reading, "How Is Religion Studied?" by Robert Crawford. It is an approach rather than a definition. Modern scholarship

The following are definitions of religion that convey the previous points.

Peter Berger: "Religion implies that human order is projected into the totality of being. Put differently, religion is the audacious attempt to conceive of the entire universe as being humanly significant."

Ambrose Bierce in *The Devil's Dictionary*: "Religion: a daughter of Hope and Fear, explaining to Ignorance the nature of the Unknowable."

Concise Oxford English Dictionary: "The belief in a superhuman controlling power, especially in a personal God or gods entitled to obedience and worship."

Clifford Geertz: "Religion is (1) a system of symbols which acts to (2) establish powerful, pervasive, and long-lasting moods and motivations in men by (3) formulating conceptions of a general order of existence and (4) clothing these conceptions with such an aura of factuality that (5) the moods and motivations seem uniquely realistic."

William James: "Religion … shall mean for us the feelings, acts, and experiences of individual men in their solitude, so far as they apprehend themselves to stand in relation to whatever they may consider the divine. Since the relation may be either moral, physical, or ritual, it is evident that out of religion in the sense in which we take it, theologies, philosophies, and ecclesiastical organizations may secondarily grow."

The Random House Dictionary of the English Language: "A belief system that includes the idea of the existence of an eternal principle that has created the world that governs it, that controls its destinies or that intervenes in the natural course of its history."

Paul Tillich: "Religion, in the largest and most basic sense of the word, is ultimate concern. It gives us the experience of the Holy, of something which is untouchable, awe-inspiring, an ultimate meaning, the source of ultimate courage."

in disciplines such as history and psychology provide a particular way to study religion. Therefore, instead of creating a definition, this book utilizes the idea of how to approach the study of religion.

Approaches to Studying Religion

The approaches to defining religion that you will be reading about are historical, theological, philosophical, psychological, sociological, phenomenological, and feminist. These have been the areas in which scholars have seriously looked at the religious experience and tried to bring comprehensive understanding, albeit from particular angles. Each of these approaches will be briefly discussed below.

Historical. History is a narrative of the past. It also strives for a neutral presentation of facts about the past. It relies on resources from which to draw information about what happened, why it happened, and when it happened. A historical approach tries to demonstrate a particular experience and provide a cause-and-effect connection. Religion is one of many subjects studied in the discipline of history. There is no essential difference between a historical study of religion conducted by a scholar in a history department or one in the religious studies field. The historical approach applies a variety of theoretical tools and resources.

Theological. Theology is the study of God. It is human beings giving expression to their understanding of God. Traditionally, theology was at the heart of higher education, established in Europe. It was known as the "queen of the sciences." It is a science, because the original meaning of *science* is knowledge. Theology was about seeking the knowledge of God and God's relationship with humanity. Theology is still an important aspect of education, and it continues to shape religious understanding. The theological approach leans heavily on understanding doctrine, ethics, interpretation of sacred texts, guidance for people, and reflections on a variety of philosophical and spiritual questions.

Philosophical. The term *philosophy* means the love or the pursuit of wisdom. The philosophical approach means to pursue something by examining it in a logical way. This is done by gaining knowledge about it and looking at the patterns it has formed. This approach has generally been seen as asking the big questions, known as metaphysical questions, such as who is God, what is a human being, and what is the universe? These questions do not have final answers but probe the mind to continue searching for answers. The philosophical approach is also conditioned by the culture it is studied in—that is, there are Western and Eastern philosophies. These different perspectives provide a richer approach to religion.

Psychological. Psychology is the study of human behavior. A psychological approach to studying religion focuses on the mind, perception, and consciousness of the religious person. Some approaches have been described as explaining away religion, saying that it is just an illusion or all in the mind. But others illustrate how existing beliefs influence the way in which religion is experienced. The focus of psychology is the human experience and how that has been influenced by childhood, memories, and other factors. The psychological approach to religion often differs in the type of religious experience, practice, or belief it focuses on. This results in different explanations of religion's origins, function, future, and positive or negative effects.

Sociological. Sociology examines human societies and how the people in societies operate. A sociological approach studies what effects a religion has on a society. This approach also employs a scientific method to studying religion that is rooted in observing actions, events, and trends that occur within religion. The sociological approach has gone from making grand theory and universal explanations to studying from a particular perspective, such as women in religion. The sociological approach examines the function, structure, and form of religion within human society.

Phenomenological. Phenomenology is the study of human consciousness through the subjective experience of its interaction with things. The phenomenological approach examines the phenomena that are the objects of a person's perceptions of things. What a person perceives is their reality even if may be actually real or not. This is their experience of their world. The phenomenological approach starts with the idea that religion is something unique and not reducible to anything else. Thus, this approach accepts the way other disciplines, such as anthropology, psychology, and sociology, study religion. A phenomenological approach states that religion cannot be fully explained and that other approaches simply add to the importance of religion.

Feminist. Feminism is a movement of women and men who are interested in achieving genuine equality for women with men on all levels—culturally, legally, and socially. The feminist approach to religion scrutinizes and deconstructs assumptions, privileges, and dominant approaches to the study of religion. This approach tries to not only recover women's historical involvement in the creation and development of the different religious traditions but also to provide a woman's interpretation of the events, cultures, and traditions of a particular time period. The feminist approach adds women's voices to a history that has ignored them.

These are not the only approaches to studying religion, but they provide an example of how many different ways a person can study it. The approaches highlight how religion is so influential in human society that its study cannot be exhausted by one perspective. These approaches also do not provide the complete definition of religion; rather, together, all of them create a fuller picture of what religion is and, more importantly, what is the experience of the sacred.

Religious Studies and the Study of Religion

After discussing definitions of religion and the approaches to studying religion, it is important to distinguish what *religious studies* is. This is a discipline that has taken off in the late twentieth century and is present in the majority of colleges and universities. It is considered a rather young discipline within higher education. In this way, many people do not know exactly what religious studies does. The discipline of religious studies is at heart an interdisciplinary study. Religious studies examines everything within the purview of humanity's conception of and relationship to reality. This reality includes the recognition of a sacred or ultimate beyond the human person. It is also a reality of experiences that are not easily explainable and need reflection and interpretation.

Another way to explain religious studies is by examining what it is not. Religious studies is not learning about a religion in order to be become a practitioner of that religion. It is not a faith study. It is not religious education, because religious education teaches those who share the same faith. In religious education, the believer is trying to learn more about his or her tradition and to become a better believer.

Religious studies looks critically at religion in an objective manner in order to fully understand all aspects of the religion. It employs various approaches, such as historical, philosophical, ethical, psychological, and theological points of view. Even though religious studies is objective, many religious studies scholars will engage in a religion to gain a subjective perspective or an insider's point of view. This provides a fuller picture of the religion.

Religious studies has been shaped by the different approaches to studying religion. It continues to develop its role in the academy, as it provides academic rigor to studying religion. But also, religious studies will help students better understand what an experience of the sacred is.

INTRODUCTION

The Contents of the Book

This textbook is a compilation of articles written on the different religious traditions. The articles provide particular views of the religions. Since it is an introduction, many of the terms may be new; thus, it is important to take time to understand these terms.

This book will cover seven religious traditions. These traditions can be broken down into three major categories: Dharmic traditions (Hinduism and Buddhism); Chinese traditions (Confucianism and Daoism); and Abrahamic traditions (Judaism, Christianity, and Islam). The Abrahamic traditions trace their foundations to the time of the patriarch Abraham. He is considered the founder of these three traditions. Even though they are different in many ways today, they each claim a connection to Abraham. The Dharmic traditions have the universal principle of *dharma*, which can mean either the duty or the essence of life. Dharma helps people understand and structure their worlds. The Chinese traditions were created in China from the philosophical and healing arts. They influenced all sectors of Chinese life and now continue to be practiced even beyond the borders of China. These two traditions have shaped Chinese culture.

The readings on these religions will be introduced by the cultures in which they were created. You will see a brief introduction on India, China, and the Middle East. These are areas of the world in which the major religions were developed. Then there is a brief introduction to the religions. A few of these are followed by longer essays and descriptions. The shorter introductions will be supplemented by suggestions for further readings and resources. Even though these are brief, you will be given means to go further into the study of these religions. Some of the chapters will have questions for further reflection. These will highlight points from the chapters but also help you to think about how these religions affect you personally.

Readings in the Textbook

The first reading is "How Is Religion Studied?" by Robert Crawford, in which he discusses the approaches to studying religion. You will read further about the approaches that were highlighted in the preface. These approaches will also lay the foundation for how religious studies examines religion. The next reading, "The Relationship between God and Humans" by Fritz Wenisch, looks at the relationship between the Abrahamic God and human beings. This short article focuses on how God is experienced by the three religions of Judaism, Christianity, and Islam.

An important element in studying religion is understanding the culture and place in which it originated. Before the readings discussing each of the three major traditions—Dharmic, Chinese, and Abrahamic—there will be a reading on the culture and place of origination. This will be followed by readings on the religions in each of the places.

The first reading focuses on India, where the Dharmic traditions were created and developed. The rich religious tradition of India laid the groundwork not only for Hinduism and Buddhism (which you will study) but also for Jainism and Sikhism, which are not covered in this course but are traditions you may be familiar with. This is followed by a reading on the history of Hinduism, which is considered to be one of the oldest religious traditions in the world. In the next reading, we move on to the tradition that came from Hinduism, which is Buddhism. It originated with Siddhartha, a prince, who stepped away from his privileged life to find the meaning of life. His search helped him create Buddhism.

The next three readings turn to China and the Chinese traditions. The first reading, a brief excursion into China, provides a quick history of the country and its beliefs and practices. The long history of China has been witness to many different religious traditions and philosophies. The two that will be discussed in this text are Daoism and Confucianism. The reading on Daoist traditions and practices is longer than the others. This is a relatively unknown tradition in the Western world; thus, a longer reading is appropriate. The next reading focuses on the other religious tradition that grew out of China, Confucianism. This tradition has been challenged by some scholars, who do not deem it strictly a religion but rather a philosophy. Since the definition of religion is cast widely, we categorize Confucianism as a religion.

From the study of China, we move to the Middle East. In the first reading here, we learn about the foundational place of the Abrahamic religions. In the Middle East, the journey of Abraham to the Promised Land describes God's intervention, support, and relationship with him. This underscores how religion is also about movement. It is moving from one place to another in order to fulfill God's will. Going to another place brings people to encounter other people with rich cultural traditions and beliefs. The encounter stimulates dialogue and the exchange of ideas, customs, and beliefs. The result of these encounters also influenced how the Abrahamic religions crafted beliefs about God and religious practices that are similar to one another. Their tradition of one God created a community of believers, and the importance of constant worship created some salient points of Western religion.

The first reading on Judaism discusses the different branches of Judaism and how they developed. The branches are Reform, Orthodox, and Conservative. These separate branches of Judaism were a result of how believers interpreted their practices in light of their reading of scripture and other canonical texts. The branches of Judaism can be described as liberal or conservative based on their interpretation and adherence to traditional practices. The liberal or conservative leanings can be attributed to the congregations' stances toward social concerns.

In similar ways, there are also branches within Christianity: Orthodox, Catholic, and Protestant. These are the three main branches, and within each of these, there are other communities that splintered from them. For instance, Catholicism has several different branches: Eastern Rite, Old, and Latin Rite, which are based on the way they culturally celebrate the liturgy. The first reading will examine the history of Christianity from its beginning through its current configuration. The discussion will focus on not only the main figures of Christianity but also how it became the major religion in human history.

The next reading on Christianity examines how Christian ethics are informed by the Gospel and tradition. It also gives attention to the role of politics within Christianity. Even though the idea of separation of church and state is strong within the United States, it is not a historical reality. In the early formation of Christianity, the church was very much a part of the political scene of the day. As a matter of fact, the church demanded a lot of power and was revered for its role in society. Thus, as politics developed into a more secular function, the church lost its importance within the society. But as contemporary politics indicate, the role of religion in the political arena is not completely lost.

The reading on Islam will focus on the holy text, which is the Qur'an. Before discussing that, it is important to remember that since Islam is an Abrahamic tradition, it also has some similar traits to Judaism and Christianity. One of these is that of having branches. Islam has two major branches: Sunni and Shi'a. There are also small communities within these branches that are grouped by culture and practice. Islam was founded by the Prophet Muhammad, who was visited and given direct recitations by Allah. These are written down in the Qur'an. These recitations are what helped the Prophet to gain disciples to follow Allah. His devotion to Allah and strong communal building fueled the growth of Islam throughout the Middle East. It is God speaking in the Qur'an that inspires and motivates believers.

UNIT 1
The Study of Religion

The Study of Religion

Editor's Introduction

In this unit, you are introduced to the study of religion. There are two readings: "How Is Religion Studied?" by Robert Crawford and "The Relationship between God and Humans," by Fritz Wenisch. They provide an introduction to the study of religion.

The first reading describes approaches to the study of religion. These approaches are as follows: historical, theological, philosophical, psychological, sociological, phenomenological, and feministic. These disciplines are definitely not the only approaches but they are foundational ones and do provide a broad perspective to studying religion.

The second reading, by Wenisch, considers the experience that human beings have with the scared. The concept of the experiences of the sacred naturally leads to examination of the relationship between the divine and human. The traditional understanding of God has focused mainly on the Judeo-Christian God, which has influenced much of contemporary society. This history is key to understanding how the definition of religion has developed and how other religions are measured. It is from the Christian religion that the term *religion* and also understanding of it developed.

Reading 1 How Is Religion Studied?

By Robert Crawford

There are various methods of study and we begin with the evolutionary approach which developed in conjunction with anthropology. Societies evolved from the lower to the higher. 'Primitive' man saw his world in terms of magic and impersonal forces (animatism) and then came to think of spirits dwelling in trees, mountains and rocks (animism). Animals were worshipped as the symbol or emblem of a tribe (totemism) and the spirit of an eminent chief would be venerated with sacrifices. His grave became a shrine (ancestor worship). A sense of awe in the presence of nature led to the worship of nature gods and this polytheism became the religion of ancient Greece and the Romans, and is still a feature of Hinduism.

Scholars in the nineteenth century believed in a progression from animism, totemism, polytheism to monotheism, a belief in one supreme God. Auguste Comte (1798–1857), the father of sociology, detected three stages: theological, metaphysical and scientific. In the first, things were explained by a supernatural cause, in the second reason took over, and in the third by a scientific understanding of natural causes. Despite his scheme, Comte saw the need for religion and founded the Religion of Humanity which was shortlived. Soon exceptions to the evolutionary development were noted, for progress is not so simple and straightforward. The scenario was too tidy and neat and did not allow for deviations and complexities. Tribes were discovered worshipping one God when they should have been committed to many. Andrew Lang (1844–1912) referred to it as the 'High God among Low Races'. Many of the investigators were 'armchair anthropologists' who had not ventured into the field and wanted to see everything as part of a grand evolutionary plan.

The nineteenth-century idea that we were morally and spiritually better than previous generations, moving upwards and 'letting the ape and tiger die', received a devastating blow in the two world wars of the twentieth century. So-called civilized nations behaved in a savage way and released weapons of inconceivable destructive power. Science and technology can be misused and there is no guarantee that an advance here will be accompanied by ethical progress. While it is not denied that religion does develop in its understanding of God, humanity and the world, the so-called 'primitive tribes' can surprise with subtle ideas about spirituality. Societies must be studied in their own terms, not placed in a higher or lower level, or placed in frameworks that we erect. Eric Sharpe points out that some anthropologists refused to go and look at the Palaeolithic cave paintings in France because such artistic expression did not fit into their views of 'primitive' culture! Such prejudice is not acceptable in any area of study.[1]

Historical

The history of religion approach relates what has happened and tries to interpret it. It examines primary sources such as literary and archaeological material (inscriptions, monuments, artefacts, etc.) connected with a religion and compares its development with other religions without any thought of one religion being superior to another. Secondary sources are considered but not treated with the same respect as the primary. The question of truth is usually left to the philosopher, though judgements of value often occur. The methods used are scientific and objective and the sacred books of the faiths are treated like any other book. Thus an historian writes concerning Sikhism that little can be known about its founder, Guru Nanak. Sikhs join Jews and Christians in deploring the radicalism of some scholars in their approach to the scriptures.

But one of the difficulties is that the sources are the response of believers and are considered subjective. There is little attempt to relate events to the contemporary culture or the forces that moulded the religion, so the conclusion is that they are theological rather than historical. We shall return to the problem when discussing the scriptures of the various faiths but comment here that the writings, though often related to history, particularly in the Semitic traditions (Judaism, Christianity, Islam), do not stress it. They are doctrinal, philosophical, impressionistic and imaginative. Such narrative does convey truth and therefore the historical must be wedded to other approaches to understand the significance of the writing. The theologian may fasten upon the patterns which the historian discovers in history and speak of the purpose and revelation of God, but the historian is likely to think of it as showing a progressive understanding by humanity.[2]

The history of religions developed in the nineteenth century with the desire to compare different religions. But it was based on the evolutionary idea from the false to the true instead of a concern with religions per se. And it was the policy to compare other religions with Christianity to show their limitations, but such a procedure is not acceptable today.[3]

Theological

There are many theologies in the various religions based on the sacred writings and traditions. Doctrines may be explicit in the scripture or implicit. Thus, it is contended that the Christian doctrine of the Trinity, while not in the Bible, can be deduced from various statements of the relation of Father, Son and Holy Spirit. Unitarians and Muslims believe that such a deduction is not valid and it becomes a point of issue in inter-faith dialogue. Theology is derived from *theos*, meaning God, and it tries to explain and validate His existence and revelation. Doctrines are established which form the basis of the ministry, sacraments, authority and organization of a religion. They can cause divisions within the community and discord with other religions.

Theology produces creeds and confessions of faith. To take Christianity as an example, there is the Nicene (325 CE), which is concerned with the status of Jesus Christ, and Chalcedon (451 CE), dealing with his human and divine natures. Confessions of faith are the Thirty-Nine Articles (1574) and the Westminster (1643), which clergy of the Anglican and Presbyterian Church subscribe to but today are signed with mental reservations. In each faith there is a theology which is theoretical and practical, with the latter trying to understand the devotional and mystical writings. Other faiths such as Judaism and Hinduism pay little attention to creeds and see religion as a way of life.

The theological approach traditionally rested on a given faith position, but during the last two centuries has adopted a more liberal stance with a freer interpretation of scripture and a much greater interest in religions other than Christianity. But revelation in its various forms—free inquiry, truth claims—continues to be a subject of debate. An impact on theological methodology has been made by the rise of Religious Studies which considers religion in general and each religion in particular and uses the various approaches that we are describing in this [reading]. Religion is seen as part of the history of ideas.

Philosophical

Philosophy can consider the methods employed in the study of religion, evaluate the evidence and arrive at the truth or otherwise of belief statements. In the past, philosophy asked ultimate questions about the purpose in the world, the existence of God, evil, morality, immortality, and so on. These questions went beyond science and were called metaphysics. In reaction, modern philosophy emphasized observation, experiment and induction (moving from particular experiments to formulating a general law), so religious statements were often treated as meaningless. The logical positivist philosopher said: 'I do not understand what you theologians are saying, it is non-sense because we cannot verify or confirm it by the senses'. In such a method there were difficulties too for morality and aesthetics. If I say, 'You stole that money', I am referring to a fact that can be verified by witnesses, but if I say, 'You ought not to have stolen it', I am merely expressing an emotion or moral disapproval. Moral approbation or censure statements were treated as 'Hurrah' or 'Boo' utterances.[4]

But within philosophy itself there has always been a scepticism about the ability of the senses and Immanuel Kant (1724–1804) was driven to declare that there was a reality behind things (things-in-themselves) which we could not grasp. He distinguished between the world of appearance which we could observe and the world of reality which we could not. The question becomes: 'Am I really seeing the world as it actually is or is it just an image or representation in my mind?' The problem will surface again when we consider the Indian religions. But in reply it could be asserted that we could check one sense against another: it may look like cheese but taste will show that it is butter. With science, observations are checked by experiments.

But what of mathematics, which is not based on sense observation? The Greeks who did so much in this area (we all remember the horrors of Euclid at school!) spoke of an unseen dimension and an invisible world of ideas and forms. The reply of the school of Logical Positivism was that both mathematical statement and statements of logic were valid because of the acceptance of the meaning of numbers and concepts. Thus, 'All husbands are married men' is true given the definition of the terms. They are analytic statements, validated by analysing the words used. But the philosophy failed to do justice to the fullness of human experience, though it had drawn attention to the importance of language and meaning.

The enquiry into religious language came to prominence in the work of Ludwig Wittgenstein (1889–1951). Language is compared to a bag of carpenter's tools, each with its particular function and technique of use or with a range of games each with its own rules and equipment and criteria of success or failure. We have to understand these if we are to know the game. Language is social, it cannot be uprooted from the life of the community in which it originated. A stranger in a foreign country needs not only to master the rules of the language but also to study the culture, customs and traditions if he wants to fully understand the people. The language of religion is intelligible within a mosque, temple, church or gurdwara, and is subject to internal rules. It is personal and cannot be reduced to what is connected with objects.

This means that we cannot define religion as a private affair as it takes place in a community and has rules for the interpretation of sacred texts and for the regulation of the behaviour of its members. The social dimension of religion must be recognized. Also, as Wittgenstein pointed out, while games have their own rules they need to be brought into relation with other games and similarities in language and rules observed. A religion needs to consider its relation to other religions and areas of knowledge for there are family 'resemblances' as well as family 'differences'.

Empiricism is not ruled out by many of the religions for they make the empirical claim that the sacred books are based on the evidence of eyewitnesses who kept company with the founder. It was the experience of the founder of the religion which led them to believe in God and pass on to others what they had experienced. The historian needs to sift out the kernel of experience from the later additions and the theological viewpoint of the writers of the Gospels or the Adi Granth or the Qur'an and so forth. While the development of religions shows change, we cannot imagine Christianity without Christ or Islam without Muhammad or Sikhism without Guru Nanak. Otherwise we make the followers greater than the founder himself! But all of this means that the philosopher has to turn to the historian to see what the critical interpretation of the texts is and he will find that they vary from the conservative through to the radical.

The language of religion has a great variety of expression: metaphor, simile, analogy, symbol, allegory. In speaking of God we are limited, for we are using human language to describe what is beyond the human. But this does not mean that such figures of speech do not impart information, for at times they can be more effective than literal statements, just as a poem can startle and arouse in a way that a factual statement cannot. We can sum up the problem of empiricism and verification by a simple example used by John Wilson. If I say, 'Mary is sweet', I am not going to confirm it by trying to taste her! But if I say 'Sugar is sweet', I can taste to verify. The two statements are different though having points of contact by the use of the same word. How I verify a religious assertion has some contact with empiricism, but there are other ways of verification.

Psychological

The emotional aspects of religion cannot be ignored so psychologists examined religious experience. Many psychologists treat religious experience like any other human experience and religious writers have followed the procedure by arguing that it is normal experience in depth. But some people contend that they have had extraordinary trances, ecstasy and visions. Ninian Smart thinks that a religious experience involves a perception of the invisible world or of some person or thing which reveals that world. Psychologists tend to be sceptical about this and explain such states as psychological conditions of the mind. The scepticism appears in the religions: Catholicism, for example, is distrustful of individual claims of conversion and direct communication with God and relies more on the sacraments of the Church and other mediating channels extended to the faithful. But much study is now devoted to mystical experience which appears in all the religions.

Many have written on religious experience. One of the most notable was William James (1842–1910) who thought it was better to believe in God since it often produced good results. This stemmed from his pragmatism which did not concern itself with the truth of a belief but its effect on our lives. Religion, he thought, is the belief that the world is part of a more spiritual universe and has the goal of achieving harmony with it. The result is a zest for life and a sense of inner peace. He distinguished between the religion of the sick soul which seeks salvation from sin and is reborn by conversion and the religion of healthy-mindedness which is less pessimistic about its spiritual condition and feels no need of conversion. There are the 'once born' and the 'twice born'.

Rudolf Otto (1869–1937) argued that the numinous or uncanny could be experienced, and that religious experience was beyond normal experience. It was a unique experience based on the awesome (*tremendum*) but attractive (*et fascinans*). It was the essence of religion and he had observed it in Hinduism and Islam as well as in Christianity. The awareness of the numinous results in a feeling of unworthiness, as Isaiah experienced in the Temple (Isa. 6), but it is difficult to describe in rational terms since it is super-rational. Otto does not attempt to prove the existence of such a Subject or Supreme Creator since this is the rational way and does not make contact with the numinous. It was enough for him to conclude that the experience of the numinous conveys its existence.[5] Such an experience could be envoked through nature, music, ritual, architecture, art, the use of a language which is mysterious and sacred, and chanting. Fear, majesty, energy, mystery, are all elements in the experience of the 'Wholly Other'. It would seem to imply a negative approach to God, since He is so unlike us we are only able to say what He is not, but Otto introduces the fascination or attraction of God and thereby agrees with Thomas Aquinas: 'We are only able to say what God is not if we also know in some sense what he is.' It can be experienced in nature as Wordsworth said: 'a presence that disturbs me with the joy of elevated thoughts'. But it can also be awakened by the Spirit of God in Judaism and Christianity and the suppression of the rational in Zen Buddhism to reach satori.[6] It is done by enigma and riddles; for example, what is the sound of one hand clapping? There are questions which have no answer and the rational mind collapses in trying to solve them.

Sigmund Freud (1856–1939) was not convinced and thought that such experiences can be explained psychologically. He wrote of God as an illusion or a projection of the father image whom the son respects but hates because he is jealous of his love for the mother. Repression of such ideas gives way to exalting the father into a divine figure. The theory may reflect more Freud's own experience, for it is difficult to establish it on a general basis. It could hardly apply to Muhammad since his father died a few days before his birth and his mother died when he was only six years old! Carl Gustav Jung (1875–1961) differed from Freud, seeing religion as having great practical value for it gave people hope and a happier outlook on life. Thus he would have agreed with William James. It was not an illusion but a natural function which affects humanity just as much as the will to power (Adler) or sexuality (Freud). He propounded 'the collective unconscious', images or archetypes which we experience in dreams and religion and the God image was one of them. He insisted that a religious outlook on life was essential.

In more recent times the question has been raised of whether drugs can induce a religious experience, but psychologists differ on this and produce many conflicting theories about religion. With regard to defining religion, most psychological attempts are rather negative, implying that it is based on fear or an attempt to escape from the demands of life or wish projection of a better time. Guilt is regarded as a neurosis which can be dealt with by realizing that we are the product of heredity and environment, so why blame ourselves? Problems of free will are often not attended to, nor are reasons given for the continuance of the fear of death.

The whole question of religious experience is important, and psychology is a useful and relevant tool. It can examine what has been called the religious instinct, the charisma of the religious leader, and the effect of suggestion in mass evangelism. But it is argued that the psychologist cannot settle the difficult question of whether or not there is a God or a transcendental dimension to which many think religion refers. But it must ally itself to sociology since religion is social as well as individual.

Sociological

The approach tries to avoid personal commitments and prejudices and formulates hypotheses which can be tested empirically. It stresses that the understanding of another society requires knowledge of the culture which influences behaviour. Questions are raised: How does religion function in a society? Does it bind together or cause division? Will it last? Augustus Comte believed religion would disappear but his sympathy with it is shown by his tribute to theologians whom he thought were aware of what human nature was like. He commented that but for them, 'human society would have remained in a condition much like that of a company of superior monkeys'.[7]

Émile Durkheim's work based on the Australian aborigines showed that the totem, a sacred object, points to an impersonal force in objects and of the tribe itself. In his *Elementary Forms of Religious Life* (1912), he argued that religion is society itself and by its rituals cements social unity. It pertains to the sacred aspects which can be distinguished from the profane. Durkheim's definition of religion is both functional and substantive: beliefs provide the substance and the practices are their functional aspects. But beliefs can divide as well as unify, and was he right in thinking that the sacred and profane are so distinct? The view is challenged in the religions, but even in such ceremonies as the coronation of a monarch or the swearing in of the President of the USA, nationalism and religion are blended. Durkheim was right in seeing religion as social but it can also be individualistic.

Max Weber opposed Durkheim, arguing that it was religion that produced social groupings. Capitalism owed much to Christian Calvinism which insisted on hard work and thrift as a sign of faith in God and His election. Ambition, saving and hard work were pleasing to God and since money was not wasted on dress or adornment or entertainment, the Calvinist invested it, leading to more capital. Sociologists are often limited in their findings because they concentrate only on the Christian religion, but Weber studied world religions and showed the nature of ethical and exemplary prophecy. The former encouraged social change while the latter held on to tradition. The traditional forms of religion supported the status quo whereas the sect could upset it. His work ranged over the area of bureaucracy and types of authority and charismatic leadership. While some of his arguments are regarded with scepticism by sociologists of religion, it is clear that his influence has permeated their writings today.[8]

Karl Marx followed Durkheim's view that religion was a human construction, though he went on to an interpretation which was quite different. [...]. More recent work such as that of Peter Berger refers to the sacred canopy: beliefs in the sacred providing an overall explanation of existence and supplying meaning in a confusing world. In his book, *A Rumour of Angels* (1971), he reacted to the general idea that religion is human in origin by pointing to signals of transcendence found in humour, hope, justice and play, and our sense of order in the world.

Sociologists are interested in how institutions react to changing circumstances: a religion founded by a charismatic figure can develop into an institution which seeks the power to consolidate and spread the faith. There are a number of examples. One is the peaceful religion of Sikhism, founded by Guru Nanak, which developed a military style of organization called the Khalsa. Another was the development of papal power in Christianity, which sent the crusaders to take the Holy Land from the Muslims. A third is the military power of Islam, which developed from Muhammad's defence of his revelation to worldwide conquest. Even in normal times, religious organizational structure can exchange spiritual power for temporal with a diminishing of spontaneity and enthusiasm as arguments continue about ritual or beliefs or leadership. The worst scenario occurs when the faith fails to adapt to society and retreats into a religious ghetto with little social outreach. Conversely, the religion may so conform to the values of the society that the original message virtually disappears. Every religion is faced with conserving the best of its past with accommodation to the present. How it balances these factors is not easy.

Many Sikhs when they migrated to Britain abandoned their turban. The Punjabi word for turban is *sikhna*, meaning to hear, hence the Sikhs listen to the word of the Guru and are continual learners. When their wives and families arrived in Britain religious ties were renewed, and the turban reappeared. The first gurdwara (Sikh temple) was built in 1958 in Yorkshire and regular attendance observed. Where there was no temple a religious service (*diwan*) was held in the home. It was a social event as well as religious and helped to strengthen the Sikh ethnic identity. But with them and other religious groups such as the Muslims, there is often a tension between the values inculcated in the schools and their religion. The stress on individualism and choice comes into conflict with the family loyalties and the tradition of arranged marriages in accordance with parental control and religious belief. Racial discrimination is evident still in Britain and elsewhere, and a secular society makes little attempt to understand religious values. In connection with Sikhism, the transport authorities tried to force Sikhs to wear the regulation cap and it was a long time before Parliament agreed to Sikhs wearing their turbans instead of crash helmets when riding motorcycles. The wearing of the turban also reasserts the ethnic pride of the Sikhs in the face of white rejection of their colour and treating second and third generations of them as foreigners.

While religions have to accommodate to survive it is obvious that a society needs to know something about the culture and customs of migrant people if racial discrimination is to be eliminated. One factor that would help is more religious education in schools so that children will know something about and learn to appreciate the customs and beliefs of everyone living in their society.

The sociologist is aware that only by participation in a religion and its culture, language, customs and values can it be understood. Many go to live with communities to gain their trust instead of standing away from them as objects to be examined. The discipline tries to be scientific, using statistical methods and surveys. Secularization is a main theme with some saying that it has occurred and others disagreeing. Much work has been done in connection with sects by J. M. Yinger, David Martin and Bryan Wilson. But there does not seem to be any single model created by sociologists to fully explain the role of religion in society.[9]

Phenomenological

The method is descriptive, looking at similarities and dissimilarities, and tries to be free from value judgements and to show empathy with the culture and beliefs. It endeavours to 'walk in the moccasins of the faithful', looking at the phenomena from the viewpoint of the people themselves, and tries to discern patterns in the religions.[10] Limitations are imposed on the investigation in that it is the observed data which are interpreted and no attempt is made to deal with the truth or otherwise of the faiths. But it cautions about seeing what we want to see or expect to see and calls for imagination to enter into the lifestyle and mind-set of those who differ from us. It draws on all the other approaches but favours participation or 'field work' studies. The approach is a good one for it is difficult to understand the conflict in Northern Ireland or Israel or other parts of the world without living among the people there. Yet while the phenomenologist does not project her own views but maintains a neutral viewpoint, it is difficult to escape one's own background and presuppositions and not exercise some judgement on what is observed.

Feministic

We shall be thinking in detail about this approach in a later [reading] but comment here that it opposes masculine assumptions about the inferiority of women in leadership roles. It contends that the scriptures of the religions are male orientated and neglect the proper place of women. The continual use of the masculine gender in referring to the deity is to be deplored and in some cases feminists have campaigned for a new edition of scriptures and prayer books which will deal with the problem.

In conclusion we note that the different approaches blend in various ways so in any study of religion all must be taken into account. No one approach gives a total view of religion and its characteristics. We will attempt to use all of them as we proceed. In the next [reading] we begin our study of six religions by considering the importance of rituals.

Notes

1. Eric Sharpe, 'Seekers and Scholars'. AD208 units 1, 2, 3, p. 62, Open University, Milton Keynes, 1981.

2. Ibid.

3. Eric Sharpe, 'The Comparative Study of Religion in Historical Perspective', in W. Foy (ed.), *Man's Religious Quest: A Reader*, Croom Helm, London, 1978, pp. 7ff.

4. Connected in particular with A. J. Ayer's book, *Language, Truth and Logic*, Penguin, Harmondsworth, 1971.

5. Paul Williams, 'The Sense of the Holy'. A101 unit 20, pp. 76ff, 87f, Open University, Milton Keynes, 1980. William James, *The Varieties of Religious Experience*, Penguin Classics, Harmondsworth, 1985. See lectures 4 and 5 for the distinction between 'once-born' and 'twice born' pp. 78ff.

6. P. Williams, op. cit., p. 93. Satori means enlightenment, the goal of Zen Buddhism.

7. A. Comte, *Positive Philosophy*, Chapman, London, 2 vols, 1853. E. Sharpe, op. cit., p. 17.

8. Peter Connolly (ed.), *Approaches to the Study of Religion*, Cassell, London and New York, 1999, pp. 199ff. See Max Weber, *Protestant Ethic and the Spirit of Capitalism* (trans. T. Parsons), Allen & Unwin, London, 1930; *The Sociology of Religion* (trans. Ephraim Fischoff), Beacon Press, Boston, 1963.

9. Bryan Wilson, *Religion in Sociological Perspective*, Oxford, OUP, 1982, deals with sectarianism and secularization. Steve Bruce (ed.), *Religion and Modernisation: Sociologists and Historians Debate the Secularization Thesis*, Clarendon Press, Oxford, 1983. It has the approaches of David Martin, Bryan Wilson and Peter Berger.

10. Clive Erricker, 'Phenomenological Approaches', in P. Connolly, op. cit., Chapter 3.

Reading 2 The Relationship between God and Humans

By Fritz Wenisch

Doing God's Will?

What does revelation say about the relationship between God and Humans?

Humanity does have a definite beginning—it began with Adam. Each and every individual human being also does have a definite beginning. While many contemporary nonreligious people believe that each and every individual human being also does have a definite end—at the moment of death, Jews, Christians, and Muslims disagree. For them, death is not the end of the human personality; rather, it is through death that one finally and definitely is enabled to enter into the very relationship with God for which one has been created in the first place, for which this life is supposed to be something like a "practice," a "preparation."

This leads us on to the "purpose of human existence" point. What have humans been created for? For entering into a relationship with God. What kind of a relationship?

Some of you might respond, remembering what you have heard in religion courses not taught according to the Fox principle, "We are to do God's will," and some of you might add, "That means, for the most part at least, not doing things we would like to do, and doing things that are hard or boring."

Judaism, Christianity, and Islam might respond, "True, we are to do God's will; but he does not want us to obey his commands in a legalistic manner. God's will is that we enter into an intimate, close relationship with him—that our hearts respond appropriately to him in view of who he is, but also in view of the intimate and close relationship he has toward us. True, doing his will in the sense of obeying his commands, even when it is hard to do so, is a part of it—it is the 'training' for responding as we are supposed to; but it is not the 'heart of the matter.'"

How Does God Relate To Humans?

What, then, is the "heart of the matter?"

Judaism and Christianity would once again take recourse to the "it is somehow like this" argument—remember the thought of humans being in the image of God. They would call attention to a relationship among humans we are familiar with and say, "God relates to us 'somewhat like this' already now; and we are to respond in kind."

What is that relationship?

Jews and Christians might tell you, "Read the book (part) of the Bible called 'Song of Songs' (or 'Song of Solomon' or 'Canticle of Canticles')—this might give you a clue about how the relationship between God and humans is to be."

Following this advice might initially confuse you, for that book is a poem describing a passionate love between a man and a woman, a man and a woman who are, as someone lacking the proper understanding of this kind of relationship would say, "madly in love" with one another, "just plain crazy" about each other. How is this to help?

Jews and Christians would say, prefacing their explanation with a reminder that wherever God is similar to humans, there are even greater differences, "God's relationship to each individual human being is, of course, totally different from all relationships between humans known to us; but the human relationship coming closest to the way he relates to us is that of a man to a woman with whom he is 'madly in love.'"

"Come again?"

"Yes, that's how it is."

"You mean to tell me that God is 'in love' with me?"

"That's what Judaism and Christianity would say; although they would add the, 'in a manner of speaking' qualification."

The "Song of Songs" is to give us an inkling of how God relates to each and every human being—with a love characterized by an intensity going beyond anything we can imagine; and of all human experiences, the love of a man for a woman with whom he is in love is most similar to this love. Muslims might be a bit squeamish about that comparison; but that God loves humans, they would agree with.[1]

How Humans Are to Relate to God

How it should be, and how it really is

This might help us understand what Jews, Christians, and Muslims believe about the purpose of human existence. In prosaic terms, we exist "to do the will of God." To get at the non-prosaic side: What does a man wish of a woman with whom he is in love? Why, for her to love him back, of course—to love him more than anyone else.

What, then, does God want, given how he relates to us?

If you say, "for us to love him back," you got it.

But given the nature of the love with which he loves us, try to understand what "He wants us to love him back," really includes: That you love him back with a love that compares favorably in intensity and intimacy with the love a woman has for a man with whom she is in love.

That's how your love for God is to be.

So I invite those among you who happen to be religious to compare their actual relationship to God with how it is supposed to be, according to the religions this course deals with. Does the intensity and intimacy of your relationship to the God you believe in compare favorably to the intensity and intimacy that exist between persons in love with each other? If LOL ever was a proper response to a question, it likely is so at this point. I am sure that many in this room who believe in God must admit that their relationship to God hardly even deserves to be called love; those bold enough to say, "I do love God," will probably have to add, "But in intensity and intimacy, it falls far short of what exists between a man and a woman in love with one another."

This makes us "stumble" from considering the purpose of human existence to our task on earth—at least according to Judaism, Christianity and Islam.

First, to repeat, the purpose for which we have been created is to experience an intensive and intimate love relationship with God, and to be forever happy in this experience. Our task is related to the realization that love is a two-way street. This love exists already from the side of God. But what is there from your side leaves a lot to be desired—and that is once again the "understatement of the millennium." Thus, your task is learning to requite God's love; changing yourself into a person who truly loves God back—this is your task during this life, according to Judaism, Christianity, and Islam.

This task is spelled out in a passage of the Jewish Holy Scriptures, considered by many Jews as the most important part of their Bible—a passage known as the "Shema Israel," two words meaning, "Hear O Israel." The passage derives its name from the first two words of the Hebrew version of the passage:

> Hear O Israel, The Lord our God, The Lord is One! **Therefore, you shall love the Lord, your God, with all your heart, and with all your soul, and with all your strength.** Take to heart these words which I enjoin on you today. Drill them into your children. Speak of them at home and abroad, whether you are busy or at rest. Bind them at your wrist as a sign, and let them be as a pendant on your forehead. Write them on the doorposts of your houses and on your gates. (Dt 6:4–9)

How to get oneself to accomplish the goal of human existence

Love is an emotion, a feeling, a response of the heart. There is hardly anything concerning which there is more confusion today than about emotions and feelings. If this would be one of my day job courses, I would now go into many details concerning a clarification of the nature of "feelings" as one can find them in the philosophical writings of one of my heroes, Dietrich von Hildebrand.

For the purpose of this course, I must confine myself to some essentials, and mention first the fickleness of the human heart; how difficult it is for us to respond with the appropriate emotions to the persons, things, and events around us.

Here are some examples:

Imagine meeting someone who is even better than you in an area in which you excel (sports, mathematics, playing an instrument, whatever—fill in what corresponds to your situation). What *should* your heart's response be? Isn't it admiration, being happy for that person? How does your heart *actually* respond, though, in many such cases? Isn't it with envy, jealousy, and resentment—maybe even hatred?

Or think of Irving who is looking forward to a baseball game on TV. There are some holdups at work, though, and he leaves later than usual. A glance at his watch lets him know, "If I drive fast, I will be home when the game starts." He steps on the gas, hoping that no cops will be lurking by the side of the road.

On the interstate, there is a traffic tie-up. He gets angry as it becomes clear that he will miss the beginning of the game. Now, several emergency vehicles, including three ambulances, make their way past the traffic on the shoulder of the road, and Irving must squeeze to the left.

"All of this will take forever," he curses.

Three ambulances—does that not tell Irving that something terrible must have happened a couple of hundred yards ahead of where he is? Several people must have been injured; maybe there was even loss of life!

Compare missing part of a ballgame—or even all of it—with several people being involved in a serious accident. What is worse? Isn't it clear that the first one does not even deserve to be mentioned in comparison to the second?

If Irving's heart was "in the right place," would he not be full of compassion for the people who must be suffering very much through what seems to be a serious accident? Instead, all his heart manages is anger about being made late for a ballgame.

Also, often, when our heart *should* respond in a certain way, it seems to be dominated by the "who cares" attitude. Think about the many cases in which you remained unmoved when you learned about other people's misfortunes, including those of acquaintances, relatives, even friends.

With regard to God, the "my heart is unmoved" phenomenon is especially frequent.

What to do? If my heart is unmoved, it does not help for me to decide, "Be moved"; my heart is not under the direct control of my will. It is, however, not entirely removed from that control either: My will does have some indirect influence over it. Think of people in poverty. Appropriately, we should feel compassion for them; but actually, our hearts may be cold. However, what if we acted toward them *as if* we had compassion with them; that is, if we actually were to go out of our way to help them when we can? We might then notice that slowly—ever so slowly—our hearts would limp after our will; and over time, something like a genuine feeling of compassion might develop.

This also works with regard to other matters; Judaism, Christianity, and Islam claim that it also works with regard to God.

Tell your will to make the kinds of decisions you would make if you would love God, admitting to yourself (and to others, if indicated) that actually, your heart is cold (otherwise, you would be a hypocrite); and slowly, over time, your heart's coldness will diminish, and maybe even genuine love for God will develop.

That's where doing God's will comes into the picture.

Remember: To move ourselves into the direction of loving God, we must act "as if" we loved God.

Think about a man at work who has a task he dislikes. Whenever he can skip it without his boss noticing, he skips it; whenever he must do it, he does it with inner resentment. One day, he finds out, however, that the woman he loves finds it important for him to carry that task out. From now on, he will never skip it again and will even do it with joy, knowing that it will make his beloved happy. Generally, if a person loves someone else, he or she will do what the other person wants him or her to do.

Remember: The person whose heart is cold with regard to God is to act as if he or she loved God—which means, as the example shows, doing what God wants him to do, or, expressed in a more formal way, "doing God's will."

Doing God's will is, for the cold-hearted person, the surest way to learn loving God.

What does doing God's will involve?

Jews reply, "Follow the law as stated in the Torah." (Details will be provided when we get to Judaism. Then, we will also see that the chief groups of Judaism differ from each other with regard to the laws of the Torah they continue to find mandatory.)

Christians state, "Follow the moral laws stated in the Torah as interpreted and amplified by Jesus." (Again, details will be provided in the Christianity segment.)

Muslims would say, "You must carry out the duties spelled out in the Qur'an; especially important are those known as the 'Five Pillars of Islam.'" (Their nature will be explained in the Islam segment.)

Let me end today's class with a real question and an answer that is, in light of the importance of the question, rather awkward—but we are "stuck" with that answer, given the role of religion at secular schools in the United States:

Question: Does God exist? (Given what we have gone over, can you think of a question more important than that one?)

Answer: "Not for me to say as a part of this course."

Tom, Beth, and Jake left the auditorium together. Tom remarked, "The kind of God he talked about in there is very different from what I got out of my Sunday school class. I was made to think about him more as someone 'out to get me' rather than someone ... someone who ... " Beth asked, "Someone who loves you?" "Precisely," Tom replied. Beth said, "Wouldn't it be awesome if such a God really existed?" "Kind of," Jake said. "'Kind of?' Only 'kind of?' What do you mean?" Jake did not reply. "Do you think he exists?" Beth asked. "Do you?"

Note

1. "Surely Allah loves those who turn much (to him) and loves those who purify themselves" (Qur'an 2.222, based on Ali). "Yes, whoever fulfills his promise and keeps his duty—then Allah surely loves the dutiful" (Qur'an 3.76, based on Ali).

References

Bible: For quotations from the Bible, the following translations are used: (1) *The New American Bible* and (2) the *New International Version*. For quotations from (1), only the book of the Bible, the Chapter, and the Verse are given (e.g., Lv 19.18); for quotations from (2), the book, chapter, and verse indication is followed by "NIV" (e.g., Mt 25.31–46 NIV). The abbreviations for Bible books are the same as those given in the Bible segment of the Christianity part of this text.

Qur'an: Quotations from the Qur'an are taken from the following English editions: (1) *The Holy Qur'an—English Translation of the Meaning and Commentary* by Mushaf Al-Madinah An-Nabawiyah, revised and edited by the Presidency of Islamic Researchers, IFTA, Call and Guidance; (2) *The Holy Qur'an, Arabic Text with English Translation and Commentary* by Maulana Muhammad Ali, first edition 1917, redesigned 2002, Dublin/Ohio, 2002. Both editions are in an old-fashioned language; I have taken the liberty of updating it, for example, by replacing "thee" with "you" and by similar changes. Quotations from (1) are identified as "based on An-Nabawiyah"; quotations from (2) are identified as "based on Ali."

END OF UNIT QUESTIONS

Directions: Use what you have learned in Unit I to respond to the questions below.

1. What are the approaches to studying religion? How do these help you better understand religion?

2. Which approach to studying religion provides you the best u understanding of religion? Provide reasons.

3. Describe the relationship that humans have with God. What are the requirements?

4. Is there an unbridgeable difference between humanity and divinity?

5. Compare and contrast the notion of the divine in the Abrahamic religions.

FOR FURTHER READING

Ellwood, Robert S., and Barbara A. McGraw. *Many Peoples, Many Faiths: Women and Men in the World Religions.* 10th ed. Upper Saddle River, NJ: Prentice Hall, 2013.

Esposito, John L., Darrell J. Fasching, and Todd Lewis. *World Religions Today.* 5th ed. New York: Oxford University Press, 2014.

Hinnells, John R. *A Handbook of Living Religions.* 2nd ed. Ringwood, Australia: Penguin, 2000.

UNIT II

The Dharmic Religious Traditions

The Dharmic Religious Traditions

Editor's Introduction

In this unit, our attention turns to the Dharmic traditions, specifically Hinduism and Buddhism. These two religious traditions both see dharma as essential to their tradition, but they have slightly different understandings of dharma. Their practices, rituals, and beliefs are clearly different. This section includes three readings. It is organized so that you are first introduced to the place and culture where these religious traditions developed, which is India.

The reading "India: History, Beliefs, Practices" by Eloise Hiebert Meneses provides a look at India's rich and long history in the world. It has one of the oldest civilizations that continues to thrive today. You will learn a little bit about the history, beliefs, and practices of this country that has created and nurtured both Hinduism and Buddhism. While both of these religious traditions are from India, they have migrated to other parts of the world.

Hinduism is a religious tradition that stems from the very beginning of India. The name *Hinduism* derives from a Western designation rather than from the local people who practice the tradition. Hinduism has many different elements in its development. There is no founder, there is not one text, and there is no central office. There are many different sects, and it is usually labeled henotheist rather than polytheist. Henotheism states that there are many gods and goddesses but only one is given attention (at a time). Polytheism is defined as the belief in many gods. Hinduism is also considered a monotheistic religion, because Brahma is the creator and supreme God. Other gods and goddesses are considered representations of Brahma. The history of the development of Hinduism will be discussed in the reading "Hinduism: History, Beliefs, Practices" by Richard Fox Young. Hinduism is a very rich religious tradition, with many different layers that have developed over time.

Buddhism is a religious tradition that was founded by Siddhartha Gautama. He was dissatisfied with the religious practices of his lifetime and sought to find another approach to understanding the purpose of life. Through observation, meditation, and fasting, he embraced a middle path that helped him achieve enlightenment during his lifetime. Since he grew up in a Hindu setting and society, many of the terms used in Buddhism are similar to those of Hinduism, but they have taken on a Buddhist interpretation. The history of the development of Buddhism will be discussed in the reading "Buddhism: History, Beliefs, Practices" by Terry C. Muck. Some people consider Buddhism a way of life or a philosophy rather than a religion, but it does have elements that are essential to religion. The history of the founder will be discussed, as well as the development of the religion after his death.

Reading 3 India: History, Beliefs, Practices

By Eloise Hiebert Meneses

History

India has been the birthplace of two world religions—Hinduism and Buddhism—and has received significant influence from a third—Islam. It is also the primary locale of a number of midsized religions, including Sikhism, Jainism, and Parsiism (Zoroastrianism), as well as of a multitude of smaller tribal religions. Throughout its history, the current of what has come to be called "Hinduism" today has held the center, requiring all other world or indigenous religions to interact with its beliefs and practices. [...] But new ideas that were spawned at the margins, along with invasions from outside the subcontinent, have required Hinduism to continually adjust or lose ground to competitors.

Hinduism is one of the oldest religions in the world. Archaeological remains from the Indus Valley Civilization show evidence of gods, priests, and purification rituals as early as 3000–2500 BCE. With the arrival of the Aryans from central Asia in 1500 BCE and their establishment over local populations (collectively termed "Dravidians"), an early pantheon of gods and goddesses was constructed, and the first outlines of a caste structure were put into place. This history has become legitimizing mythology to contemporary conservative Hindus in the defense of the superiority of high castes over low (Aryan over Dravidian), and Hinduism over other religions.

Early Hinduism was dominated by the Brahmin (priestly) caste. Brahmins had a cosmology that included an impersonal supernatural force, *Brahman*, that could be manipulated through the magical use of sound. Chanting verses of poetry and sacrificing animals to the gods were the means of influencing life's circumstances.

These verses were eventually codified in the Vedas (twelfth–eighth centuries BCE). Later, in a period of disillusionment with magic, the Upanishads were written (seventh–fifth centuries BCE), providing the philosophical foundation for much of contemporary Hindu belief and practice. The Upanishads declared attachment to earthly life to be the cause of suffering, equated the soul with God, and commended various forms of asceticism to release the soul from this life.

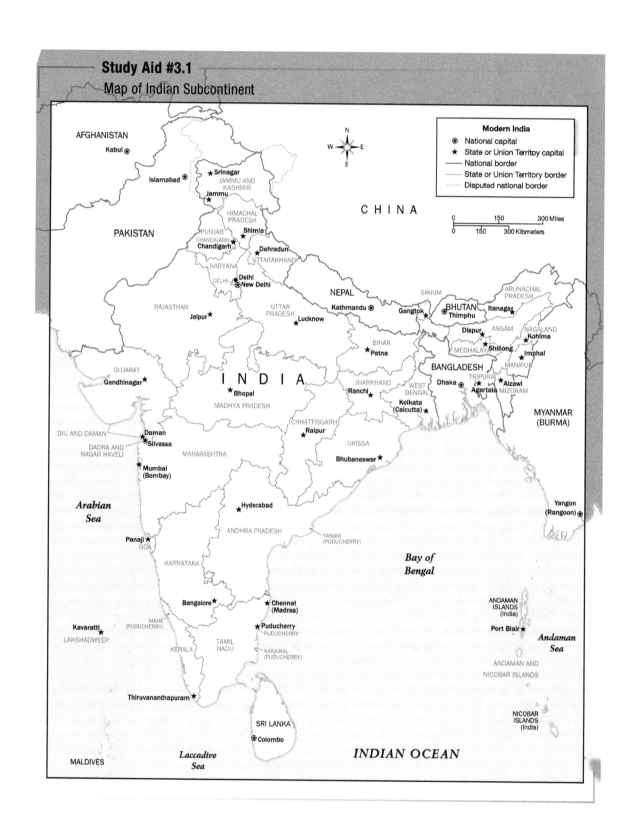

Study Aid #3.1

Map of Indian Subcontinent

Modern India

⊕ National capital
★ State or Union Territory capital
—— National border
—— State or Union Territory border
---- Disputed national border

AFGHANISTAN

Kabul ⊕

Islamabad ⊕

★ Srinagar
JAMMU AND KASHMIR
★ Jammu

HIMACHAL PRADESH

CHINA

PAKISTAN

PUNJAB
CHANDIGARH
Chandigarh

★ Shimla

★ Dehradun
UTTARAKHAND

HARYANA

DELHI
● Delhi
⊕ New Delhi

NEPAL
Kathmandu ⊕

SIKKIM

ARUNACHAL PRADESH

Gangtok ★
★ BHUTAN
Thimphu

Itanagar ★

RAJASTHAN

UTTAR PRADESH
★ Lucknow

Jaipur ★

Dispur ★
ASSAM

NAGALAND
★ Kohima

MEGHALAY Shillong ★
Imphal ★

BIHAR
★ Patna

BANGLADESH
MANIPUR

GUJARAT
Gandhinagar ★

Dhaka ⊕
JHARKHAND
Ranchi ★
WEST BENGAL
TRIPURA
Agartala ★
Aizawl ★
MIZORAM

INDIA

★ Bhopal
MADHYA PRADESH

Kolkata (Calcutta) ★

MYANMAR (BURMA)

DIU AND DAMAN
★ Daman
★ Silvassa

CHHATTISGARH
★ Raipur

DADRA AND NAGAR HAVELI

MAHARASHTRA

ORISSA

Bhubaneswar ★

Mumbai (Bombay) ★

Arabian Sea

★ Hyderabad

ANDHRA PRADESH

YANAM (PUDUCHERRY)

Yangon (Rangoon) ⊕

Bay of Bengal

Panaji ★
GOA

KARNATAKA

ANDAMAN ISLANDS (India)

Kavaratti ★
LAKSHADWEEP

MAHÉ (PUDUCHERRY)

Bangalore ★

★ Chennai (Madras)

★ Puducherry
PUDUCHERRY

Port Blair ★

Andaman Sea

KERALA
TAMIL NADU
KARAIKAL (PUDUCHERRY)

ANDAMAN AND NICOBAR ISLANDS

Thiruvananthapuram ★

SRI LANKA
⊕ Colombo

NICOBAR ISLANDS (India)

MALDIVES

Laccadive Sea

INDIAN OCEAN

0   150   300 Miles
0   150   300 Kibmeters

In the sixth century BCE, Buddhism was founded in North India by Siddhartha Gautama, in part as a reaction against excessive asceticism. Buddhism thrived in India for over seventeen centuries. But following a period of decline, it was largely driven out by the Muslim invasions of the twelfth century CE. It remains the dominant religion of Sri Lanka. Also in the sixth century BCE, Jainism was founded by Mahavira, in a strong affirmation of asceticism. Jains are found throughout India living side by side with Hindus now. Later, in the tenth century CE, India received the followers of Zoroastrianism when they were driven out of their homeland by the Muslim invasions of Persia. Known as "Parsis," they are now a highly respected and indigenized community in the western part of the country.

Following a few peripheral trading contacts by sea, Islam entered India in the tenth–eleventh centuries CE with the invading armies of the Turko-Afghans (including Mahmud of Ghazni). Over the next five centuries, successive waves of Muslims from central Asia raided, established kingdoms, overthrew one another, and ruled the Hindu populace of North India. The greatest of these kingdoms was the Mughal Empire, one of the largest and wealthiest empires in the world at the time. Muslim overlords were variously ruthless or relaxed in their treatment of their non-Muslim subjects. But resentment was strong in the Hindu population and continues to this day.

Caught between the influences of Hinduism and Islam, Guru Nanak (1469–1539) founded Sikhism in the fifteenth century CE. The Sikhs were initially peaceful but gradually developed a militant stance after centuries of persecution that included the torture deaths of two of their leaders at the hands of the Mughals. Currently, they are a politically organized and wealthy community concentrated in the northern state of the Punjab.

Throughout this history, there have been tribal peoples living in the mountainous areas of the country who have retained their traditional religions. They are known by Hindus on the plains as *adivāsis*. Some have been progressively absorbed into Hinduism as Dalits, or "untouchables" (*āvarnas*), at the bottom of the caste structure (see Bailey 1960). But significant pockets remain, especially in the far northeast of the country (Nagas, Assamese, Tripuris, Mizos) in the central Vindhya Mountains

Study Aid #3.2

Nations of Indian Subcontinent

India: 80 percent Hindu
Pakistan: 96 percent Muslim
Bangladesh: 88 percent Muslim
Sri Lanka: 70 percent Buddhist
Nepal: largely Hindu
Bhutan: Buddhism state religion
Maldives: Islam state religion

(Santals, Khonds, Bhils), and in the Andaman and Nicobar Islands. Virtually every part of India still has *adivāsis* practicing traditional religions, sometimes in syncretism with popular Hinduism.

The following sections will segment religious belief and practice by categories: (1) popular Hinduism, (2) Jainism, (3) Parsi, (4) Sikhism, and (5) tribal religions. But it is important to note that there is tremendous diversity within each category, and a great deal of syncretism at the local level, even between Hinduism and Islam (see Beals 1980).

Beliefs

Popular Hindu beliefs are focused on village life. Local cosmology is replete with a wide variety of spirits, ghosts, demons, and *devas* (gods). Propitiation of low-level goddesses is particularly important because they are believed to cause disease. Over time, local gods and goddesses become incorporated into the larger Hindu pantheon. For example, Murugan, a regional warrior god of the south, has come to be identified as the "first" son of Shiva and Parvati, despite the prior claim of the elephant god, Ganesh, for that role in mythology. Such contradictions do not disturb ordinary people, but over time some consistency is achieved by the simple device of identifying the same god as having different forms. The result is that nearly every village and town claims the epic events of the Hindu gods to have happened in their own place, and local beliefs and practices have become increasingly "Sanskritized"—that is, dominated by the ubiquitous language of the epics, Sanskrit, which in some ways is the "ecclesiastical" language of India.

Jain cosmology shares much with Hinduism, including modified beliefs in *dharma*, *karma*, and reincarnation. Mahavira (599–526 BCE) taught that the world consists of a multiplicity of souls (*jīvas*) at various levels (gods, humans, animals, plants, even microbes), weighed down by *karma*, but moving upward toward release into *moksha*, or blissful omniscience. Three "jewels" are needed to get there: right knowledge, right faith, and right conduct. Time is eternal and cyclical. Those souls who have purified themselves through severe asceticism are known as *tīrthaṅkaras* and can become *gurus* or teachers before they die and are released. Jains value education and have a well-defined philosophy of multiple perspectives on the truth.

Zoroaster, the founder of the Parsi religion, lived in Iran at about the time of Abraham, 1400–1200 BCE (Boyce 1988, 18). The religious environment shared features with early Brahminism such as polytheism, fire sacrifice, and religious intoxication. But Zoroaster preached monotheism and a radical distinction between good (order, truth) and evil (chaos, falsehood). He declared one of the gods, Ahura Mazda, to have been the Creator and predicted his triumph over evil at the end of time, along with a new creation. In the meanwhile, humans are caught up in a cosmic battle and have a responsibility to actively promote the created good over the uncreated evil and decay.

Guru Nanak (1469–1539 CE), founder of Sikhism, rejected the polytheism, idolatry, and caste hierarchy of the Hinduism into which he was born. He taught that God is one and should be worshiped by that name, *Ek* ("One"). Rejecting excessive asceticism and ritual, and possibly influenced by Hindu *bhakti* (see below) and Muslim Sufism, Nanak stressed devotionalism and purity of heart toward God. By such worship, the soul might be released from its attachment to worldly desires, and attain *mukti*, or release from reincarnation and union with God.

Tribal peoples (*adivāsis*) have a wide variety of indigenous religions, but there are some commonalities that are the result of tribal social organization and relationship to the environment. Unlike the ranked Hindu castes, tribes are egalitarian. And unlike the highly specialized agricultural villages and urban areas of the plains, tribal communities involve all members equally in productive work. Religious beliefs tend to be animistic and closely linked to the forest environment. In addition to spirits in nature, there may be ancestor spirits, gods and goddesses, and a remote supreme God. Mythology centers on the origins of the group, legendary figures, and animal stories. Tribals typically do not believe in reincarnation unless they have been in contact with Hindu beliefs. Their lives are circumscribed by the day-to-day practical needs and events of their foraging, horticultural, or pastoral economies.

Practices

Popular Hindu religious practice is centered on a magical notion of worship. That is, gods are propitiated in order to bring good luck and avoid bad luck. *Puja* (worship) is conducted at home by offerings of food, incense, vermillion, lamplight, and prayers to *murtis* (idols) in household shrines or to iconic posters on the walls. By visiting temples, near and far, pilgrims can contribute to the *puja* being offered by priests. Both the offerings (often money) and the *darshan* (seeing the god) return blessings to the devotee. Propitiation at small local shrines, and to ant- and snake-hills, is also done. Astrologers are consulted for every major occasion and many minor ones. Rites of passage are numerous and are celebrated with prescribed rituals conducted by priests. And *bhakti*, or devotionalism, includes singing, poetry, and impassioned prayer to personally chosen gods.

Study Aid #3.3

Religions of India

Hinduism: 2500 BCE?
Tribal religions: 2500 BCE?
Buddhism: 6th century BCE
Jainism: 6th century BCE
Christianity: 1st or 2nd century CE
Parsiism: 10th century CE
Islam: 11th century CE
Sikhism: 15th century CE

A Jain's life is circumscribed by the purity rules that will ultimately release his or her soul from karmic bondage. Five vows must be taken: nonpossession (of material goods), truthfulness, nonstealing, celibacy, and nonviolence. Because of the stringency of the vows, the community is divided into monastics and laity, with the latter performing the vows only in modified form. The vow of nonviolence requires all Jains to be vegetarians. Monastics (male and female) take more extreme measures, such as wearing masks to avoid breathing in insects. They are strictly celibate and wear only simple white clothing, or none at all, to avoid having possessions (Mahavira wandered naked). Fasting is highly valued, potentially culminating in the supreme ascetic act of *santhara*, or suicide by starvation. Laity give alms to monastics and venerate icons of *tīrthaṅkaras* in order to meditate on their purity and to emulate them in life.

Parsis are a close community, widely respected in India, but segmented off by their endogamous marriages and rejection of conversion. Because human action is needed to defend creation against the forces of decay, asceticism is frowned upon as an irresponsible fleeing from the world. What is needed are good thoughts, words, and deeds. Earth, fire, and water, as parts of creation, are sacred. Fire is particularly important, in homes and in temples, as a center of worship. Regular daily prayers and purification rites allow humans to advance the cause of good in the world. Traditionally, at death, bodies are laid on the top of "Towers of Silence" (round, open-air stone structures) to protect the earth from pollution. The scriptures, the Avesta, consist of a compilation of hymns for liturgical use. Parsi communities in India have relative gender equality and are active in education, industry, and philanthropy.

Unlike Hindus, Sikhs create local congregations through the practice of having communal meals eaten at *gurdwaras* (temples). Sikh communities stress relative caste and gender equality. Worship is centered on reverence for the scriptures, the Guru Granth Sahib ("the last *guru*"), verses of which are sung as hymns and memorized. Guru Nanak was succeeded by nine other gurus. The tenth, Guru Gobind (1666–1708), declared himself the last, left behind the scriptures, and formed a brotherhood of warriors, the Khalsa. Members of the Khalsa must be baptized, take the name "Singh" ("lion"), and wear the "Five K's": *kesh* (uncut hair), *kangha* (wooden comb), *kara* (metal bangle), *kachera* (cotton underclothes), and *kirpan* (dagger). The center of Sikh religion is the Golden Temple in Amritsar.

Tribals hold feasts, sing and dance, and sacrifice to spirits. They celebrate the rites of passage (especially for boys), perform rituals to appease and control nature, and prepare for war with magical means. The cult of manhood can be strong, as in the far northeast where head-hunting was once practiced. Many tribals are now converted to Christianity, and some are in conflict with the government of India over their marginalization by the Hindu majority.

The Indian subcontinent consists of India, Pakistan, Bangladesh, Sri Lanka, Nepal, Bhutan, and the Maldives. India itself is 80.5 percent Hindu, 13.4 percent Muslim, 2.3 percent Christian, 1.9 percent Sikh, 0.8 percent Buddhist, 0.4 percent Jain, and 0.7 percent other (2001 Census of India). Pakistan, which was formed to be an Islamic state, is largely Muslim now (96 percent). Bangladesh, the former

East Pakistan, is also predominantly Muslim (88 percent). Sri Lanka has been tragically divided by a civil war and its aftermath between the Sinhala Buddhists (70 percent) and the Tamil Hindus (15 percent). The smaller countries have state religions: Hinduism in Nepal, Buddhism in Bhutan, and Islam in the Maldives.

Sources

F. G. Bailey. *Tribe, Caste and Nation*. Manchester University Press, 1960.

Alan R. Beals. *Gopalpur: A South Indian Village*. Harcourt Brace, 1980.

Mary Boyce. *Zoroastrians: Their Religious Beliefs and Practices*. Routledge, 1988.

Fred W. Clothey. *Religion in India*. Routledge, 2006.

Paul Dundas. *The Jains*. Routledge, 2002.

Ainslie Embree, ed. *Sources of Indian Tradition*. Vol. 1. Columbia University Press, 1988.

C. J. Fuller. *The Camphor Flame: Popular Hinduism and Society in India*. Princeton University Press, 2004.

Eleanor Nesbitt. *Sikhism: A Very Short Introduction*. Oxford University Press, 2005.

Reading 4 Hinduism: History, Beliefs, Practices

By Richard Fox Young

Years ago, when I began my studies of "Hinduism" (quotation marks seem called for, since many things go by that name), I wanted to get inside of it (insofar as I possibly could) through the life of an individual whom I felt that I knew rather intimately. This, perhaps, was my historian's conceit. The individual had long since passed on, but I had ample material to work with, biographically, opening a window (widely, I thought) onto what it was to be a "traditional" Hindu in Varanasi, the most sacred site of all in Indian geography. The individual I have in mind lived in the nineteenth century and was called Nilakantha, a name for Shiva. Born into a Shaiva family surnamed Goreh, he was a Brahmin of impeccably high status, a Chitpavana. Raised religiously, Nilakantha immersed himself in the Ganges each morning, recited prayers invoking divine blessing, and spent his days mastering a vast corpus of sacred texts, the Vedas. Akin to Greek and Latin, Sanskrit is the language of divinity; for Vedic hermeneutics, Nilakantha needed linguistic tools, grammar, and lexicography. Though born Shaiva, through his studies he became concerned that Shiva lacked virtues that the divine ought to have and devoted himself to Vishnu instead. True to form, his was a life lived Vedically (as a Christian might aspire to live biblically).

Later, I learned of another Hinduism, less Sanskritic, more vernacular, and as enthusiastically Shaiva in orientation as Nilakantha's had been Vaishnava. Here, my historical interlocutor was Arumuka Pillai, a contemporary of Nilakantha's down on the northern tip of Sri Lanka (Jaffna), where Brahmins of any kind were few and far between. As a Vellala of the cultivator caste (which ranks near the bottom of the Hindu social hierarchy), Arumuka was ineligible for Vedic studies, technically. Regionally, however, the Vellala were dominant (being propertied landowners) and pretty much able to do as they pleased. As assiduous in his ablutions as Nilakantha, Arumuka (whose name also gives him away as a Shaivite) immersed himself in a different corpus of sacred texts; these were largely vernacular texts, in Tamil: the *Agamas*. Centered on Shiva, the apical divinity who will brook no rival, they prescribe a temple-based worship that Arumuka was an avid proponent of. This was an alternative universe

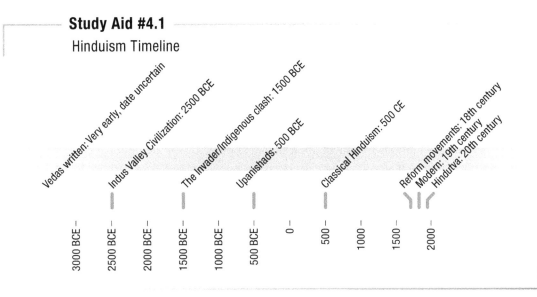

of *Agama*-centric Tamil Hinduism, unlike Nilakantha's Vedic, Sanskritic universe, and it had quite a different kind of gravitational pull.

Later still, back to the north, in a village off the beaten track near Jaipur in Rajasthan, I became acquainted (this time personally) with a woman known locally as Bhawani Ma (Mother Bhawani). Here, outside a small, brightly painted shrine, tended by her husband, a truck driver, in his off-hours, Bhawani Ma enters a deep state of trance, possessed by a goddess, originally (no one can say when) a woman of the Rajput (warrior) caste who had immolated herself on the funeral pyre of her husband, a casualty of snakebite. Villagers approach Bhawani Ma for help; finding lost objects is a specialty of hers, but so too is advice on lost affections. After all, as the perfect wife (perfectly devoted, that is, to her husband), Bhawani Ma knows a thing or two (when possessed) about keeping husbands and wives together. Rajasthan knows of many women like her. Vehicles of the divine, as it were, they embody Shaktism (from *shakti*, literally, "power," associated with goddess worship), the third of India's most prevalent theisms after Vaishnavism and Shaivism.

Much as I would like, one simply cannot cover, globally, all that wears the label "Hinduism" in the overview above. And so, before anything else, one needs clarity on how the phenomena are to be sorted out, which things included and which excluded. Like any religion, Hinduism lives only in the concrete, temporally, and not in the abstract, timelessly. In striving to be an unbiased observer (who, alas, is never fully transparent, even to himself), I aspire to rise above all Hindu normativities by which other Hinduisms are judged (Vaishnava versus Shaiva versus Shakta). That being said, the believer's self-understanding provides an indispensable point of departure; naturally, one's perspective may pose a challenge (and probably will) to one's self-understanding, theologically. One must reflect on such differences, deeply, once the possibility of interreligious understanding exists. Until that point, the rules of engagement are to be construed empirically. Accordingly, when Hindus find it difficult to recognize themselves in each other, I am much impressed (and feel that I may have something to learn from them) that they do not utterly and absolutely deny that the Vaishnava, Shaiva, or Shakta "other" is a Hindu. But I am also content to think of Hinduism (as I do of Christianity) as an agglomeration of things (beliefs, practices, etc.) that can be named "Hinduism" for convenience, but ought not to be treated as an invariable substance. Substance (or essence) is a philosophical concept and, as such, is best left to philosophers; as a historian of religions, I am agnostic on all such questions. In a brief overview, one must also avoid an abracadabra approach, as if the doors of comprehension might magically open up if one could only get the password right. Sufficient unto itself is the task of disagglomeration, and being clear on how it is to be accomplished.

Of my three Hinduisms, here I can include only two, that of Nilakantha and Arumuka; Bhawani Ma cannot make the cut, but only because her "Hinduism" centers on beliefs and practices that have no "orthodox" analogue. Having such analogues is why Hinduisms of the other two escape being cut. In history of religions, orthodoxy simply has to be situational and variable; on another occasion, it might be a good exercise to have a second look at orthodoxy, from Bhawani Ma's point of view. That cannot happen here, however, which is unfortunate. Though not of the mainstream in terms of Vedic respectability, her orthodox rivals, Nilakantha and Arumuka, are clearly a sideshow, demographically. From the time of Robert Redfield, social science and religious studies scholars have denominated Bhawani Ma's "Hinduism" the "Little Tradition," reserving the "Great Tradition" for the likes of my two other "specimen" Hindus. Numberwise, the nomenclature might be reversed; between them, one might imagine the Little Tradition as an ocean, out of which, here and there, Great Tradition islands rise. To go with that image, it helps to think of Great Tradition Hinduism as Sanskritic as opposed to the vernacular Little Tradition; as pan-Indian instead of local; and as a tradition that fosters ambitious goals, soteriologically (e.g., *moksha*, release from transmigration), instead of conjugal harmony and other lesser goods that Bhawani Ma is good at arranging. Neither, though, is sealed off from the other hermetically, and between the two their relationship might be described as a loose-fitting hypostatic union. Hereafter, however, I leave Bhawani Ma aside (but with brief comments, later, on goddesses in "traditional" Hinduism). And with these clarifications, the quotation marks around "Hinduism" can come off.

In one's approach, it helps to be alert to the uneven playing field Hinduism competes on, as it were, when taken out of its natural linguistic medium (Sanskrit or any of the Indian vernaculars). English is up to the task, but any interreligious literacy is going to need a foreign-language vocabulary. To start with, talk of Hinduism as a "religion" seems unavoidable; the very term, however, skews our understanding in ways that are actually very European (and, indeed, Christian). Having used the term, I need to backtrack and correct the misapprehension that Hinduism is about holding Hindu beliefs in a correct—that is, orthodox—way. Nothing could be further from the truth, although Hinduism is not utterly laissez-faire, beliefwise. "Faith," if one can call it that (*shraddha*), has a grammar, and religious claims cannot be made willy-nilly. Still, one has to understand that orthodoxy in Hinduism is

Vaishnava	642 million
Shaiva	250 million
Shaktism	30 million
Neo-Hinduism	20 million
Reform Hinduisms	5 million

mainly about orthopraxy, the norms of right conduct. Behavior is, or ought to be, guided and regulated, punished and rewarded by *dharma* (from a verb meaning to "uphold" or "sustain"), making it a poor candidate to carry the heavily cognitive, belief-oriented burden of the word "religion." This, however, it has been made to do (Hinduism now being called *Hindudharma*, Christianity *Khrishtadharma*, etc.), and so to recover a clear sense of it, one needs to strip it of any vestige of normativity with respect to belief. There is pushback from this in the complaint one often hears from Hindus who say that Hinduism is not so much a religion as a "way of life."

Norms for the Hindu "way of life" have been derived from the sacred corpus called Veda ("knowledge"), of hoary antiquity. The oldest collection, dating to the early second millennium BCE, is the *Rig*, containing "hymns" of praise to gods (*deva*) and goddesses (*devi*). In today's pantheon, few of these retain a place. Nor are the later collections, the *Sama* (songs), *Yajur* (ritual formulas), and *Atharva* (hymns and incantations) living texts, except in a rather attenuated sense. The priestly (brahminical) cultus of which they were the mainstay found itself gradually superseded by the Hinduisms remaining to be mentioned. Still, the basic morphology of Hinduism is discernible in the Veda. One can trace back to this—including the Upanishads, the last stratum of all, which predates the Christian era—the origin of notions having to do with *karma* (the postmortem fruition of human actions, good and evil), of beginningless rebirth and redeath (*samsara*), and of final liberation or release (*moksha*) from, as it were, a cosmic merry-go-round that never stops, eschatologically. Populating this cosmos, the Veda talks of four categories of persons (*varnas*): the quartet of Brahmins (ritualists), Kshatriyas (warriors and rulers), Vaishyas (commoners), and Shudras (serfs). Ideally, life was envisioned as involving, sequentially, youth and study, adulthood and householdership, old age and renunciation in quest of final liberation. Note, though, that *dharma* was unexchangeable; neither universal nor individualized, one's *dharma* was defined by birth. Therefore, there was no single Hindu "way of life."

Impressive as it looks, a society of this description may not have existed, actually; the description is less a real morphology *of* ancient India than an ideal morphology *for* it. Hinduisms taking shape from the Christian era onward began to emerge with specificities of their own. One myth that has to be punctured is that the Veda offers a template for understanding Hindu society today. To start with, the social hierarchy on the ground is vastly more complicated than one might imagine, extrapolating from ancient texts. Overall, castes number in the thousands; in any locality, one finds several dozen. Interactions between them (involving commensality, marriage, etc.) are regulated, biosocially, by complex notions based on purity and impurity unrelated to the social functions of priest, warrior or ruler, commoner, and serf. The textual prototype omits any mention of "untouchability," even though much of the Indian population still carries that stigma (modern constitutional safeguards notwithstanding).

Hugely important for the impact it had on Hinduism's social profile, the exclusion of "untouchables" from the temple-based cultus was mitigated by the rise to prominence of *bhakti*, a less structured form of devotional theism more open to all and less regulatable, brahminically. Arising in tandem are three sectarian formations (called *sampradayas*) oriented toward one of the three divinities already alluded to, whose rise to prominence can be seen in the Veda: Vishnu; Shiva; and Devi, the goddess (whose followers are called, respectively, Vaishnavas, Shaivas, and Shaktas). Though deeply sectarian, such Hinduisms are monolatric, overall; that is to say, though centered on a particular divinity, the reality and even the limited efficacy of other divinities are not absolutely denied (yet they may be inferiorized, intentionally and more or less publicly, depending on context).

A last difference of note is the existence of an extensive body of extra-Vedic sacred texts barnacled onto each of the three sectarian formations already mentioned, but playing a huge role in Hindu religious life, down to the present. Of my three "specimen" Hindus, Nilakantha and Arumuka lived largely within this extra-Vedic realm (Arumuka more than Nilakantha); Bhawani Ma's ties even to extra-Vedic texts are far looser. Best of all would be to dispense with the notion of "canon" as too restrictive (and Christian). The Bhagavad Gita ("Song of the Blessed Lord") is a case in point. Nowadays considered the Hindu scripture par excellence, the Gita is actually a chapter in the Mahabharata, one of the great Vaishnava epics in which Krishna, one of Vishnu's *avatars* (from a verb meaning "descend"), instructs Arjuna, a warrior, on the indestructibility of the *atman* (literally, "self," derivatively, "soul"). Being extra-Vedic makes no difference to its popularity, even beyond Vaishnavism.

Study Aid #4.3

Hindu Beliefs

Brahman: The Oneness of all.

Brahman-atman: The division of the world we see into *Brahman* and individual selves; or a unity that includes all.

Samsara: The endless round of rebirths that all experience.

Karma: The value (positive and negative) one accrues for doing (or not doing) one's duty.

Dharma: Duty, determined by birth, caste, *jati*.

Moksha: Freedom or release from *samsara*.

Time rolls on, but religions do too, and among the newer Hinduisms having distinctive orientations, neo-Hinduism is perhaps the foremost. Emerging first in Calcutta (Kolkata) in Bengal in the early 1800s (but also elsewhere on the Indian periphery where Europe converged on India most palpably), neo-Hinduism pushes beyond the parameters of Vedic and even extra-Vedic sacred texts and manifests a remarkable receptivity to religions that, historically, were altogether extra-Hindu—Islam and Christianity in particular. Beginning with Ram Mohun Roy (1772–1833), who acted as a conduit for both Islamic and Christian influence, a movement gained momentum that came to be called the Bengal Renaissance, an efflorescence of cross-cultural and interreligious interaction. An ardent proponent of Hindu "reform," Roy called on Hindus to renounce their monolatric ways and worship the *one* true God, the Unconditioned *Brahman*, aniconically. Though his "Society of [Friends of] Brahman" (the Brahmo Samaj) lasted but a few years, Roy was a seminal figure who inspired many, including the preeminent neo-Hindu of all, Mahatma K. Gandhi (1867–1947). Genealogically, all neo-Hinduism enjoys an affinity of outlook that might be called universalistic to the nth degree, making it averse to being labeled an "ordinary" religion on a par with others. As Wilhelm Halbfass (1991, 51) observes:

> Instead, it is—according to this view—a framework, a concordance and unifying totality of sects … . It is said to be the "eternal religion," religion in or behind all religions, a kind of "metareligion," a structure potentially ready to comprise and reconcile within itself all the religions of the world, just as it contains and reconciles the so-called Hindu sects, such as Shaivism or Vaishnavism and their subordinate "sectarian" formations.

Nowadays, most of the Hinduisms introduced above flourish abroad wherever the South Asian Diaspora is found. That being so, an exclusively book-based—even or especially an iHindu internet-based—interreligious literacy ought to be discouraged. Around the corner or down the block, one has in one's neighborhood unparalleled opportunities for observing "living" texts—believers themselves—making theology "visible" in worship at the different temples that now dot our landscapes. "The history of religions," as Diana Eck (2001, 22) says, "is unfolding before our eyes."

Sources

Wendy Doniger. *Hindu Myths*. Penguin, 2004.

Diana Eck. *A New Religious America: How a "Christian Country" Has Become the World's Most Religiously Diverse Nation*. HarperSanFrancisco, 2001.

Wilhelm Halbfass. *Tradition and Reflection: Explorations in Indian Thought*. SUNY Press, 1991.

Arvind Sharma. *Classical Hindu Thought: An Introduction*. Oxford University Press, 2001.

Reading 5 Buddhism: History, Beliefs, Practices

By Terry C. Muck

History

Buddhism is a cross-cultural religion founded in India by a man named Siddhartha Gautama (563–483 BCE). After extensive sampling of all the religions India of his day had to offer, from high-caste Hindu wealth and privilege to a wide range of ascetic practices in the forest with other holy men (*sannyasin*), he discovered the Middle Way. Henceforth known as the Buddha (the Enlightened One), he spent the remaining fifty years of his life as a traveling mendicant preacher, teaching and preaching in the northeastern Indian and Nepali provinces of his birth and early life.

Gautama Buddha's teaching was successful. He quickly gained a following that continued to grow after his death. His immediate followers held two councils shortly after his death, one to rehearse all they could remember of his teaching and his rules for monastic practice, the other to discuss divergent opinions that had arisen as to teaching and practice since his death. This second council is usually seen as the beginnings of sectarian Buddhist schools developing. This diversity was both a response to the shape the teaching took as it spread into cultures different from its culture of origin and also an enabler of that same geographical spread.

Buddhism's widest diffusion, however, came as a result of the coming to power of the Mauryan political dynasty, which managed to unify much of the Indian subcontinent. The third ascender to the dynastic throne, Asoka, advertised his beloved Buddhism by chiseling messages on rock pillars throughout and especially on the borders of his kingdom. He culminated this work by calling a council of Buddhist leaders, a meeting that resulted in the sending of Buddhist missionaries, called *mahadhammarakkhitas* or *dharmadhatus*, to the surrounding countries such as Sri Lanka, Myanmar, Thailand, Cambodia, Pakistan, and central Asia.

In the succeeding centuries, Buddhism continued its spread into central, northern, and East Asia. It reached China in 40 CE, Korea in 350, Japan in 575, Tibet in 640, and Mongolia in the 1300s.

The Buddha's teaching had obvious cross-cultural appeal, and its capacity, typical of Asian religious systems, to form relatively functional partnerships with whatever indigenous religions it came in contact with—Taoism and Confucianism in China, shamanism in Korea, Shinto in Japan, Bon in Tibet—proved to be uniquely effective.

Buddhist ideas spread to Europe and the West (during and after the eighteenth century) by means of two of the three traditional modes of religious diffusion: military, merchants, and missionaries. (The diffusion of Buddhism has been remarkably free of military attachments, at least when compared with the other missionary religions of the world.) The British East India Company came in contact with Buddhists in India and Southeast Asia. Roman Catholic, Reformed, and Wesleyan missionaries followed in the traces dug by Portuguese, Dutch, and British traders. Missionaries did the first translations of Buddhist texts, and their influence created a demand for "Oriental" studies at Cambridge and Oxford. Soon after those academic programs were established, Ivy League universities in the United States followed suit, teaching courses in Eastern philosophies and religious ideas, resulting in a form of philosophical thinking called transcendentalism.

In the twentieth century it wasn't just Buddhist ideas that came West, but Buddhists themselves. Three waves of Asian immigrants washed across American shores. The first came as laborers necessary to build the infrastructure to support the California gold rush in the late nineteenth and early twentieth centuries. The second wave, in the post–World War I years, was so successful that it created a backlash in the form of a series of restrictive immigration laws in the 1920s. The third wave came as a result of a revising of those immigration laws. The New Immigration Act of 1965 was Asian-immigrant friendly and had the effect of encouraging migration from Asian countries. Of course, a steady growth of South and Southeast Asian, Chinese, and East Asian immigrants in the last quarter of the twentieth century made United States Buddhism in the twenty-first century a religious denomination of significant size, perhaps two to three million strong.

Beliefs

What Siddhartha Gautama discovered sitting in deep meditation under the Bo-Tree at the age of thirty—what made him a Buddha, an Enlightened One—was based on the common Indian worldview that assumed everyone is enmeshed in a series of rebirths (*samsara*) that are based in quality on the positive or negative value of one's actions (*karma*). But whereas most Indian religious traditions taught that the value of one's *karma* was based on strict adherence to caste duty (*dharma*), the Buddha taught that it was recognition through trial and error of the truth of his teachings—what came to be known as the Four Noble Truths—that determined the positive or negative value of one's karmic deeds.

The First Noble Truth—that all is suffering (*dukkha*)—is the linchpin of the entire system. We suffer, the Buddha taught, because we see permanence where there is only impermanence (*anicca*). We want to rely on things—fame, money, honor, achievement—that only have fleeting value. Even

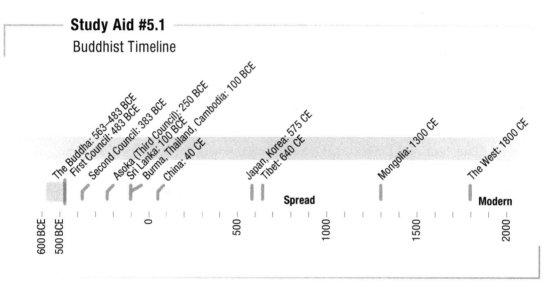
if we retreat to belief in only one enduring entity, our human self or soul, we are mistaken. Gautama Buddha taught that even our own selves, while real, are only temporary constructs, or no-self (*anatta*). Everything is impermanent. But because we desperately want to cling to some enduring reality, we suffer.

The Second Noble Truth explains the origin of our suffering, of our intractable desire to hold on to something lasting. We are caught, the Buddha said, in an ongoing spiral of existence that operates on the simple basis of cause and effect. He called the spiral *paticca samuppada*, the circle of dependent origination. Our existence is made up of a repeating cycle of twelve links in a chain of cause and effect, moving from birth to becoming to craving to clinging, through personhood to ignorance and death—and back to birth again. The cycle of dependent origination displays a sophisticated understanding of human psychology unmatched in the other cultures of the world.

The Third Noble Truth teaches a way out of the endless round of rebirths. One breaks the cycle of existence by controlling one of the links of the chain, the desire (*tanha*) link. A full intuitive understanding of suffering and impermanence leads to a cessation of desire for an eternal self. Once desire for such an existence ceases, rebirth ends. The state that follows is called enlightenment when referring to an individual. But since the enlightened individual ceases, another term, *nirvana*, sometimes translated as "emptiness," is used to designate the eventual end of karmic existence.

The Fourth Noble Truth, the Noble Eightfold Path, implicitly acknowledges that most of us do not become enlightened in this lifetime and continue on in conditioned existence. We are reborn. The dynamics for living in conditioned existence sometimes seem at odds with the overall goal of *nirvana*. One lives as if this life matters, as if a good rebirth based on acquiring good *karma* through merit-making activity leads to a permanent, enduring existence. But the Noble Eightfold Path—right livelihood, speech, action, energy, concentration, mindfulness, thought, and wisdom—is an interim ethic, a way of living here and now that will most likely enable us to make spiritual progress in understanding the first three Noble Truths, and will eventually in some future life lead to enlightenment.

Three different schools of Buddhism have traditionally been identified, although each of these three major schools has many subschools. *Theravada* Buddhism is the Buddhism of Southeast Asia, countries such as Sri Lanka, Thailand, Burma (Myanmar), Cambodia, and Laos. Theravada means "words of the elders," and Theravadins often claim—with some justification—that they are the oldest of the Buddhist schools. *Mahayana* means "great vehicle" and is the Buddhism of China, Japan, and Korea. Their defining characteristic is the *bodhisattva* ideal (see below). *Vajrayana* means Diamond Vehicle and is the school primarily located in Tibet and Mongolia.

Practices

In practice, then, Buddhists seem to cope with existence on two levels, the level of *samsara*, or conditioned existence (rebirth), and the level of *nirvana*, or enlightenment (release from rebirth). At the samsaric level, Buddhist laypeople do things that earn them positive *karma* (merit) such as feeding and clothing monks (*bhikkhus*), and attending temple services for protection and veneration of the images of the Buddha. Such merit-making activities, if assiduously followed, lead to better rebirths, the theoretical aim of which is to enable the people leading those lives to continue to work on the more important problem of their enlightenment.

In order to do the more ethereal work of enlightenment, meditative skill is required. Two dominant schools of meditation have developed. In Theravada (southern) Buddhist countries, insight (*vipassana*) meditative practice was/is the method of choice. In the Mahayana (northern) Buddhist countries of China, Japan, and Korea, an a-rational approach called Zen meditation became popular. In Vajrayana, Tibetan, and Mongolian countries, other types of meditative practice utilizing mandalas and visualization developed. Although quite distinctive in terms of practice, all Buddhist meditative practices aim at enabling the practitioner to enter into the oneness of being—or the nothingness of nonbeing. All of these various types of meditation have become mainstays of Buddhism in Western countries, where it appears a lack of sophisticated meditative traditions have made Buddhism appealing.

In Mahayana Buddhist countries, an important social ethic of sorts grew up around a concept known as the *bodhisattva* ideal. The *bodhisattva* is an almost-enlightened person who instead of going on to achieve the final extinction within his or her grasp chooses to devote his or her considerable spiritual resources to helping others make progress on the spiritual path. *Bodhisattvas* take on the aura of divine helpers to whom one can turn for spiritual succor. They tend to become known for particular core virtues such as compassion (e.g., Kuan Yin) or wisdom (e.g., Manjusri).

Historically Buddhism flourished under political monarchies where a symbiotic relationship between king and religion flourished. Monarchs provided Buddhist monastic orders with patronage and protection. Monks provided kings with religio-spiritual advice and, when necessary, divine mandates for rule. This traditional partnership has been tested in more modern democratic pluralisms and nationalisms where religious plurality has replaced established religions. A similar symbiosis has traditionally existed between laypersons and monastics, who together formed the spiritual hierarchy. Again, in modern egalitarian Western cultures, privileged monastic orders are not seen as a benefit to societal function. Laypersons, therefore, have had to find alternative arenas for gaining merit and spiritual altruistic outlets. Some have turned to social service in a movement known as Engaged Buddhism.

As a cross-cultural, missionary religion, Buddhism has always exhibited an exemplary capacity to shape itself to fit into an existing culture and its mores without losing its essential core. In modern times, a globalized, urbanized Buddhism has taken root across the globe; it is a Buddhism that is characterized by individualized meditative practice, a portable metaphysic congenial to global culture, and an epistemology that fits postmodern thought very well. This has not been done to the exclusion, however, of more culturally specific Buddhisms across Asia.

Buddhism is a growing religion in the world today. Although it is not growing as fast as Islam and Christianity, it has spread into the traditionally Christian populations of Europe and North America. It is probably the fourth-largest religion in the world (behind Christianity, Islam, and Hinduism) with as many as 350 million members worldwide (excluding Chinese Buddhists, who are difficult

---

Study Aid #5.3
Buddhist Divisions

Theravada: 177 million
Mahayana: 264 million
Vajrayana: 28 million
Western: 10 million

to count). It is the dominant religion (more than 50 percent of the population) in eight countries around the world.

Sources

Edward Conze, ed. *Buddhist Scriptures*. Penguin, 1959.

Peter Harvey. *An Introduction to Buddhism*. Cambridge University Press, 1990.

Damien Keown. *Buddhism: A Very Short Introduction*. Oxford University Press, 2000.

Donald Lopez, ed. *Buddhism in Practice*. Princeton University Press, 1995.

John Powers. *Introduction to Tibetan Buddhism*. Snow Lion, 1995.

Walpola Rahula. *What the Buddha Taught*. Grove, 1974.

Paul Williams. *Mahayana Buddhism*. Routledge, 1989.

END OF UNIT QUESTIONS

Directions: Use what you have learned in Unit II to respond to the questions below.

1. What is the Hindu understanding of divinity?

2. What is dharma, and how does it differ between Hinduism and Buddhism?

3. Should Buddhism be called a religion if it does not profess faith in a supreme being?

FOR FURTHER READING

Bhaskarananda, Swami. *The Essentials of Hinduism: A Comprehensive Overview of the World's Oldest Religion.* 2nd ed. Seattle: Viveka, 2002.

Eck, Diana L. *India: A Sacred Geography.* New York: Harmony, 2012.

Flood, Gavin, ed. *The Blackwell Companion to Hinduism.* Oxford: Blackwell, 2003.

Keown, Damien. *Buddhism: A Very Short Introduction.* 2nd ed. Oxford: Oxford University Press, 2013.

Harvey, Peter. *An Introduction to Buddhism: Teachings, History, and Practices.* 2nd ed. Cambridge: Cambridge University Press, 2012.

UNIT III

The Chinese Religions

The Chinese Religions

Editor's Introduction

This section includes three readings that are similarly organized as those in the previous section. The first reading, "China: History, Beliefs, Practices" by Jonathan Seitz, introduces you to the place and culture of China, where Daoism and Confucianism developed. The country of China has a rich history of empires and kingdoms, as well as a strong tradition of beliefs and many religious practices. Even though China now has a communist government, this reality does not hinder the development and practices of various religious traditions. Historically, the Chinese people developed many different religious traditions and also accepted many new ones, such as Buddhism and Christianity, into their country. The religions that are in China are not stagnant. They continue to meld with the culture and in turn shape China's culture today as well.

The reading "Daoist Traditions and Practices" by Mario Poceski describes the history and development of Daoism. This religion is unique to China; however, today it has found its way into popular culture worldwide, with such popular symbols as the yin/yang and I Ching. There are many different elements in Daoism that inform its development: dynastic empires, politics, alchemy, spirituality, philosophy, and religion. But some people have defined Daoism by one of these rather than seeing how all of these elements are part of the whole of the tradition.

The reading "Confucianism" by Archie J. Bahm provides a perspective on this tradition. It helps us understand Confucianism as a tradition, a philosophy, a religion, a way of governing, or simply a way of life. Confucianism developed from what was later called the Hundred Schools of Thought, from the teachings of the Chinese philosopher Confucius (551–479 BCE), who considered himself a codifier and transmitter of the theology and values inherited from the Shang (c. 1600–1046 BCE) and Zhou (c. 1046–256 BCE) dynasties. Confucianism continued to develop alongside the changes within Chinese society and history.

Reading 6 China: History, Beliefs, Practices

By Jonathan Seitz

"C hinese" may describe a nation, civilization, ethnic group, or one of many linguistic groups; and Chinese religions include most of the major world religions, as well as a variety of local, popular, or folk religions. In popular culture and some scholarship, it is common to speak of the "three religions" or "three teachings" (*sanjiao*): Confucianism (or Ruism), Daoism, and Buddhism (*rujiao, daojiao, fojiao*). These traditions find parallels in Korea and Japan, where Daoism as the indigenous religion is replaced by the system of mediums or Shinto. Chinese themselves often describe the three teachings as complementary, using expressions such as *sanjiao guiyi* ("the three teachings derive from the same source"). Chinese religion more broadly is shaped by shared life rituals, a coherent Chinese cosmology, and family and government traditions that have shaped contemporary Chinese religion.

History and Beliefs

One of the earliest records of Chinese religious practice was oracle bones, which dated to the Shang dynasty and were used for divination. The bones provide much of the earliest information on Chinese writing. During the following centuries a rich religious culture grew and developed. Chinese religion is sometimes seen as being based on *qi* (breath, air, or energy), complementary duality (*yin* and *yang*), and the five elements that were seen as constituting life. Early writings, including the Yijing or Book of Changes, were eventually incorporated into a Ruist/Confucian canon. Other practices, including purification rituals, healing rites, and regional festivals, were aggregated into Daoist and popular religious schools or sects.

Confucianism is the Jesuit Latinized rendering of the name of Confucius (Kongzi), which may give the mistaken impression that Confucianism is the distillation of a single person's teachings. Scholars now often prefer Ruism ("the learned or scholarly teaching"), which better respects the diversity of Confucian belief and practice. Kongzi (Confucius: 551–479 BCE) helped systematize the Chinese classics and according to tradition assembled the five classics (wujing), composed of the Book of Changes, the Book of Poetry, the Book of Rituals, the Book of History, and the Spring and Autumn Annals. His own writings, collected in the *Analects* (Lunyu), provided greater coherence to the project. Kongzi developed a number of earlier concepts, most notably humanity (*ren*), righteousness (*yi*), loyalty (*zhong*), reciprocity (*shu*), and propriety (*li*).

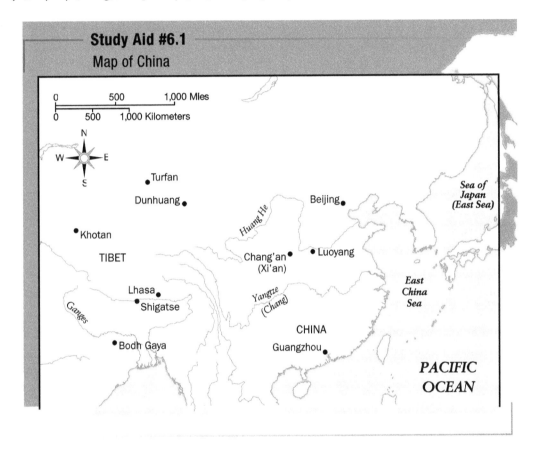

Study Aid #6.1
Map of China

Near contemporaries Mengzi (Mencius: 372–289 BCE) and Xunzi (312–230 BCE) became associated with Confucius as part of a shared school or approach. By the Han dynasty (206 BCE–220 CE), Confucianism garnered political support and became associated with the state ideology of the dynastic system. Later movements are sometimes dubbed neo-Confucianism, and Confucianism is understood to include practically any system related to the state or Chinese culture. While it has often been associated with a single ethnicity, Confucianism also profited from the innovation of foreign-led dynasties, such as the Yuan, which created the national examination system, China's version of civil service exams. Confucianism is closely aligned with state ideology, but in the modern period, advocates have employed it in seeking an ethnic identity that is not dependent on communist ideology or in expressing an authentic identity apart from a single government. The Confucian program took on renewed vigor with the neo-Confucianism of Zhuxi, Wang Yangming, and the Cheng brothers. Under Zhuxi (1130–1200), the four books were codified alongside the five classics. The four books are *The Great Learning*, *The Doctrine of the Mean*, *The Analects* (of Confucius), and the *Mencius*.

Daoism ("the teaching of the way") drew on earlier Chinese cosmology, including the ideas of yin-yang complementary duality and a physical world composed of five elements. The two principal works of the formative period were Laozi's *Daodejing* (*Classic of the Way and Righteousness*) and the *Zhuangzi* (named after its author). Both books include Confucius as a minor character, and Daoism is often seen, in contrast to Confucianism, as a return to the pristine natural order that exists apart from civilization. Daoism is sometimes separated into philosophical and religious Daoism (*Daojia* and *Daojiao*), although such a distinction should not be overdrawn. Significantly, religious Daoism grew out of a set of early cosmology, rituals, and practices, often seeking to deal with the daily concerns of life, life transitions, or the ideal of a long life. In time, Daoism was organized into schools. The Daoist canon, once passed down exclusively through ritual communication and ordination, is now available in libraries, although it includes nearly five thousand texts.

Buddhism ("teaching of the Buddha") has existed in China for almost two millennia; it was carried along the Silk Road during the Eastern Han dynasty (25–220 CE). Buddhism is unique among the three teachings in its foreign origins, a fact that made it an occasional object of censorship or persecution (early notable persecutions occurred 452–66 and 547–78). The name of the Buddha is the transliteration of a non-Chinese word. Buddhism arrived in China in several successive waves, bringing missionaries from south and central Asia who gradually translated the scriptures. Chinese

Buddhism, even from the early years, was largely Mahayana. Monastic structures and the written canon helped institutionalize Buddhism in China, but ideals of celibacy and poverty (including relying on others for alms) added to the foreign association. Nonetheless, Buddhism found patrons and developed key forms of devotion, including festivals, pilgrimages, the construction of monasteries and stupas, and the printing of tracts and other materials. Translation was a prized activity and accompanied the proliferation of texts, from the smaller Pali and Sanskrit canons to the much larger Chinese and Tibetan canons.

Study Aid #6.3
Dynasties of China

Ancient
  Xia: 2100–1600 BCE
  Shang: 1600–1046
  Zhou: 1045–256
Imperial
  Qin: 221–206
  Han: 206 BCE–220 CE
  Three Kingdoms: 220–80
  Jin: 265–420
  Southern/Northern: 420–589
  Sui: 581–618
  Tang: 618–907
  Five Dynasties and Ten Kingdoms: 907–60
  Song: 960–1279
  Yuan: 1279–1368
  Ming: 1368–1644
  Qing: 1644–1911
Modern
  Republic of China: 1912–49
  People's Republic of China: 1949–present

Scholars of Chinese religions have sometimes challenged the three teachings emphasis. The *sanjiao* approach is itself an innovation of an earlier *erjiao* approach that predated Buddhism, and there have been proposals for a *wujiao* understanding of the religions, adding Christianity and Islam to the traditional three religions. There has also been major debate within these traditions. The complexity of Chinese religion may also be reflected in the difference between what Robert Redfield called the great and little traditions. An early influential essay by Arthur Wolf spoke of

Chinese religion as including "gods, ghosts, and ancestors." Gods were beings who could answer petitions or respond to needs and problems. Ghosts were usually malevolent beings. Ancestors, if well cared for, could protect and preserve the present generation. Each was seen as a distinct category of supernatural activity.

There is considerable debate over the "Protestantization" of Chinese religions, including the tendency of modern interpreters to philosophize and textualize Chinese religions, prioritizing or creating a canon that may not reflect the broad sweep of Chinese religions.

Practices

With massive canons and a high tolerance for heterodoxy, Chinese religion has rarely taken a creedal form. Instead, official schools, local practice, and mystic rites sometimes coalesce. China is often described as having a coherent cosmology. Chinese practices draw heavily on the yin-yang, five-elements cosmology. Consequently, years follow a sixty-year cycle (twelve months or elements repeated five times). Rituals may be based in the family system (veneration of ancestors) as well as the human life cycle (birth, death) or various community rituals (anything related to temple life, especially festivals). There are also important days during the year when the ancestors deserve special attention. The major traditional Chinese holiday is the New Year, which is still based on the lunar calendar.

Chinese gods—Buddhist, Daoist, or other—are organized within pantheons, or collections of gods, which vary according to geography and period. The pantheon system mirrors the broader Chinese bureaucracy, with gods holding distinct rank and positions in the larger pantheon. Appeals may be made to a god to help with specific problems or tasks, to reduce suffering in hell, or to aid the ancestors. Major Buddhist buddhas and bodhisatvas, including Mañjuśrī, Avalokiteśvara, and Maitreya, all became subjects of devotion in China. Historical figures from the religions have developed popular cults also, and there are often temples or statues to figures such as Kongzi, a popular figure for students taking exams; or to Guangong, the Daoist god of war; or Mazu, a popular goddess for sailors and those by the ocean.

Chinese Buddhism is principally Mahayana, with a wide variety of tantric practices included. An important minority movement is tantric Buddhism of Tibet (arrived in the seventh century CE) and Mongolia (where it was adopted by the Mongol rulers of China in the thirteenth century). Beyond the contemporary implications, central Asian Buddhism exerted a strong influence on China proper through empire (Mongol and Manchu), tribute relations (where vassal nations brought tribute to the emperor), and pilgrimage. Tibetan Buddhism includes several distinct practices, including lineages of enlightened beings (the lamas), as well as a Tibetan canon and a variety of monastic and lay traditions.

There are a variety of pantheons (collections of gods) that may be influenced by time, geography, or tradition. Thus Buddhist and Daoist canons have substantial overlap. In one exceptional case, Jesus and Mary were interpolated into an eighteenth-century Daoist book of gods. Daoists also perform a wide range of rituals, including the *jiao*, a community-based purification rite. Priests might also perform rituals for the dead, help with healing and health issues, or assist in divining the best response to a problem.

Because of the size of China (as civilization, empire, or nation), communities from virtually all world religions have been present in China, including the Abrahamic religions as well as transplant communities from central Asian religions. Jews, Christians, and Muslims have all had major communities in China, although usually they have been understood as different ethnically from the Han majority. There are now two major Muslim populations, the Hui, who live throughout China, and the Uyghur, who tend to live in the northwest (Xinjiang). Today the People's Republic of China religion bureau regulates five official religions (Buddhism, Catholicism, Daoism, Islam, and Protestantism).

Sources

Catherine Bell. "Religion and Chinese Culture: Toward an Assessment of 'Popular Religion.'" *History of Religions* 29, no. 1 (August 1989): 35–57.

Kenneth Ch'en. *Buddhism in China: A Historical Survey*. Princeton University Press, 1964.

Donald Lopez, ed. *Religions of China in Practice*. Princeton University Press, 1996.

Daniel Overmyer, with Gary Arbuckle, Dru Gladney, John McRae, Rodney Taylor, Stephen Teiser, and Franciscus Verellen. "Chinese Religions: The State of the Field. Part II, Living Religious Traditions: Taoism, Confucianism, Buddhism, Islam, and Popular Religion." *The Journal of Asian Studies* 54, no. 2 (May 1995): 314–21.

Daniel Overmyer, with David Kneightley, Edward Shaugnessy, Constance Cook, and Donald Harper. "Chinese Religions: The State of the Field. Part I, Early Religious Traditions: The Neolithic Period through the Han Dynasty (ca. 4000 BCE to 220 CE)." *The Journal of Asian Studies* 54, no. 1 (February 1995): 124–60.

N. Standaert, ed. *Handbook of Christianity in China*. Vol. 1. Brill, 2001.

C. K. Yang. *Religion in Chinese Society: A Study of Contemporary Social Functions of Religion and Some of Their Historical Factors*. University of California Press, 1961.

Fenggang Yang. *Religion in China: Survival and Revival under Communist Rule*. Oxford University Press, 2011.

Reading 7 Daoist Traditions and Practices

By Mario Poceski

In This [Reading]

This reading continues the historical survey of Daoism [...], covering the medieval and late imperial periods. The first two sections focus on Shangqing (Supreme Clarity) and Lingbao (Numinous Treasure), the main scriptural corpuses and traditions of medieval Daoism. That is followed by coverage of other key traditions and elements of Daoism, including ritual, sacred texts, political involvement, monasticism, and contemplative practice.

Main Topics

- Origins of the Shangqing revelations and the teachings of the Daoist tradition that grew around them.
- Emergence of the Lingbao tradition and the scope of Buddhist influences evidenced in its texts.
- Codifications of Daoist ritual and contributions made in that area by the Lingbao tradition.
- Formation of the Daoist canon and functions of the texts contained in it.
- General patterns of imperial patronage and the relationship between Daoism and the Chinese state.
- Interreligious debates and interactions among representatives of the three teachings.
- Formation of Daoist monastic orders and the basic character of their institutions and ideals.
- Prominent roles of women and their status in Daoist history.
- Practice of meditation and cultivation of interior alchemy.

The Shangqing Revelations

During the 364–370 period a medium called Yang Xi (330–386) reportedly received a series of divine revelations, which became foundations for a new school of Daoism. The divinities, said to have appeared to Yang at night, were members of a celestial class of beings superior to the legendary immortals of earlier Daoist lore. They were new-fangled celestial spirits or "perfected" beings (*zhenren*) that descended from a high heaven named Supreme Clarity (Shangqing, also known as Highest Clarity or Highest Purity). That became the name for the whole corpus of revealed scriptures and the school of Daoism that grew around them. The celestial spirits that purportedly communicated to Yang a variety of novel Daoist teachings included Lady Wei, who in her last earthly existence was a libationer in the Celestial Masters tradition with the name Wei Huacun (251–334), while others among them had never experienced imperfect human existence. Yang, who was a talented calligrapher, then wrote down the revealed teachings in a form that could be shared with the rest of humanity.

Yang Xi was employed by the Xu family, which was a member of the southern aristocracy and was related to the family of Ge Hong [...]. The Shangqing revelations were initially communicated via Yang to the Xu family, whose members addressed a variety of queries—some spiritually oriented, by others of a more prosaic or pragmatic nature—to the divine beings that revealed themselves to Yang. Eventually other families of similar standing became involved in the same process. Accordingly, the new movement initially grew within a fairly narrow social milieu constituted by elite southern families. While proud of their illustrious ancestry, at the time these families felt marginalized by the recent arrival of emigrants within elite backgrounds from the North, who moved south together with the imperial court of the Jin dynasty after the fall of its capital to foreign invaders in 316 CE.

As the northerners established their political control in the South, they also set up their own cultural traditions and religious institutions. That included Celestial Masters Daoism, which initiated a program of suppression of local religious movements. The initial rise of the Shangqing tradition can be seen as a particular mode of Southern response to the loss of sociopolitical power and the encroachment of alien culture. By introducing new Daoist teachings, allegedly revealed by superior deities than those of the Celestial Masters, segments of the southern aristocracy turned the tables around. Effectively, they upended the northern interlopers by establishing themselves as possessors of a superior Daoist lore.

Notwithstanding claims made regarding the newness of the revelations, the Shangqing scriptures did not represent a revolutionary break from preceding Daoist traditions. Basically they incorporated a range of teachings and practices derived from the major strands of Daoism that existed at the time. That included doctrines and techniques associated with seekers of immortality such as Ge Hong, although with a changed emphasis, as external (laboratory) alchemy was deemphasized at the expense of contemplative practices or reinterpreted in a metaphorical manner. There were also substantial borrowings from Celestial Masters Daoism and popular religion. There were even traces of Buddhist influences, which are indicative of the growing clout of the foreign religion. The Buddhist influences, however, were relatively superficial, especially when compared with the extensive borrowings of Buddhist elements evident in later Daoist texts and traditions.

The scriptures of the Shangqing corpus—which collectively represent a coherent body of canonical literature—were at the center of the Shangqing school. The texts' popularity was to a large extent based on their considerable literary value, which reflected the importance and high respect attached to writing within elite Chinese culture. As Yang Xi attempted to replicate in literary Chinese idiom the arcane and rarefied speech of his celestial interlocutors, he created ingenious literary works that are remarkable for their poetic language, abstruse vocabulary, resourceful use of metaphors, and rich symbolism. The texts' literary qualities inspired and influenced later generations of poets and writers, as can be seen from the copious allusions that appear in a range of writings composed during the medieval period.

At its core, the Shangqing school was a tradition of Daoism based on sacred texts, which were deemed to have divine origins. At first the scriptures were carefully transmitted from master to disciple within a limited socioreligious milieu, primarily constituted by persons with upper-class background. They were meant only for a select group of people, who by virtue of possessing the texts were given access to the sacred realms of the perfected. Consequently, there were rules that regulated their transmission, which contained prohibition of their dissemination to unworthy recipients. These select groups of well-educated individuals, often linked by family ties, gradually evolved into religious confraternities dedicated to study of the scriptures and cultivation of the practices explicated in them. The expansions of the movement led to increased institutionalization. That encompassed the development of distinctive rituals, ecclesiastical hierarchy, and monastic communities supported by the faithful, all of which became integral parts of the Chinese religious landscape. By the sixth century the Shangqing school became the most influential and respected tradition of Daoism, and it retained that status well into the tenth century.

Among the leading figures within the early Shangqing movement was the famous scholar Tao Hongjing (456–536)—sometimes depicted as the de facto founder of the school—who collected, edited, and disseminated the Shangqing scriptures, as well as writing commentaries on them. Coming from the familiar social milieu of southern aristocrats—his family was related to the Ge and Xu families—Tao led a monastic community, whose organization was loosely modeled on that of the Buddhist monasteries, at Mao mountain (Maoshan). His friends and supporters included Emperor Wu of the Liang Dynasty (r. 502–549), the prominent pro-Buddhist monarch. Located in the vicinity of Nanjing, Maoshan became a famous center of Daoist practice (the Shangqing school is also known as Maoshan Daoism, from the name of the mountain). Tao was concerned with establishing criteria for authenticating genuine Shangqing scriptures, as the popularity of the corpus, along with the high value attached to the possession of individual texts, led to the production of spurious scriptures. That went along with the circulation of fraudulent and unauthorized copies, some of which were stolen or sold for profit.

By rearranging and modifying the constituent parts of medieval Daoism, the Shangqing school presented a fresh approach to spiritual cultivation, marked by an overriding concern with exploration of the inner world. Communal observances and rituals largely gave way to contemplative practices and visualizations performed by individual adepts, preferably in the solitude of mountains or in meditation chambers. The interior practices described in the texts of the Shangqing corpus supposedly mirrored those performed by the perfected beings,

Figure 7.1 Meditating adept visualizes the arrival of celestial deities.

who as a result of their spiritual cultivation acquired sublime bodies and came to reside in rarefied celestial abodes. The meditative visualizations (often accompanied with invocations) engaged the Daoist adepts' faculties of religious imagination and mental pliability. They involved the conjuring up of eidetic images of various gods and divinities, including those that reside within the body and control its functions (see box below and Figure 7.1). The ultimate goal of salvation entailed removal of all boundaries between the individual and the universe, as the adept's inward journey culminated in his/her coalescing with ultimate reality.

Box 7.1 Shangqing Depiction of the Spirits Inhering Inside The Body

The body of a person contains the spirits of the Palaces of the Three Primes. Within the Gate of Destiny are the Grand Sovereign of the Mystic Pass and the spirits of the three cloudsouls. Altogether there are seven spirits within the body who desire that the person live a long life. These are the greatly propitious sovereigns of kindness and benevolence. The seven white souls are also born within the same body, but they are thieves who attack the body. That is why they must be controlled.

The Upper Scripture of Purple Texts Inscribed by the Spirits;
translated in Bokenkamp 1997: 326.

The spiritual practices depicted in Shangqing literature also include spiritual journeys that evoke the ecstatic wonderings described in *Zhuangzi*. Advanced adepts are allegedly able to travel to mythical places, such as the famed "islands of immortality," or Kunlun (the *axis mundi* according to Chinese tradition) and other sacred mountains. During these journeys they encounter an assortment of divinities and uncanny creatures, many of them previously depicted in Chinese mythology. Moreover, on occasion these inspired mental or mystical journeys take the adepts beyond the reaches of the terrestrial realms, as they sojourn to the sun, the moon, the stars, and variously heavenly realms. According to canonical accounts, there they commune with the gods and obtain celestial nourishments that foster bodily sublimation, leading to the procurement of a subtle and luminous body of an immortal.

The Lingbao Scriptures

Within a few decades after the advent of the Shangqing scriptures, around 400 CE, a new corpus of Daoist texts appeared in southern China. Declared to be divine revelations and collectively known as the Lingbao (Numinous Treasure) scriptures, these disparate texts initially surfaced in the vicinity of Nanjing. Not only was their place of origin not far from the site of the earlier Shangqing revelations, but the new texts also initially circulated in similar aristocratic circles. The emergence of these texts can be seen as another attempt at reformulating or reforming Daoism.

The core of the Lingbao corpus contains some earlier materials, generally ascribed to notable Daoist adepts of previous eras, most notably Ge Hong's relative of an earlier generation Ge Xuan (164–244), as well as scriptures composed during the early fifth century. In these texts we find a noticeable shift in attitudes and priorities: a move away from the elitist concerns with interior exploration typical of the Shangqing revelations, which are largely replaced with a focus on communally-oriented, liturgical forms of worship. These ritualistic features are somewhat analogous to the ceremonial practices of the Celestial Masters, which had broad appeal and resonated with the religious needs and predilections of wider audiences.

The Lingbao scriptures represent a prominent synthesis of the major traditions of medieval Daoism, including those of the Celestial Masters and the Shangqing school, which were combined with copious borrowings from Buddhist texts and practices. The Buddhist influences are especially noteworthy, as this was the first wholesale introduction of Buddhist ideas and imagery into mainstream Daoism, with lasting ramifications for the subsequent religious history of China. From a traditionalist or normative perspective, the majority of the texts in the Lingbao corpus were earthly manifestations of celestial writings, based on revelations primarily communicated by a high divine being known as Heavenly Worthy of Primordial Origin (Yuanshi Tianzun). In some contexts, the primordial genesis of this powerful divinity is associated with the creation of the universe. Similarly, the cosmic point of origin is depicted as a principal source for the Lingbao scriptures and the talismans associated with them. From a historical point of view, the initial revelation of the texts—and perhaps also their compilation—is attributed to Ge Chaofu (fl. c. 400 CE), an obscure member of the southern aristocracy, who was a descendant of Ge Hong.

Box 7.2   Benefits of possessing and reciting a Lingbao scripture

Whoever possesses this scripture is able to mobilize its powerful merits on behalf of heaven and earth, the thearchial rulers, and the masses of people. When, in times of calamity, you arouse your faith and practice retreats, burning incense and reciting this scripture ten times, your name will in all cases be recorded in various heavens and the myriad spirits will guard you. In contradiction to the aforementioned whose grasp of the Dao is shallow, those who excel in its study will serve as ministers of the Sage Lord in the Golden Porte.

The Wondrous Scripture of the Upper Chapters on Limitless Salvation; translated in Bokenkamp 1997: 430.

A major step towards the formation of a distinct tradition of Daoism centered on the Lingbao scriptures and took place during the middle part of the fifth century, when the prominent scholar and ritual specialist Lu Xiujing (406–477) organized the disparate scriptures and systematized their teachings. An important part of that process was Lu's compilation of the first catalogue of the scriptures and his standardization of the rituals depicted in them. His efforts paved the way for the creation of a coherent school of Daoism, renowned for its codification of communal rituals. That was accompanied with the production of additional scriptures and the writing of commentaries.

Although subsequently it was largely overshadowed by the Shangqing school, the Lingbao school continued to occupy an important position within Daoism. Its elaborations and codifications of Daoist liturgy were especially significant, as they became the predominant liturgical frameworks and ritual templates for the whole of Daoism. The lasting influence of Lingbao Daoism is still evident in the common forms of ritual practiced within contemporary Daoism.

As was the case with the Shangqing school, the amalgamation of diverse elements of medieval Daoism into the Lingbao texts and the teachings associated with them involved notable shifts in emphasis and that implied selective rearranging of the priorities of religious life. The Lingbao school continued a trend towards relegation of physical exercises, use of herbs and potions, and laboratory alchemy to a relatively marginal position within the broad array of Daoist practices, even if the quest for immortality remained a predominant theme, albeit in a reformulated form. The solitary meditations and visualizations of the Shangqing school were also not a major focal point of attention. Instead, the Lingbao school is renowned for its pervasive emphasis on ritual as the primary form of practice and the central element of Daoist religious life. The liturgical framework adopted and promulgated by the tradition's adherents was predominantly communal in character, even though some of the original scriptures might have been meant for solitary recitation performed in a meditation chamber.

One of the novel ideas brought into Daoism by the Lingbao schools is the notion of universal salvation, which is a prime example of the previously noted Buddhist influences. Other notable developments were the introduction of the Buddhist concepts of merit, reincarnation, and karma, which came to exert great influence on Daoism and popular religion. Buddhist ideas also creep into discussions of morality, where they are typically mixed with traditional Confucian virtues. Furthermore, concepts derived from Buddhist texts play a role in the reconfiguring of Daoist cosmological schemes, including the depictions of various hells and heavens, some of which are given Buddhist-sounding names.

For instance, the threefold division of the heavens introduced in Lingbao texts was based on the Buddhist notion of three realms (or worlds): the realm of desire, the realm of form, and the formlessness realm. Even the main deity associated with the Lingbao scriptures, Heavenly Worthy of Primordial Origin, had notable Buddhist overtones. Not only was his title derived from Buddhist sources, but the deity himself can be seen as a Daoist recasting of the cosmic Buddha Vairocana. Moreover, in a manner reminiscent of the Buddhist scriptures, Heavenly Worthy was provided with a disciple who also served as his interlocutor, a potent deity called Supreme Lord of the Dao (Taishang Daojun).

The authors or editors of some Lingbao scriptures took the additional step of directly appropriating whole sections from Buddhist canonical texts. In addition, the mysterious celestial language reproduced in some of them is modeled on Chinese transliterations of Sanskrit words found in Buddhist scriptures, effectively functioning as a pseudo-Sanskrit concoction that is meant to evoke a sense of otherworldliness. Nonetheless, the infusion of Buddhist ideas and imagery into Daoism needs to be put into a proper perspective. There are palpable elements of superficiality in many of the borrowings, which were primarily based on popular forms of Buddhism, rather than on the rarefied intellectualizations of the clerical elite.

The process of appropriating Buddhist elements within Lingbao Daoism was complex and multi-faceted. Buddhist ideas were often subjected to significant modifications as they were integrated into indigenous theoretical and ritual templates, and they were often used for somewhat different purposes. Even so, the pervasive influence of Buddhism, readily observable throughout Lingbao literature, marks an important point in the ongoing reconstitution of the Chinese religious landscape. The infusion of Buddhist concepts and imagery enriched and expanded the contours of Daoism, precisely at a point when Daoism was entering a golden age of unparalleled flourishing and influence, which reached its apogee during the Tang era.

Codification of Daoist Ritual

Daoist ritual is essentially concerned with bringing about social harmony and cosmic accord. It is meant to foster integration with the Dao, at the individual and the communal levels. On the whole, the liturgical observances formulated and enacted by the Lingbao school were marked by structural complexity and multidimensionality. They simultaneously operated at three different levels: the

Figure 7.2 Daoist priests perform ritual bows, Hong Kong.

heavens, the earthly realm, and the individual person. The primary focus on ritual also brought about significant institutional changes. Most notably, it facilitated the growth of Daoist priesthood that specialized in the performance of rites and ceremonial functions. The members of the clergy secured their privileged status—which also carried notable economic benefits—by adopting the prominent role of mediators between the gods and humanity.

The main element of the Lingbao school's liturgical program was the communal recitation of sacred texts, which to this days remains a focal aspect of Daoist practice. Central to the ritual observances were intricate purificatory rites (*zhai*), of which there were nine main categories. Together with the "offerings" rites (*jiao*), sometimes also referred to as "rituals of cosmic renewal," these rites form the two main categories of Daoist ritual. Staged in carefully designated sacred space that contained a central altar, the rites involved public confession of past transgressions, as well as communal chants, prayers, and petitions directed towards the heavenly realms and the gods that reside there (see Figures 7.2 and 7.3).

The main part of the ritual was preceded by preliminary purification observances, including bodily cleansing and fasting. The formal ceremonies were often followed by communal feasts. The assorted

Figure 7.3 Daoist priests participate in the Grand Ceremony of Luotian, Hong Kong.

ritual observances adopted a solemn tone and were supposed to mirror central Daoist principles. Key ritual elements were purportedly grounded in contemplative experiences; to that effect, short periods of silent meditation were imbedded in some of the rituals. At the same time, the rituals also possessed striking theatrical traits. They featured conspicuous dramatic elements, such as dance movements and the playing of musical instruments, and made extensive use of ceremonial paraphernalia that included colorful banners and incense. These exterior traits, along with the belief in the spiritual potency of the rituals, doubtlessly contributed to their remarkable popularity and staying power.

In terms of their primary function, the rituals of Lingbao and other Daoist traditions were understood as potent vehicles for return to a primordial order, in which the faithful arrive at a union with the Dao. Within this soteriological scheme, the primary means for the attainment of salvation was ritual practice grounded in sacred texts, situated into a larger cosmological framework. The texts were also credited with talismanic power, as they were believed to bestow protection and possess salvific efficacy. Because of their importance, the sacred texts were to be carefully safeguarded by assuring that they only landed in the hands of legitimate owners. That meant they were to be transmitted only in a properly authorized manner.

The Lingbao rituals were often used for the achievement of prosaic goals, such as the prevention of natural calamities. However, their self-professed ultimate aim was the salvation of all beings. The salvation of the individual (and by extension the group) was therefore closely linked with the salvation of all beings in the universe, an idea adopted from Mahāyāna Buddhism. The prospect of collective salvation from the suffering and imperfection of earthly existence was also extended to the dead. In an apparent bow to Chinese traditions and prevailing sensibilities, the Lingbao texts and rituals make special references to the salvation of the ancestors. That seemingly superfluous move points to an ongoing preoccupation with ancestor worship, which reflected deeply felt religious needs and prevalent cultural sentiments.

Canon Formation and Functions of Texts

One of the defining features of Daoism is that it is a religious tradition grounded in texts or writings. At the core of its textual corpus are scriptures alleged to be revealed by gods and other celestial divinities, which are meant to disclose the inner structure of reality and the mysterious workings of the Dao. Daoist myths of origin trace the initial formation of the scriptures back to the primordial time of cosmic creation, as the original logograms were formed spontaneously from primal breaths or vapors. The gods then wrote down the celestial prototypes of the scriptures—on jade tablets, according to some accounts—which refracted and crystallized the fundamental cosmic patens of the Dao. The scriptures revealed to humanity are deemed to be second-order versions derived from the heavenly archetypes, but they are still greatly revered as sources of sublime knowledge and immense power. This kind of accounting of scriptural genesis resonates with deeply-ingrained notions about the mystical origins of the written graphs that comprise the Chinese script, reflected in the reverential attitude towards writing that infuses Chinese culture.

When used properly, the scriptures are believed to be able to bring about reordering of the world, at the everyday and the otherworldly levels, as well as lead to the realization of sublime states of transcendence. In accord with prevalent beliefs about their primeval and divine origins, the texts are seen as ageless repositories of precious knowledge, with universal import and common meaning, intended for all of humanity. Consequently, their creation is traditionally decoupled from the temporal contexts and historical exigencies that were implicated in their initial manifestations and ensuing modifications. In contrast, critical scholarship sees the Daoist scriptures predominantly as products of the religious and social worlds of medieval China, akin to the canonical collections of other religious traditions. That makes the texts fascinating sources of information about the social worlds and the religious milieus that produced them.

With the ongoing increase in textual production in medieval China, exemplified by the divine revelations surveyed above, there arose a need to assemble together the expanding body of Daoist writings and organize it into a coherent canon. Significant efforts in that direction were the compilations of early catalogues of Daoist texts, such as a catalogue compiled by Ge Hong during the third century. The basic structure of the Daoist canon is already evident by the time of Lu Xiujing, who created an

Figure 7.4 *Huangting neijing jing (Scripture of the Inner Radiance of the Yellow Court)*; calligraphy by Bada Shanren (1626–1705) (Freer Gallery of Art, Smithsonian Institution, Washington, D.C.: Purchase- E. Rhodes and Leona B. Carpenter Foundation in honor of the 75th Anniversary of the Freer Gallery of Art, F1998.29.1-12)

inclusive catalogue of Daoist texts, the second version of which he presented to the imperial throne in 471. Lu divided the catalogue into three broad categories, called "caverns" (*dong*). The gradual process of canon formation was an important step in the creation of a common Daoist identity, as diverse groups were brought together within the broad confines of a relatively cohesive religious tradition. The process of common identity creation was influenced by the increased popularity of Buddhism, whose religious and institutional identities were fairly stable, and to a substantial degree were linked with the prominent status of its voluminous canon.

Besides their normative roles as repositories of timeless knowledge, guides for spiritual cultivation, and manuals for liturgical practice, Daoist scriptures were also perceived as powerful talismans. Some texts were deemed appropriate for broad dissemination (e.g. *Laozi*), but many texts were meant to only have limited circulation. With the increased institutionalization of Daoism, the later group of texts was supposed to be transmitted in carefully defined ritual contexts. That contributed to the

Box 7.3 The "Three Caverns" of the Daoist canon

- Cavern of Perfection (Dongzhen)—Shangqing scriptures
- Cavern of Mystery (Dongxuan)—Lingbao scriptures
- Cavern of Divinity (Dongshen)—Three Sovereigns (San huang) scriptures

formation of transmission lineages, which to a large extent served to solidify the power and authority of clerical elites. Consequently, scriptural transmissions became key elements in the ritual initiations and ordinations of Daoist priests, some of which were also extended to other practitioners. Daoist adepts were able to go over a series of increasingly higher ritual empowerments and ordinations, each linked with the transmission of a particular scripture. The process ended with the transmission of texts recognized as forming the apex of the canonical hierarchy, which usually meant scriptures belonging to the Shangqing corpus.

The Daoist canon is known as *Daozang* (Repository of [texts about] the Dao), a designation that was originally based on its Buddhist counterpart. Within the threefold division of Daoist texts introduced by Lu Xiujing, the scriptures of the Shangqing school were placed in the first cavern, those of the Lingbao school in the second cavern, while the third cavern comprised a smaller body of texts centered on the *Three Sovereign Scripture* (see box). This kind of arrangement involved hierarchical ordering of the various traditions of Daoism, with the Shangqing school occupying the highest position. Gradually this arrangement grew in complexity, as each of the caverns was further divided into twelve sections. The tripartite division of the canon was probably based on Buddhist models: either the original threefold division of the Buddhist canon (scriptures, texts about monastic discipline, and scholastic treatises), or the three vehicles of Mahāyāna Buddhism (those of hearers, pratyekabuddhas, and bodhisattvas). It is notable that the three vehicles model in Buddhism involves hierarchical ordering of teachings that is analogous to the one implicit in the Daoist canon.

The Daoist canon was an open collection of sacred texts. Consequently, it continued to grow over the centuries, as newly-composed texts were added to it, while older texts were subjected to alterations and ongoing exegesis. In light of such growth, the original division of the canon into three caverns proved inadequate. Consequently, four supplements were added to it during the sixth century. The fourth supplement, named Orthodox Unity (Zhengyi), contained the scriptures of the Celestial Masters school. In addition to the aforementioned scriptures, the Daoist canon came to include a wide range of other materials: scholastic and exegetical treatises, historical texts (including collections of hagiographies), and above all ritual manuals, which in terms of their number became the largest genre of texts in the canon.

The production of various editions of the canon was customarily undertaken under imperial auspices, as was also the case with the Buddhist canon. During the early eight century, Emperor Xuanzong (r. 713–756) ordered the collection of all Daoist texts circulating throughout the vast empire. The texts were then put together into a canonical collection, copies of which were distributed to Daoist temples across the country. Similar undertaking was ordered by emperor Taizong (r. 976–97), as part of efforts to consolidate central imperial authority after the reunification of China under the Song dynasty. The version of *Daozang* used today was compiled in 1445 under the imperial auspices of the Ming dynasty; it is thus known as the *Ming Canon of Daoist Scriptures* or the *Zhengtong Daoist Canon* (from the name of the reign era during which it was published). It is a vast collection of texts, numbering some 1,500 separate titles, to which a supplement was added in 1607.

Daoism as Official Religion

We already noted a few instances of the long-standing connections between Daoism and the exercise of political power in ancient China. Pertinent examples include the political readings of *Laozi* and the ideas about rule by the way of non-action articulated by the Huanglao movement in Han times. The incipiency of Daoism as an organized religion had prominent sociopolitical dimensions, as evidenced by the formation of a theocratic mini-state in Sichuan by the Celestial Masters. The subsequent move of the Celestial Maters to the North was accompanied with their official recognition in the early third century. That represented a momentous shift in political and ideological orientation, a clear move away from the origins of religious Daoism in millenarian movements, which were predominantly peasant-based and thrived at the social margins.

From the third century, the adoption of court-oriented outlook became a predominant concern within the nascent Daoist church, paving the way for rapprochement between the religion and key power-brokers in medieval Chinese society. An early culmination of that process was the institution of Daoism as de-facto state religion under the Northern Wei dynasty (386–534), whose Toba rulers were of non-Chinese extraction. At the time, the promotion of Daoism was perceived within elite circles as a way of Sinicizing the Toba. The central figure in this transformation of Daoism into an elite religion closely alighted with the imperial government and the aristocracy was Kou Qianzhi (365–448). He was a prominent Daoist leader with aristocratic background, who claimed to be a recipient of divine revelations. This procurement of elevated status as Northern Wei empire's official religion was a first event of its kind in the history of Daoism, sometimes interpreted as the establishment of Daoist theocracy.

As a reward for Kou Qianzhi's valuable efforts at providing religiously-based sanction to the Northern Wei dynasty, he was awarded the official title of Celestial Master. The Daoist endorsement and legitimization of dynastic rule, reflected in the emperor's adoption of a Daoist title for himself and the official institution of Daoist rituals at the court, sanctified Wei's authority and bolstered the dynasty's claim to be the rightful inheritor of the Mandate of Heaven. Under Kou's leadership, the

Daoist church expanded its footprint and influence at the court, adopting a conservative ideological stance and aligning itself closely with the interests of the state and the ruling elites. The consolidation of Daoism as an official religion under Wei rule was accompanied with the surfacing of exclusivist attitudes. That was given concrete expression in a government-sponsored persecution of Buddhism and other religious groups that were labeled as heretical cults.

The Northern Wei experiment with the institution of Daoism as state religion was short-lived, roughly taking place during the 425–450 period. Following Kou Qianzhi's death, by the mid-fifth century the dynasty shifted its main focus of religious allegiance and political patronage to Buddhism. Nonetheless, on the whole Daoism continued to prosper during the subsequent centuries, as Daoist institutions were recipients of state support under a number of dynasties. That was especially the case during the Tang era, when Daoism achieved the peak of its development and influence on Chinese culture and society. The Tang dynasty afforded great prestige to Daoism and extended generous patronage to the Daoist church. At the same time, the dynasty relied extensively on Daoist ritual, imagery, and cachet to bolster its prestige and enhance the legitimacy of its rule.

The roots of the close connection between the Tang dynasty and Daoism go back to the early seventh century, when the imperial family tried to bolster its standing vis-à-vis the better established aristocratic families of northern China by tracing its ancestry back to Laozi. This ploy at aggrandizing the ancestral pedigree of the new imperial family, as part of an overall strategy of bolstering its claim to have received the Mandate of Heaven, was based on the fact that their family name Li was the same as the one that was traditionally ascribed to Laozi. The purported familial connection with the ancient sage was also linked with a popular prophecy about the pending rule of a sagely ruler surnamed Li, which circulated within millenarian circles. Accordingly, in 625, seven years after the official founding of the dynasty, its first emperor proclaimed that Daoism will be officially ranked first among the "three teachings," ahead of Confucianism and Buddhism.

Picking up on the notion of ancestral connection with Laozi, subsequent Tang emperors offered substantial political and economic patronage to the Daoist clergy and their temples, although the level of official support varied according to political circumstances and reflected the personal pieties of individual emperors. The Tang era is usually celebrated as a remarkable period in Daoist history, marked by imposing consolidation of principal Daoist teachings, practices, and institutions. From a religious perspective, it was a golden age that saw the formation of a grand Daoist synthesis, formed to a substantial degree by the incorporation of copious elements from Buddhism.

Key aspects of the ingenious Tang synthesis were manifested in rarefied philosophical speculations, splendid rituals, and vibrant religious institutions, which secured Daoism's prominent position and its central role in the transmission of traditional Chinese culture. At the same time, throughout this period Daoism had to contend with the greater popularity of Buddhism, whose clergy and religious establishments greatly outnumbered those of the Daoists. The parallel flourishing of both religions is a testimony to the grandeur and openness of Tang culture, in which all three teachings participated and interacted with each other. On the whole, the cosmopolitan and pluralistic outlook generally characteristic of the Tang era proved well suited for the flourishing of multifaceted religious and intellectual life, marked by their sophistication, creativity, and embrace of diversity.

During the Tang era, the height of the status of Daoism as official state religion occurred under the rule of Emperor Xuanzong, which was marked by unparalleled economic prosperity and cultural effervescence. Although like other Tang rulers Xuanzong continued to support Confucianism and Buddhism, throughout his reign he exhibited distinct pro-Daoist sympathies. His extensive patronage of Daoism was to a large extent grounded in personal beliefs and predilections, although pragmatic political consideration also played an important part. The emperor was a student of Daoist literature—he even "authored" a commentary on Laozi's classic—and was an ardent believer in miracles and omens. He associated with a number of prominent Daoist prelates, especially those affiliated with the dominant Shangqing school, often inviting them to lecture and perform rituals at the imperial court. In addition, Xuanzong received a Daoist ordination.

Xuanzong's support of the Shangqing school is evident in a decree that the local gods associated with the five sacred mountains, traditionally linked with the state cult, were to be put under control of Shangqing divinities, who were to be worshiped at temples situated on each of the five mountains. Xuanzong also established a system of state-supported Daoist abbeys, which were required to perform officially-sanctioned liturgies for the benefit of the imperial family and the state. His patronage of Daoist learning included the setting up of Daoist schools and the institution of official Daoist examinations, which made mastery of the Daoist classics an alternative avenue for entry into the imperial bureaucracy. These policies went along with the already-mentioned compilation of a Daoist canon and its distribution throughout the empire.

Following a recognizable historical pattern, this kind of generous patronage was linked with policies aimed at controlling the religion. For instance, Xuanzong and other Tang emperors issued decrees and instituted regulations that restricted the clergy's freedom of movement and the scope of its activities, aimed at the Daoists and the Buddhists alike. Clerics had to register with the government, which also controlled the system of monastic ordinations and influenced the selection of abbots. Their freedom of movement and association were also restricted, and the government had a system of punitive laws and harsh punishments for those who misbehaved or violated its directives. Various emperors also asserted the governmental prerogative to adjudicate the inclusion (or exclusion) of texts into the canon, which gave them an important say in the delineation of religious orthodoxy. From the Song dynasty onward, another aspect of the relationship between Daoism and the imperial state was the Daoist canonization of popular cults that were recognized by the state.

Interreligious Debates

One of the remarkable features of religious life in medieval China was the staging of interreligious debates that featured prominent representatives of the three teachings. The formal enactment of such public events—which highlighted both the distinctive features and the points of convergence among the doctrines of Buddhism, Confucianism, and Daoism—was a potent symbol of China's embrace of a broad framework of religious pluralism. This kind of ecumenical stance stood in stark contrast to the interreligious strife and intolerance that at the time prevailed in Europe and elsewhere. A number of these debates were held at the imperial courts of various dynasties, including the Tang, often in front of the emperor and his senior officials, some of whom took part in the proceedings. Beside their religious and educational functions, at times the debating performances had certain entertainment value and were integrated into larger imperial celebrations.

Typically the official interreligious debates were carefully staged events, often set in convivial ambience and performed in accord with formulaic patterns of courtly ritual. Nonetheless, at times the stakes were real and the outcome of the debate had substantial repercussions for individual religions. That was especially the case with the Buddhists and the Daoists, who occupied conterminous social and religious spaces, and were often in direct competition for status and patronage. There was often a sycophantic undertone to the debates, as each tradition tried to score points by establishing its greater usefulness to the imperial state.

A major point of argument put forward by Daoist leaders in their intellectual duels with the Buddhists was a well-known theory that the emergence of Buddhism was outgrowth of a "conversion of the barbarians," undertaken by none other than Laozi. This notion was given canonical sanction by *Huahu jing* (Scripture on the Conversion of Barbarians), an apocryphal text initially composed around 300 CE and greatly expanded over the subsequent centuries. This spurious scripture was widely circulated in Daoist circles and often evoked in the debates with the Buddhists. According to *Huahu jing*, the Buddha was an incarnation of Laozi, who traveled to India in order to edify the ignorant foreigners. This idea was based on the well-known legend about Laozi's final journey to the West. It essentially insinuated that Buddhism is little more than a diluted form of Daoism, devised for the benefit of culturally inferior people.

The formulation of this kind of religious and pseudo-historical lines of argument, presented in *Huahu jing* and other similar polemical tracts, seems to have been initially animated by a spirit of inclusiveness. They also reflected a concern for accounting the seeming similarities between the teachings and practices of the two religions. Before long, however, the tone of the arguments, as evidenced in later versions of *Huahu jing* and other texts with similar message, became more combative and defamatory. In effect, the original contention about the putative relatedness of Buddhism and Daoism deteriorated into scratchy polemical assertions about the inferiority of Buddhism and triumphant declarations of the superiority of Daoism, tinged with xenophobic sentiments about innate Chinese superiority. That annoyed many Buddhists, who vehemently objected to what they perceived to be slanderous remarks about their religion's founder and open affront to his teachings.

The choice of the conversion of the barbarians theme as a debating point turned out to be a losing proposition and a source of considerable grief for the Daoists. The Buddhists were repeatedly successful in discrediting *Huahu jing* as a ludicrous forgery, even if in the process of doing that they themselves used far-fetched sources and dubious arguments about the greater age of the Buddha and the like. Some fringe Buddhist texts even put forward a curious theory that Laozi was a disciple of the Buddha, as was Confucius. The string of debates lost by the Daoists—a number of which incorporated the *Huahu jing* and its tenets, but also covered other areas of difference or disagreement—started during the early sixth century, although it is worth noting that at times the Daoists were successful in making their case and gaining an upper hand.

The last series of formal debates took place at the Mongol court of Kubilai Khan (r. 1271–1294) during the Yuan dynasty. The Daoists were primarily represented by the Complete Perfection school (see below). According to traditional accounts, they were defeated at the last debate of 1281 and suffered disastrous consequences. Not only was there an imperial decree that all copies of *Huahu jing* must be destroyed, but the same fate was to befall all other Daoist texts, with the sole exception of *Laozi*. At the same time, severe restrictions were placed on the Daoist clergy, although it is unclear how strictly the imperial decree was actually enforced on the ground.

Monastic Orders and Institutions

Even before the emergence of Daoism as organized religion, various forms of reclusion—withdrawal from society that usually involved (temporary) renunciation of social status and worldly pleasures—were familiar features of the Chinese religious landscape. Examples of religiously-inspired abandonment of conventional norms and adoption of alternative lifestyles during the Han era, often linked with eremitic ideals, are evident among the *fangshi* practitioners of magical arts and the seekers of immortality. Nonetheless, the fully developed ideals and institutions of monasticism were essentially unknown in China before the advent of Buddhism. Although the Celestial Masters instituted comprehensive communal structures and formal rules that governed the behavior of their followers, their movement did not adopt a monastic orientation. Their priests were married householders with distinct ranks and ritual functions, unlike the Chinese followers of Buddhism, the most fervent among whom adopted a monastic ethos imported from abroad; however, during later periods some of the Daoist clergy choose to lead a celibate life.

The monastic vocation involves observance of celibacy as part of a distinctive religious way of life, ideally oriented towards the pursuit of spiritual perfection. Entry into a monastic order is effectively an expression of individual commitment, but it usually takes place within a structured communal setting, meant to provide optimal conditions for a religious quest, ostensibly directed towards the pursuit of ultimate truth and self-realization. The emergence and codification of Daoist variants of the monastic vocation was a gradual process that unfolded over several centuries. The evolution of Daoist monasticism involved extensive borrowings from the Buddhist monastic order, which brought to China longstanding models of monastic institutions with evolved organizational structures, systems of communal rules, and established patterns of interaction with the surrounding society and the state.

The Buddhist monastic models were selectively adapted in accord with Daoist ideas and practices. Gradually they coalesced with the communal ethos of the Celestial Masters and the previously-mentioned eremitic ideals. By the fifth century we already encounter quasi-monastic communities led by noted Daoist leaders such as Kou Qianzhi and Lu Xiujing, whose members practiced celibacy and embraced reclusive lifestyles. A similar trend is observable in the Daoist community on Maoshan that was led by Tao Hongjing during the early sixth century, paving the way for the emergence of two parallel—though not necessarily radically disjoined—vocational patterns for the Daoist clergy that continue to the present day: as celibate monastics (male and female) or married priests (typically male).

The flourishing of fairly developed monastic tradition was a prominent feature of Daoism during the Tang period. This was an integral part of the overall consolidation of Daoism during its heyday, which went along with its mature assimilation of elements from Buddhism. During this period we find a large number of monastic establishments situated across the Tang empire, from large and imposing abbeys in the two capitals to small temples and hermitages scattered across scenic mountains. In these establishments thousands of Daoist monks and nuns pursued their religious vocations, which in addition to various forms of spiritual discipline also included the performance of liturgies for their patrons and the imperial state. The abbeys and convents developed elaborate institutional structures, with extensive administrative offices, comprehensive sets of regulations, and evolved liturgical programs. They served as important centers of Daoist practice and learning, but they also performed important cultural roles and were frequented by commoners and literati alike.

Daoist monasticism underwent further development and formalization after the Tang era. A prime example of monastic Daoism from the late imperial period is the Complete Perfection (Quanzhen) school, which initially emerged in the twelfth century and by the thirteen century became the dominant tradition of Daoism in northern China. The clergy of the Complete Perfection school were celibate, followed vegetarian diet, and lived in well-ordered communities. They practiced mendicancy and led austere lifestyles; a focal point of their spiritual regiment were contemplative practices aimed at realizing one's true nature (see last section). The school's founder Wang Zhe (1113–1170) was a scion of a wealthy family who entered religious life as a middle-aged person; prior to his conversion he was an eccentric figure prone to heavy drinking. After a series of visionary experiences, during which he purportedly established communion with distinguished immortals and celestial beings, Wang came to prominence as the charismatic leader of a band of dedicated and talented disciples, some of whom became notable figures celebrated in popular Daoist lore.

The Complete Perfection school is sometimes described as the first fully-developed monastic order within Daoism, within evolved structures and distinctive communal way of life that paralleled those

Figure 7.5 Daoist monks and laypeople in front of a shrine room, Baxian (Eight Immortals) Abbey, Xi'an.

of the Buddhist monastic order. Especially noticeable are the similarities with the Chan school, the predominant tradition of elite Buddhism, evident across the areas of monastic discipline, doctrine, and practice. Notwithstanding the movement's monastic orientation, its leaders also cultivated a close relationship with numerous lay supporters. The laity was organized in associations that provided support for the monastic communities.

Wang is also notable for his syncretic tendencies and ecumenical attitudes, including his advocacy of the unity of the three teachings. He advised his disciples to recite popular Confucian and Buddhist texts, especially the *Classic of Filial Piety* and the *Heart Scripture*. Wang and his disciples were prolific writers, leaving behind a large body of Daoist literature that included poetry and essays. They also composed manuals of spiritual cultivation, transcripts of oral teachings, hagiographical collections, and exegetical works.

A key event marking the Complete Perfection school's rise to great prominence was the meeting in 1222 between Wang's most prominent disciple Qiu Chuji (1143–1227) and the great Mongol conqueror Chinggis Khan (d. 1227). The meeting took place at the Mongol court in Central Asia, and before long Qiu's epic journey became celebrated as a seminal event in the Daoist tradition's history.

The Mongol ruler was duly impressed by the Daoist master and his teachings. Consequently, Chinggis Khan issued a decree that all Daoist monks and nuns should be given tax-exempt status and placed under the control of the Complete Perfection patriarch. Subsequently the Complete Perfection school became the most powerful religious movement in northern China.

Although it subsequently lost some of its initial vigor and influence, to this day the Complete Perfection school remains the main representative of monastic Daoism, even though the majority of its clergy are in fact married. The gradual decline from its peak, achieved during the thirteenth century under the Mongol Yuan dynasty (1271–1367), parallels the overall weakening of Daoism during the late imperial period, although recent scholarship has shown that on the whole Daoism flourished during the Ming era. The religion's gradual decline is especially evident during the Qing dynasty (1644–1911). Together with the Celestial Masters—who by the fourteenth century resurfaced in the South as a major Daoist tradition—the Complete Perfection school remains one of the two main schools of Daoism. Its strongest presence is in northern China, while Celestial Masters Daoism is more prevalent in the South.

Figure 7.6 Female devotees reading scriptures, Xingtian Temple, Taipei.

Female Role Models and Adepts

Generally speaking, throughout history the pursuit of religious vocation within a Daoist milieu has been open to both sexes. For example, women were welcomed as full-fledged members in the early communities of the Celestial Masters, and they could also serve as libationers. Later women could join the ranks of the religious and enter Daoist convents. There they could lead pious lives, presumably oriented towards plumbing the mysteries of the Dao, in ways that mostly paralleled the vocational patterns of their male brethren. On the whole, Daoist methods of spiritual cultivation are gender-neutral and realization of the ultimate goals of practice is open to both men and women. Although it is true that some of the early stages in the practice of internal alchemy differ somewhat

- Queen Mother of the West (Xiwangmu), the supreme Daoist goddess, believed to rule over a western paradise from her majestic palace at mythical Mt. Kunlun.
- Wei Huacun (252–334, also known as Lady Wei), noted adept in the Celestial Masters tradition and deity that revealed the Shangqing scriptures.
- He Xiangu (Immortal Maiden He, also known as He Qiong), the sole female member of the renowned group of Eight Immortals, said to originally have been a girl that lived during the Tang era.
- Sun Buer (1119–1182), one of the seven major masters of the early Complete Perfection tradition.

between men and women, that is primarily due to the need to take into account the physiological differences between the two genders.

There were of course exceptions to the prevalent egalitarian attitudes of female acceptance and participation. For instance, in certain sexual practices male adepts used multiple female consorts as sources of vital energy that bolstered the circulation of their sexual essence, often without being overly concerned with the wellbeing of the women in question. There are also indications that Daoists were not always immune to various forms of prejudice directed towards women, which were rampant within the patriarchal social order of imperial China—as well as in virtually all other societies at the time—especially if we judge from the vantage-point of modern Western ideas about gender equity. Nonetheless, on balance it is fair to say that Daoism was especially welcoming to women, giving them unique opportunities to act as individual agents and pursue alternative avenues of personal growth and expression. That included exceptional opportunities to get away from the dominating relationships with men, which governed the lives of females in the Confucian-oriented society of traditional China.

Women attracted to Daoist life and practice had a number of positive female role models to follow. The Daoist pantheon includes many female divinities and immortals, such as the Queen Mother of the West and the female deities and perfected that inhabit the Shangqing heaven. There were also famous female adepts and priestesses, some of whom became apotheosized and turned into objects of cultic worship (see box). As a result of the veneration of notable female figures and the hospitable attitudes towards female participation, Daoist convents attracted a broad range of women into their ranks, from girls coming from peasant families to imperial princesses.

The prominent women who entered Daoist convents included the daughter of Empress Wu (r. 684–705), the only female monarch in Chinese history. Although renowned for her outstanding support of Buddhism, the empress was also a patron of Daoism. She had a Daoist convent built for her only daughter, who was installed as its abbess. Nuns also remained a prominent fixture in the Daoist orders that thrived in late imperial China, especially those of the Complete Perfection tradition. One of Wang Zhe's most prominent disciples—hailed as the "seven perfected ones"—was the female adept Sun Buer, and there were many other prominent nuns and female adepts. The tradition of Daoist nuns continues to this day.

Internal Alchemy and Meditation

One of the prominent features of the Complete Perfection school's soteriological orientation is the integration of internal alchemy (*neidan,* lit. "inner cinnabar") into its comprehensive program of spiritual cultivation. Internal alchemy stands in contrast to external or laboratory alchemy, which seeks to procure the elixir of immortality by means of chemical procedures performed in the alchemist's furnace [...]. While internal alchemy adopted much of the chemical vocabulary of external alchemy, it used it in a metaphorical manner to indicate inner essences and processes that occurred within the individual practitioner. In effect, the body and mind of the Daoist adept became the primary foci and tools of spiritual transformation, replacing the mineral substances and laboratory instruments of external alchemy.

In the context of Complete Perfection praxis, the earlier goal of transmuting the body and achieving physical immortality is largely beside the point. Instead, the primary focus within its soteriological paradigm is on bringing about inner transformation that ultimately involves transcendence of the mundane realm, in which the adept's mind/heart (*xin*) harmonizes with the primordial and ineffable Dao. While spiritual cultivation incorporates corporal aspects and physiological elements, it is essentially a meditative process guided by and centered on the mind/heart that culminates with the experience of enlightenment. At the end of the spiritual journey, the adept uncovered his or her true mind or original nature, which is unborn and is never destroyed.

Box 7.5   Realization of The True Nature in Complete Perfection Daoism

If you want to nurture your vital energy and complete your spirit, you must completely get rid of your myriad attachments. Be pure and still on the surface and within. If you remain dedicated and devoted for a long, long time, your spirit will be stable, and your vital energy will be harmonious. ... Only those who study the Dao will reach the stage where their spirit will reside together with the Dao and thereby be indestructible forever, and also have the power to raise nine generations of ancestors to the [realm of] Supreme Purity.

From the recorded sayings of Complete Perfection patriarch Ma Yu (1123–1184); translation adapted from Eskildsen 2004: 90–91.

The shift from external to internal alchemy developed gradually, over a number of centuries. Early precursors of the tenets and procedures of internal alchemy are evident in the contemplative visualizations and inwardly-oriented practices of the Shangqing school. An example of that is the meditative formula of "guarding the One" (*shouyi*), earlier versions of which circulated before the Shangqing revelations. The practice is based on the notion of correspondence between the macrocosm and the microcosm—a central idea featured in many Daoist texts—which implies close linkage of the individual with the cosmos. An important facet of that correlation is the inherence of the gods that populate the cosmos within the human body.

Like the bureaucratic pantheon of their celestial counterparts, the gods of the body have discrete areas of oversight, ensuring the proper working of bodily organs and physical processes. The contemplative practice of "guarding the One" consists of visualizing and concentrating on the One, a supreme deity that represents a divinized presence of the primordial void and controls the other gods in the body, who in turn are responsible for the proper operation of different bodily organs and functions. By means of this form of meditation, the adept is supposedly able to safeguard the bodily gods and thus ensure his or her health and longevity, while also harmonizing with larger cosmic forces and attuning to the Dao.

A major turning point in the development of internal alchemy took place during the Tang era. At the time external alchemy reached its highpoint of influence, but we also witness the first development of identifiable strands of internal alchemy. The two types of alchemy were sometimes cultivated together and had overlapping imagery and vocabulary. Another trend observable during the Tang period was the development of discursive types of meditation, which were connected with the formulation of new doctrinal schemes influenced by Buddhist philosophies. This kind of meditation corresponds to the Buddhist practice of insight (*guan*), which together with calmness (*zhi*) is one of the two basic types of Buddhist meditation. A representative example of these tendencies comes from the writings of the Double Mystery (Chongxuan) school, which flourished during the first half of the Tang era and was heavily influenced by the Middle Way or Madhyamaka philosophy of Buddhism.

The notion of "twofold mystery" denotes dual repudiation of one-sided beliefs in existence and nonexistence (or nonbeing). The first mystery entails transcendence of existence and nonexistence, while the second mystery involves obliteration of attachment to the first mystery. At the stage of the first mystery, the Daoist adept cultivates detachment from dualistic conceptions of reality that revolve around the notions of existence and nonexistence. Then, at the second stage the adept becomes disengaged from the state of detachment itself. That implies complete elimination of all desires and attachments, including the attachment to tranquil abiding in a state of absence of desires.

The process of self-cultivation followed by practitioners of mature forms of inner alchemy in late imperial China, including those of the Complete Perfection school, implies gradual ascent from coarser to more refined levels of reality or states of existence. Looked at from a different perspective, it represents a procedure of reversal or inversion of natural processes that leads back to a primordial state of perfection and wholeness, return to an original oneness that purportedly existed "before Heaven." That involves gradual move from the everyday existence of ordinary people towards the increasingly subtle and pure states of being that are ascribed to the sages. At the preliminary stage, the adept's self-cultivation mostly takes place at the level of the physical body, which is fortified and balanced by various forms of calisthenics, psychosomatic exercises, diets, and massages. Then the practice unfolds at three basic levels, represented by essence (*jing*), vital energy (*qi*), and spirit (*shen*). Often referred to as the "three treasures" (*sanbao*), these three function as basic components in the inner process of alchemical transmutation.

At the initial stage of the inner alchemical process, special attention is paid to physiological functions, especially the circulation of sexual essence—the conventional or coarse form of essence—whose leakage must be prevented at all cost. The essence is gathered and refined, and its circulation becomes regulated. This stage culminates with the transmutation of essence into vital energy. At the next stage, the adept's practice focuses on the purification and refinement of vital energy, which is enabled to circulate unobstructed inside the body. The most subtle and pure mode of vital energy is caused to rise up to the highest of the three "cinnabar

Figure 7.7 The embryo of immortality leaves the body of a Daoist practitioner.

fields" (*dantian*)—key points in the body that control physiological functions and where alchemical transmutations take place—located in the head and associated with thoughts and consciousness. This stage is perfected when the highly purified vital energy is transmuted into spirit.

Box 7.6   Key Points

- The Shangqing scriptures were originally revealed and disseminated within a southern aristocratic milieu, where they were accepted as divine revelations communicated by perfected beings. While the Shangqing tradition incorporated elements from the various strands of medieval Daoism, it placed special emphasis on exploration of the inner world and the contemplative aspects of spiritual cultivation.

- Within the Lingbao scriptures, which appeared soon after the Shangqing revelations, there is a move away from solitary forms of interior exploration and towards ritual forms of worship that are communally oriented. This is also the first time that we find a substantial infusion of Buddhist concepts and ideas into Daoism.

- Lingbao rites were central in the codification of Daoist ritual, which incorporates two main categories: rituals of purification and rituals of renewal. In their classical form, Daoist rituals are multidimensional and incorporate a variety of elements, including the chanting of scriptures, making of petitions and prayers, performance of dance movements, and playing of musical instruments; these are often followed by communal feasts.

- The various Daoist scriptures were by the fifth century organized into a coherent canon, which in its classical form was divided into three parts, the so-called "three caverns," to which additional supplements were added later. The Daoist canon was an open collection of sacred texts, which meant that over the centuries many new texts, composed in different genres, were added to it.

- During both the medieval and the late imperial periods the Daoist church was for the most part closely aligned with the imperial state. The state was an important source of patronage for the Daoist clergy and its temples; the state also asserted its authority over the religion and used it for its own purposes.

- Under the influence of Buddhism, Daoism developed its own monastic orders and institution, which came to play central roles in the religion's historical growth. A prime example of monastic Daoism is the Complete Perfection school, which was formed in the twelfth century and continues to exist to this day as one of the two main traditions of Daoism.

- Daoism was open to female participation, either as a layperson or a nun. Daoist women had numerous positive role models to follow, from various goddesses and females perfected to exemplary nuns and famous female practitioners.

- From the Tang era onward there was a shift from external to internal alchemy. In internal alchemy the focus is on an inner process of alchemical transmutation that takes place with the body and mind of the Daoist adept. The whole process culminates when the purified primeval spirit separates from the body and returns to the point of origin, becoming absorbed into the eternal Dao.

At the third stage, the spirit is gradually refined, as the adept's mind disengages from dualistic thoughts and reverts to a state of emptiness. The purified spirit constitutes an embryo of immortality that, after being properly nurtured over a period of gestation, leaves the body by way of the top of the head (see Figure 7.7). The whole process of spiritual transformation purportedly culminates in transcendence of the foregoing domains and stages, as the primeval spirit leaves the body and returns to the point of origin, merging with the primordial state of absolute nothingness and becoming absorbed into the timeless and all-pervading Dao.

Discussion Questions

1. What were the main roles of sacred texts in medieval Daoism, and what were the prevalent beliefs about the origins of the Daoist scriptures?

2. Trace the growing impact of Buddhism on medieval Daoism, as it is played out in the doctrines and practices of the three main Daoist traditions: Celestial Masters, Shangqing, and Lingbao.

3. What was/is the status of women in Daoism and how does it compare with the general status of women in traditional Chinese society?

Further Reading

[...]

Bokenkamp, Stephen R. *1997. Early Daoist Scriptures. Berkeley, CA: University of California Press.*

Bokenkamp, Stephen R. 2007. *Ancestors and Anxiety: Daoism and the Birth of Rebirth in China.* Berkeley, CA: University of California Press.

Cahill, Suzanne Elizabeth. 1993. *Transcendence and Divine Passion: The Queen Mother of the West in Medieval China.* Stanford, CA: Stanford University Press.

Despeux, Cathrine and Livia Kohn, eds. 2003. *Women in Daoism.* Cambridge, MA: Three Pines Press.

Eskildsen, Stephen. 2004. *The Teachings and Practices of the Early Quanzhen Taoist Masters.* Albany, NY: State University of New York Press.

Girardot, N. J., James Miller, and Xiaogan Liu. 2001. *Daoism and Ecology: Ways within a Cosmic Landscape.* Cambridge, MA: Center for the Study of World Religions, Harvard Divinity School.

Goossaert, Vincent. 2007. *The Taoists of Peking, 1800–1949: A Social History of Urban Clerics.* Cambridge, CA: Harvard University Asia Center.

Kohn, Livia. 2003. *Monastic Life in Medieval Daoism: A Cross-Cultural Perspective.* Honolulu, HI: University of Hawai'i Press.

Kohn, Livia. 2008. *Introducing Daoism.* London and New York: Routledge.

Little, Stephen, and Shawn Eichman. 2000. *Taoism and the Arts of China.* Chicago, IL: Art Institute of Chicago.

Mollier, Christine. 2008. *Buddhism and Taoism Face to Face: Scripture, Ritual, and Iconographic Exchange in Medieval China.* Honolulu, HI: University of Hawai'i Press.

Robinet, Isabelle. 1993. *Taoist Meditation: The Mao-Shan Tradition of Great Purity.* Albany, NY: State University of New York Press.

Schipper, Kristofer. 1993. *The Taoist Body.* Berkeley, CA: University of California Press.

Schipper, Kristofer Marinus, and Franciscus Verellen. 2004. *The Taoist Canon: A Historical Companion to the Daozang.* Chicago, IL: University of Chicago Press.

Wong, Eva, trans. 2004. *Seven Taoist Masters: A Folk Novel of China.* Boston, MA: Shambala Publications.

Reading 8 Confucianism

By Archie J. Bahm

C onfucianism is a religion. In fact, Confucianism, considered as all of those beliefs and practices attributed to Confucius and Confucians which have accumulated during the two and a half millennia of its history, may be regarded as several religions. Gradual development of ideas about the nature of man and the universe yielded varieties that may be regarded as distinct, and the name "Neo-Confucianism," for example, denotes some major shifts in doctrinal viewpoint.

The task of putting Confucianism into proper perspective for Western readers, becomes further complicated due to the fact that several misconceptions about Confucianism as a religion have grown out of attempts by theists to evaluate Confucianism in terms of their conception of "religion as belief in God or gods." These attempts have begotten several interpretations of Confucianism: as not a religion, as agnostic about religion, as an insincere animistic religion, as ancestor worship, as deification of Confucius, and as deliberate use of Confucian doctrines by ruling classes to maintain the status quo. Although some basis exists for each of these interpretations, all of them miss being accurate evaluations of Confucianism as a religion. The thesis presented here asserts that the philosophy of Confucius—even if not that of all his followers who called themselves "Confucians"—is a great religion, perhaps the world's greatest religion, and that what makes it so is a fundamental trait almost entirely overlooked by Western interpreters.

Confucius

Discussion of Confucianism must begin with Confucius, his life, his background, and his philosophy. Confucius lived between 551 and 478 B.C. He flourished during the sixth century B.C., which was also the century of Lao-tzu the Taoist, Gotama the Buddha, and Mahavira the Jain, before the time of the great Greeks, Socrates, Plato, and Aristotle, before the assemblage of the Hebrew Pentateuch, and half a millennium before the appearance of Jesus Christ. His own scholarly interests centered in the history and traditions of his and neighboring kingdoms, and the ideals he expressed were attributed by him to men of earlier times. He regarded himself as a transmitter of ancient wisdom rather than

Archie J. Bahm, "Confucianism," *The World's Living Religions: A Searching Comparison of the Faiths of East and West*, pp. 175-198. Copyright © 1992 by Jain Publishing Company. Reprinted with permission.

as an innovator. Such reforms as he proposed were pictured as a return to the more virtuous ways of old. We cannot be sure just when or how the ideas he propounded began. Furthermore, his own teachings were recorded mainly from memory by followers after his death, sketchily and with some modifications. However, a philosophy did emerge that is clear in its general outlines. Whether it is precisely what Confucius thought, we may never know. But that it flowered early as one of the great philosophical insights attained by man appears beyond doubt, and its attribution to Confucius is a practice convenient to follow.

Sketching the little we know about his life, we may infer that he had a good education for at the age of twenty-one he began to teach, by the time he was thirty he had reached settled opinions, at thirty-four he visited the capital of the empire and saw the places where the great sacrifices to Heaven and Earth were offered and the ancestral temples of the rulers. He spent much time collecting and editing available literature about ancient customs and beliefs. At fifty he became the chief magistrate of a city where he put his theory of government into practice with such telling effect that it became a model town within a year. The duke was so pleased by the transformation that be made him minister of justice. Laws fell into disuse because there were no criminals. People came from elsewhere to study his methods. Thus he became famous. But other advisers to the duke became jealous of his success and diverted the duke's attention so that he no longer paid heed to Confucius. Finally, Confucius gave up and quit in disgust. Then he traveled from court to court, offering his services, with little success. He spent the later years of his life studying and finishing his collections. He died at the age of seventy-three.

As background essential to understanding his views, the facts of rural life, family life, court life, animistic beliefs, pictographic writing, the development of hexagrams and their symbolic interpretation, and the Taoistic philosophy of Lao-tzu need to be mentioned. The role of nature and of men's arising and declining as parts of the ongoing processes of nature, described by Lao-tzu, were incorporated into the philosophy of Confucius. However, the nature of family life, which also forms a backbone of Chinese culture throughout its history and which was largely ignored by Lao-tzu, and the nature of courtly life and government, which was shunned by Lao-tzu, became central problems for study by Confucius. Animistic practices, calligraphy, scientific prognostication by means of hexagrammatic analogies, concern for music and poetry, and burial and memorial traditions that were carried on in courtly society constitute important parts of the cultural milieu within which Confucius found his task of understanding the nature and goal of life.

Since both popular and scholarly evaluations of Taoism and Confucianism typically represent them as extremely antagonistic, our first duty in summarizing the philosophy of Confucius is to demonstrate how much it is like that of Lao-tzu. Basically their philosophies remain essentially the same. Both accept the ideas of Tao or Nature, Yang and Yin as principles of initiation and completion, the cyclical character of Nature's processes, the naturalness of man and the goodness of each man's living out his own life in accordance with his own tao. Religiously, they are also similar, since both idealize spontaneity, self-activity, and an unquestioning affirmation of life. Their differences appear in ethical, social, and political philosophy, as we shall point out later. But these differences will be more accurately understood if the Taoism of Lao-tzu is pictured as roots and trunk of a tree out of which the philosophy of Confucius grows as a major branch than if they appear as separate, unrelated plants. The philosophy of Confucius was a necessary supplement to that of Lao-tzu; for as Chinese culture emerged farther from its agricultural bases, through its family and courtly systems of association and control, with their social and political principles of operation, the naturalistic Taoism had to be adapted to account for the "tao of society," that is, the nature of man in his social relationships. Faced with inescapable facts of family and courtly life, one cannot, as Lao-tzu recommended, run away and hide. If Lao-tzu's function was mainly that of describing Tao, then the function of Confucius was chiefly that of describing the "tao of society." Lao-tzu was primarily a metaphysician, Confucius primarily a social scientist. But both were in agreement about saying "Yes" to nature's way, whether as the universal Tao or as each person's own tao. Lao-tzu simply lacked comprehension of that tao which man has as a social being. Confucius, in filling this lack, was a more complete philosopher.

In describing Tao and tao, Nature and human nature, Confucius expresses ideas similar to those of Lao-tzu but in somewhat different language. The opening passages of the *Chung Yung,* one of "The Four Books" presenting Confucian ideas, summarize Taoistic ideals upon which Confucius takes his stand. "What Nature [*T'ien,* or that nature which transcends man] provides is called 'his own nature.' Living in accord with one's own nature is called 'self-realization.' Proper pursuit of self-realization is called 'maturation.' One's own nature cannot be disowned. If it could be disowned, it would not be one's own nature. Hence, a virtuous man attends to it and is concerned about it, even though it is invisible and inaudible. One's visible exterior is nothing more than an expression of his invisible interior, and his outer expression reveals only what is inside. Therefore, the virtuous man is concerned about his own self." (Section I.)

"The wise man retains his true nature. The foolish man does the opposite. A wise man retains his true nature because he is wise; and he is wise because he retains his true nature. A foolish man does the opposite because he is foolish, and he is foolish because he fails to appreciate what is good." (Section II.) "One's true nature is self-sufficient, but few people can maintain it for a long time." (Section III.) "I know why the course of one's true nature is not pursued. Men of accomplishment try to rise above it. The inept fail to come up to it. I know why the course of one's true nature is not understood. The ambitious overestimate it. The lazy fail to appreciate it." (Section IV.) "Nature's way is to be genuine. Man's way is to become genuine. To be genuine is to act truly without effort, to attain without thinking about it, and automatically and spontaneously to realize one's true nature. Such a man is wise." (Section XX.)

However, Confucius goes on to assert that mere self-concern is not sufficient for realizing the fullness of life. Man is also a social being who finds his fullest expression only through his associations with others. Section I, quoted above, concludes: "Being undisturbed by [attitudes toward others involving] pleasure, anger, grief, or joy is called 'one's true nature.' Being stimulated by [such attitudes] each in its appropriate way is called 'one's true social nature.' This 'true nature' is the primal source [great root] from which all social affairs develop. This 'true social nature' is the means for attaining happiness by all humanity. When our 'true nature' and 'true social nature' prevail uninterrupted, conditions both above man and below man remain wholesome, and everything thrives and prospers."

Section XXV reiterates: "Genuineness is self-sufficient. And its nature is self-directing. Genuineness pervades being from beginning to end. Without genuineness nothing could be. This is why the wise man values becoming genuine above everything else. Genuineness not only promotes self-realization; it is the means through which one develops his relations with others also. Self-realization involves associating with others [Jen]. Developing one's relations with others involves sympathetic insight. Both associating with others and having sympathetic insight are abilities which anyone has for realizing his own nature [teh]. One's whole nature [tao] integrates both external (social) relations and internal (individual) processes. Hence, genuineness is fully genuine when both of these abilities are appropriately integrated." (Author's versions.)

Confucius was a Taoist who believed the tao of man involved him in human association and that he was not wholly human until his social nature was fully developed also. Although he would not have spoken of a "tao of society," thereby giving society a substantial status and nature of its own, he did discriminate between a man's social tao and his individual tao as integral and continuous portions of his whole tao. Confucius devoted his life to being a social psychologist, by observing the practices of various courtly societies and studying the records of previous societies, to discover the most successful ways of organizing human relationships and the kinds of attitudes needed for conducting them. These ways were then held up as ideals for others to emulate. Thus Confucius became a teacher of customary morality as it had prevailed in the happiest kingdoms. We will not here review details of those customs which have now become obsolete. But we should investigate the ethical philosophy that he developed by generalizing upon his observations, and the general theory of human nature, which, supplementing that of Lao-tzu, remains one of the grandest and most penetrating philosophies of all time. In developing it, Confucius expounded one of the profoundest, possibly the most perfect, philosophy of religion that has ever emerged. Let us see how he did it.

We can summarize the philosophy of Confucius by developing his four characteristics of the ideal man, sometimes called the "Sage," whom we shall speak of as the "wise man." The "wise man" as here described remains an ideal that few ever attain to perfection. But it is an ideal that all may use in improving themselves. These four characteristics are referred to as *yi, jen, li,* and *chih.*

(1) YI is the best way of doing things. We must keep in mind the basic tenet of Lao-tzu and Confucius that nature and human nature are good. Whenever anything is allowed to live in accordance with its own inner nature, all will go well, provided, of course, that it does not try to overdo, underdo, or modify it artifically. *Yi* is the way things behave when they act in accordance with their own natures;

and this is the best way for all things to act. No man is wise until he understands *yi*. He may not completely understand the nature of all things, but he should grasp the fundamental truth that Nature provides each being with a nature that is self-sufficient and self-fulfilling and thus as good as it can be. To try to make it better than it is involves trying to change it; trying to change it is artificial; making it artificial will bring it to an unnatural end. Reading Lao-tzu's eulogies of behaving naturally serves as an excellent background for comprehending the presuppositions underlying Confucius' conception of *yi*.

But, since human nature is also essentially social, the best way for human beings to behave is as social beings. What, then, are these best ways? What are the principles of social behavior that each person can discover operating in his own way of doing things? We summarize these under two headings, "the principle of reciprocity" and "the principle of sincerity."

(a) *The principle of reciprocity* is a basic principle of the universe in which all activity involves both initiation (yang) and completion (*yin*). Today we formulate it as a physical principle: for every action there is an equal and opposite reaction. But early Chinese thinkers, like early Hindu ("law of karma") and European ("retributive justice") thinkers, did not separate the physical out of the natural world and castrate it of values, as European materialists have done. Whatever is natural is good. Since it is natural to come into being, so it is good to come into being. Since it is natural for what comes in to go out, so it is natural, and good, to go out of being, in due time and in proper course. To resist this reciprocal behavior of Tao, which is both the source and the culmination of the goodness of each thing, is bad because it is against one's own nature.

The principle of reciprocity not only operates throughout Nature and each individual nature but also in and through man's nature socially. One person gives and another receives. One who receives responds by giving in return. In this way, social interaction occurs. Recall how, when someone snubs you, you automatically want to snub back. If civilization has already built restraints into you, try to remember how you once responded by observing the normal behavior of little children. When someone does you an unexpected favor or pays you an undeserved compliment, do you not feel a desire not to be outdone in doing for others what they do for you? The simple psychological principle involved is obvious to anyone who takes time to observe its operation, and peoples of all cultures have formulated it in one way or another in their lore. Christians speak of it as "the Golden Rule," "Do unto others as you would have them do unto you," thereby formulating it as a "commandment" or "rule" rather than as a "principle." The Confucian way of stating the rule, unfortunately regarded as "negative" and therefore inferior by proud Westerners, is more subtle and is based in the Taoistic philosophy out of which it grows.

In addition to stating the principle as a rule—"Do not require of another what you would not have another require of you"—Confucius added a phrase that reveals his insight to be more penetrating. As we shall see, Mo Ti, a critic of Confucius, rejected this additional phrase; and it is generally neglected in other cultures. The phrase is: "if you were that person." That is, "treat another as you would be treated if you were that person." People are unequal. A child and his parent differ. A wife and her husband differ. A sick person and a healthy person are different. A mother should treat her child as a child, not as if her child were another mother. And she should treat her child as she would like to be treated if she were her child. A man is not a woman and does not wish to be treated as if he were a woman, and a woman is not a man and does not wish to be treated as if she were a man. A man should treat a woman as a woman, and treat her as he would like to be treated if he were a woman. More particularly, he should treat each person as if he were that person. This kind of treatment considers actual differences between persons and takes them into account in deciding how to act according to the principle of reciprocity. It is important to notice that greater insight, *i.e.*, sympathetic insight, is needed in order to act on this principle. For one needs to make the effort to think about the nature and feelings of the other person in order to know how he would like to be treated if he were that other person.

The Taoistic spirit upon which the philosophy of Confucius is founded presupposes that if each thing lives in accordance with his own inner nature, all will go well. Whenever one is imposed upon by others, his inner or natural course may suffer. Hence, the most "positive" way of formulating the principle of reciprocity is to say "Do not interfere with the good natures of others in ways that you do not want to have your own good nature interfered with." Each person has his own vital flow, his own tao, with his own desires, wishes, or will. Therefore, as a minimum, "do not" will to interfere with his will.

By his observing that the principle of reciprocity is an essential trait of men as social beings, Confucius was able to advance beyond the "shun all association as artificial" doctrine of Lao-tzu. For Lao-tzu, the ideal life was one in which each person would stay as far away from all others as possible, since contact with them involved impositions of each upon the other. But Confucius, steeped in the facts of living in large families, clans, tribes, and nations, recognized both the necessity and naturalness of people living together and thus "imposing upon" each other. He looked for, and found in the principle of reciprocity as he formulated it, a principle of human nature that is just as natural and necessary as any other natural principle.

A child cannot be born without depending for his conception and gestation upon his mother. A child cannot survive without milk, which must come from his mother, who, by then, is "another." A child cannot survive without protection and care, which, in practice, require many varieties of dependence upon others. Each such act of dependence upon others would be a kind of imposition if such dependence were not also natural to the inner (social) interests of the person depended upon. Thus the inner interests of a mother in her child make her already, automatically, and naturally, a social being. Her inner and outer interests are continuous with one another rather than being contradictory in nature. Hence, the principle of reciprocity grows out of a mother's own inner nature. It is not something forced upon her from the outside as "artificial." So with the child. His coming into being, his own nature, his own survival, the molding of his own interests and character, all grow naturally out of his associations with his mother. Her interests are his interests, for if she dies he dies, unless he can find someone else to take an interest in him.

The principle of reciprocity, which is so obvious in intimate family relations, continues to work as one's horizons widen, and include persons in a larger family. Discriminating observation reveals that one's relations with others vary. Consequently, one may question whether the principle is the same in relations with different people. Here again, one should observe with care. Brothers quarrel and become jealous of each other and of parental favoritism. Different families compete for the food available from a particular plot of land. Exchange of goods between families or between strangers does not always come out equally. Kings attack other kings, even when they are not attacked. Yet, what alternative is there to the principle of reciprocity? Perhaps in response to questions by his pupils, Confucius elaborated details about applying the principle to all kinds of social relationships. He was especially concerned about those between rulers and subjects. But his advice about rulers grew naturally out of the general principle, which he found working at all levels of interaction. For purposes of instruction, all such relationships were conveniently summarized into five kinds, namely, those between parent and child, between husband and wife, between an older brother and a younger brother, between a ruler and his subject, and between friend and friend. Recognition of differences among these five kinds of relations provides a foundation for extending such discrimination to grandparents and grandchildren, to a husband's brothers and to a wife's sisters, to older sisters and younger sisters, to rulers and subjects, to less intimate friends, casual acquaintances, strangers, and even to enemies. Mastery of the principle of reciprocity in these five prepares one for discriminating use of it in all social relationships.

However, since one may not be able to trust it as a general principle until he first becomes aware of its operation in his most intimate relationships, the relation between parent and child receives special emphasis. Not only may one grasp it intuitively and surely in such a relationship but if either a child or a parent fails to accept the principle here, family life will come to disaster. Hence "filial piety," as English translations customarily name the need of a child to treat his father as he would be treated if he were his father, has a basic significance. Since failure here will lead to failures elsewhere, its recognition is essential.

(b) *The principle of sincerity* (*hsin*) is a second principle of the tao of association. Some rate it as a fifth characteristic of the wise man. It follows naturally from the first for, according to the principle of reciprocity, if you are insincere in your dealings with others, the most you can expect is insincerity from them. Since you do not wish to be dealt with insincerely, you must treat others sincerely. If you merely pretend to respect others, the most you can expect in return is pretended respect. But deceit begets deceit, distrust distrust, fear fear, and you soon find yourself in a situation that is not best for yourself. Hence, being sincere is a part of *yi,* the best way of doing things for yourself in your association with others.

(2) JEN is goodwill; it is willingness to do what is best socially. Since acting in accordance with one's own nature is what is best for each person, goodwill consists basically in allowing each person to act in accordance with his own nature. This means not interfering with him or wanting him to be different from what he is. A man of goodwill accepts each person for what he is. *Jen* is simply willingness to act according to *yi. Yi* is the best way of doing things, and *jen,* goodwill, is willingness to do, or to have things done, the best way, individually and socially.

Two requirements of goodwill may be easily overlooked. The first is insight. Where persons in intimate relationships act interdependently, each can know how to treat others only if he has some insight into their natures. If, for example, a parent wants what is best for his child and wishes him to develop naturally, must he not try to put himself in the child's situation so he can realize how much or how little to require of him in the way of social behavior? If a parent works hard all day gathering ten bushels of rice, should he treat his eight-year-old son as an equal and expect the same hard work and the same ten bushels from him? Or should he develop sufficient insight into the nature and capacity of his child to recognize the child's limitations? Does not genuine goodwill require action toward another in terms of that other's own nature and ability?

The second requirement is sympathy. Insight is necessary, but it is not enough. Not only must one recognize how others feel when treated in certain ways, but one needs to try to promote good feelings if he has goodwill. One who desires to torture another may be more successful if he has insight into how another responds to such torture than if he does not have such insight, but sympathy means actually sharing the feelings of another, so far as possible. Insight *and* sympathy assure *jen* or genuine goodwill. The principle of sincerity together with the principle of reciprocity require genuine goodwill.

(3) LI is propriety, or the appropriate way of giving overt expression to inner attitudes. Involved here is a basic principle, namely, that one's inner nature and one's external behavior are correlative, or should be correlative when one's intentions are sincere. Only a deceiver or an ignoramus will behave toward others in such a way that they misunderstand his intentions. To act with good intentions in a way that others will take to be bad is a wrong way of behaving. In order to be sure that one is conveying his good intentions to others, he should, in addition, behave in such a way that the other cannot mistake his intentions. Now, do some ways convey intentions more clearly and precisely than others? Yes. At least so Confucius concluded from studying the behavior in different families and courts, both in his own time and as recorded in history. If customs have developed with regard to specific ways of expressing respect, such as bowing, saluting, or handshaking, one who wishes to be understood will automatically employ these ways. They are the best ways of behaving because they actually convey one's true intentions. Hence, understanding *yi,* the best way of doing things, involves not only having *jen,* but also *li,* or knowing and practicing the best ways of behaving so as to accomplish the intended result.

Now unfortunately, once appropriate etiquette has been formalized, deceivers may also use these forms. Consequently, one who has been deceived by use of them may come to distrust them. Also, when parents try to teach their children appropriate manners before they recognize the need for such manners, the children may feel externally forced to conform to a convention that has for them no inner meaning. To learn forms of behavior without learning their inner meanings is artificial, not natural, and so is not a part of the best way of doing things. Not only Lao-tzu but Confucius, too, advised us to shun the artificial. But Confucius conceived the artificial as behaving in any manner that fails to express inner intentions. Hence, one should avoid formalism. For each *yi,* the best inner way of behaving, there exists a *li,* the most effective external manner of behaving. *Li* and *yi* should be correlated if one seeks his fullest self-realization through his tao of association. External expression is false unless one both knows *yi* and has *jen. Hsin,* genuineness, requires the desire to be free from all such falsity.

Now *li* may also be called "propriety" or the proper way of behaving. We also speak of this as the "right way" or as "right conduct." Many of us have forgotten that "rite" and "right" have similar meanings and that rituals were originally intended to be the right, *i.e.,* best, ways of doing things. When social intercourse becomes too complicated for us to keep in mind the value of all social rituals, the latter tend to become ritualistic, *i.e.,* forms without meaning. Confucius not only warned against artificiality, formalism, or ritualism, but he also sought to discover more details about right behavior as social relations become more complicated, as they do in larger families and more intricate systems of government.

Recognizing that persons holding different political offices also require different external forms of behavior to express the different responsibilities inherent in each office, he sought to discover the forms that custom had already developed for these purposes. Then he systematized them and taught them for the purpose of expediting efficiency. Just as in science today we idealize precision in performing our experiments, so Confucius sought precision in modes of behavior, which we call "punctiliousness." "Punctiliousness" is conscientious behavior, not formalism. Unfortunately stupid formalists mistook means for ends and demanded performance of rituals even after their meaning had been lost. Consequently, Confucius, who preached *against* formalism, has come to be considered its proponent.

Another important phrase in the language of Confucius is "rectification of names." If we regard "rectitude" and "rectification" as merely stiff-necked or artificial, we will misunderstand Confucius again. His interest here is also in "the best way of doing things." Names and natures should be correlated. If two things are the same, *e.g.,* two children, they should have the same name, *i.e.,* "child." But when two things are different, *e.g.,* a child and a man, they should have two different names, *i.e.,* "child" and "man." Each different kind of thing (chair, table, house), each different kind of person (father, wife, eldest daughter, baby), and each kind of office (ruler, minister, scholar, guard) should have its own name. Use of names can be relied upon only if two principles are followed.

First, each thing, person, and office should be called by its right name. For to call a guard a "ruler" or to call a child a "man" is to use words falsely. Secondly, each person who has a name should live in accordance with it; otherwise either his life or his name is false. To call a person a "ruler" when he has ceased to look after the best interests of his subjects is wrong. Such a person should no longer be called a "ruler" but should be deposed. To call a woman a "wife" when she runs about after other men and no longer behaves like a wife is to misname her. According to the principle of the "rectification of names," fathers who neglect their fatherly duties and scholars who do not study should be treated no longer as fathers and scholars. These two principles—that persons should be called by their right names and that persons should live up to their names—together constitute the principle that names and natures should be correlated and further illustrate "knowing and practicing *li,*" the principle that external expression (*e.g.* "names") should appropriately represent inner nature and intent.

Whereas Lao-tzu advised the shunning of naming, Confucius recommended shunning the misuse of names. According to Lao-tzu, "No name can fully express what it represents." "In seeking to grasp what is, the intelligent man does not devote himself to the making of distinctions which are then mistaken to be separate existences." (*Tao Teh King, op. cit.,* pp. 11, 12.) He appears to regard all naming as artificial. Confucius, on the other hand, recognizes the social necessities of noting differences between persons and of distinctive names for those differences. But he warns that "Not acting according to one's nature and name, is to act artificially. Hence, the best way for a person to act is in accordance with his actual nature and right name." (*Ibid.,* p. 111.) Right names are thus an essential part of *li, jen,* and *yi* and of the tao of human relationships.

(4) CHIH is wisdom. No man is wise until he is happy. Wisdom consists in confident living. Living confidently involves consenting to things as they are, *i.e.,* to *yi, jen,* and *li,* three characteristics of the wise man. Wisdom does not require encyclopaedic knowledge. It does require knowing that allowing each one to act in accordance with his own nature is best for each, and that differences among the natures of the persons upon whom he depends and who depend upon him, must be respected if he is to five in harmony with them. Achieving *chih* requires knowing *yi.* If one cannot live confidently until he has, and knows he has, genuine goodwill toward others, then he cannot achieve *chih* until he fully embodies *jen.* If one cannot live confidently until he knows all of the appropriate external manners needed to express his true intentions toward others, then he cannot achieve *chih* until he knows and practices *li.* Yet merely knowing *yi,* having *jen* and knowing and practicing *li* is not enough.

Chih is an ideal to be approached by degrees. One's assurance grows as he learns more. One's confidence increases as he frees himself from fears of inadequacy. One's trust in nature's ways—Nature at large, one's own inner nature, and one's social nature—develops as he desires less and less to deviate from their inherent norms. One will achieve *chih* fully only when *yi, jen* and *li* have become embodied within him so completely that he responds in each occasion, social and private, with perfect spontaneity. In *chih,* one lives according to habit, without question or reservation. *Chih* involves *hsin,* complete unwillingness to deceive oneself or others. *Chih* epitomizes yea-saying, thereby making the ideals of Confucius among the greatest religious ideals of all mankind. It is Confucius' ideal of *chih* that makes Confucianism a great religion, not the deification of Confucius by later admirers nor his teachings about "ancestor worship." *Chih* is wisdom because a person having achieved it responds to his opportunities and responsibilities so unreservedly, so automatically and spontaneously, that he never for a moment abandons the habit of living confidently. *Chih* is such a high religious ideal that Confucius himself complained that he was never able to reach it even though he tried the best he could throughout his life.

What is "ancestor worship"—as followers and critics of Confucius call it? Did he recommend specific ways for revering ancestors? Yes. Did he believe in the continued existence of departed ancestors in some incorporeal form? To this question, as to questions about the existence of spirits of any kind, he gave no positive answer. His reply, which has become familiar to us in a stilted form of pidgin English, was "Not know life; how know death?" Why, then, should he have bothered so much about specific ways of revering ancestors? You already know the answer if you can apply *yi, jen* and *li* to your relations with your own ancestors.

Consider, for example, how the principle of reciprocity applies here. Do you expect to die and become a departed ancestor? Yes. Do you desire to be forgotten as soon as you die? No. How long do you desire to be remembered after you are dead? Should you not then, according to the principle of reciprocity, desire to remember your ancestors in the same way as you desire to be remembered when you become one? How should you express your remembrance of the goodness and greatness of your ancestors? In the same manner and for as long a time as you desire to be so remembered? Since you doubtless do not wish to be forgotten too soon, especially by those dearest to you, nor remembered too long, especially by those who were never acquainted with you, you may find some socially accepted and culturally established manner of enacting such a remembrance.

Thus what appears to others as superstitious ancestor worship was for Confucius a natural expression of self-respect by socialized individuals. When we recognize additionally that one's social tao involves *hsin* or sincerity, we will then want to remember our ancestors as sincerely as we desire to be remembered. Do our ancestors still really exist? The principles of reciprocity and sincerity require that we regard our ancestors as existing in the same way in which we now desire others to regard us as existing after we have become departed ancestors. The naturalness of this desire makes it appropriate to set up tombstones, memorial days, tablets, halls, gardens, ceremonies, etc., which flow from our nature as social beings.

Confucius did not regard men as victims of determinate processes of Nature. Men become agencies that help to determine the course of Nature. But "it is only he who is completely genuine in the affairs of this world who can develop his nature to its fullest. If he can develop his own nature to its fullest, then he can help in the full development of the natures of other men. If he can help in the full development of other men's natures, then he can help in the full development of the natures of all animate and inanimate beings. If he can help in the full development of the natures of all animate and inanimate beings, then he can help in the production and maturation activities of Nature above and Nature below. When he helps in the production and maturation activities of Nature above and Nature below, he becomes a third kind of agency in the universe." (*Chung Yung,* Section XIII, author's interpretation.)

Critics of Confucius

The most famous and perhaps most influential rival of Confucius was Mo Ti. Mo Ti was a soldier in charge of instructing and commanding those who guarded the land. A good soldier must protect all equally and so must be willing to serve all equally and to die, if necessary, for all equally. Mo Ti claimed that *jen,* or genuine goodwill, must regard all persons without discrimination. He accused Confucius of teaching, if not an immoral, then at least a low moral, doctrine, namely, "discriminating love." A discriminator refuses to treat people alike because he claims that different people should be treated differently. He will not care for his friends as much as he does for his family. Consequently, he will not do very much for his friends. But a nondiscriminator will regard all people as alike and will do everything he can to help his friends, just as in the case of his family. He will have that "all-embracing love" which alone can assure peace and tranquility.

But Mo Ti did not end his criticisms by disagreeing about the nature of *jen*. He went on to say that there are four ways in which Confucian principles will ruin the whole world. (1) Confucianists do not believe in the existence of God or of spirits. Consequently God and the spirits are displeased. Mo Ti was himself a theist who believed that both an omnipotent but loving God and lesser spirits punish men who discriminate. As a soldier, he advocated absolute rule by a chief ruler who had power to reward and punish people; and he recognized the need for a supreme deity who would reward and punish any ruler who failed to love impartially. (2) Confucianists place so much emphasis on ritual that even those living a long life cannot encompass the learning needed to become acquainted with all of the formalities, and even those with the vitality of youth cannot perform all of the ceremonial duties. For example, the elaborate preparations for funerals and the persistence of acts of mourning for three years after death of a parent require so much wealth and energy that people do not have enough left over for ordinary living. (3) Confucianists advocate learning to play and listening to music. But the time and energy devoted to music is so wasteful that not even those who have amassed great wealth can afford to do so in the way Confucius recommended. (4) Confucianists seem resigned to a predetermined fate, which makes them lazy rather than productive. This latter criticism, at least, is hardly justified, since Confucius held that only after a person has done all that he can for himself should he resign himself calmly to the inevitable.

Commentators upon the controversy between Confucianists and Mohists delight in pointing out apparent inconsistencies on both sides. Mohists believed in the existence of spirits yet failed to perform ceremonies designed to please them. Confucianists punctiliously conducted ritualistic ceremonies for spirits even though they refused to believe in the existence of spirits. Yet such apparent inconsistencies disappear when we remember certain facts. The Confucian reason for conducting these ceremonies is not based on the assurance of the existence of spirits but upon the assurance of the principle of reciprocity inherent in the tao of association; that is, one should treat the spirits of his ancestors just as he would like to be treated if he were such a spirit. Consequently ceremonial expression of respect for spirits grows naturally from an extension of self-respect. The Mohist reason for belief in spirits is not based so much on evidence for their existence or for concern about their welfare as upon need for assurance that those who fail to love everybody indiscriminatingly will be punished by superhuman powers whenever human powers fail to guarantee such love.

Another critic of Confucius, Hsun tzu, was really a follower of Confucius in most respects. But he objected to the Taoist and Confucian doctrine that nature, including human nature, is essentially good. A child is born selfish and needs to be socialized. He does not at birth have an interest in the welfare of others. This he has to acquire and he can acquire it only by being taught. Human nature is not originally good, but it has to be made good by effort. Therefore the teaching of morality must be imposed upon new individuals by an external agency. Hsun tzu argued that rules of morality originated not so much as an extension of man's internal nature as from the fact that men cannot live together without some kind of social organization that requires social rules, and that men cannot defend themselves against enemies unless they have such an organization and rules. The rules of morality are designed to set limits upon the desires of those whose natural selfishness and aggressiveness would disrupt social harmony; in order to insure order such rules must be imposed upon everyone. It is the function of *li,* appropriate conduct, to establish these rules.

Han Fei-tzu, culminator of another classical school of Chinese philosophy, studied under Hsun tzu and agreed with him that human beings are born selfish and need to be controlled if welfare and stability are to be maintained. Han Fei-tzu was an administrator or minister of internal affairs. Thus he represented the viewpoint of a civil servant. Like his predecessor, Shen Tao, he argued that without authority an administrator cannot govern no matter how good he is, whereas with authority he can govern no matter how bad he is. Therefore a ruler's power must be absolute. Like another predecessor, Shen Pu-hai, he argued that a ruler should delegate his responsibilities to ministers, who will be rewarded if they succeed and punished if they fail. Therefore a ruler need not be either a wise or a highly moral man. Like a third predecessor, Shang Yang, he argued that uncertainty concerning laws leaves people unclear about their duties and that leniency and favoritism weaken a ruler's power. Therefore laws must be enacted on all subjects, made clear, and enforced with impartiality upon those high as well as low in social rank. Thus Han Fei-tzu and his school disagreed with the Confucian doctrine that knowledge of *li,* the best way of externally expressing one's inner nature, is sufficient for good government. They insisted that rulers should have absolute authority to impose conditions upon people so that they would be forced to be good.

Another attack on Confucianism, which occurred centuries later, was that by Buddhists. Confucian naturalism offered no hope of individual survival after death, no metaphysical explanations about the nature of the universe, no doctrine of grace whereby one might obtain special favors from powerful deities, and no escape from the rigorous moral duties detailed for each position in the family hierarchy. Buddhism, as it came from India, brought ideals of reincarnation and thus hope for rebirth, survival and eventual attainment of beatific Nirvana whereas Confucius and Lao-tzu believed death to be final. Buddhism brought speculations about the ultimate nature of cosmic reality and value, including ages of the world, levels of being, psychological processes, subtle dialectic, and even hells, which stimulated imagination and expanded intellectual horizons. Confucius, on the other hand, had maintained a simple, naive picture of experienceable nature and an agnostic attitude about invisible powers. Buddhism brought doctrines of Karma, with its accumulation of merits, and of *bodhisattvas,* who graciously sought to aid all who came to them in need; Confucianism did not include special favors from invisible divinities or rewards to be collected only in a future life. Buddhism brought ideals of monkhood, celibacy, and monastic isolation from worldly, including family, affairs, which permitted those suppressed in a family hierarchy to escape to a morally freer way of life; Confucianism allowed no opportunity for relief from domination of inferiors by their elders. Buddhist metaphysical, psychological, and logical ideas about the ultimacy of indistinctness ran directly counter to Confucian ideas about the genuineness of regularity and the orderliness of natural processes, about the need for appreciating the ultimacy of one's present duties whatever they may happen to be, and about discriminating among different persons, offices, and things. Buddhism regarded interest in external affairs, including government and ritual, as illusory, and thus attacked Confucianism at almost every level. The conversion of rulers to Buddhism, and its spread and partial domination of China for almost a thousand years, was perhaps the greatest threat to the survival of Confucianism that occurred until recent times.

Defenders of Confucius

Chief defender of Confucianism in early times was Mencius (372?–?289 B.C.). Critics of Confucius, both before and after Mencius, emphasized problems connected with spirits, ancestor worship, agnosticism, ritualism, and discrimination to such an extent that the positive contributions of Confucius, which were too subtle for many of them, tended to be ignored. The teachings of Confucius constitute some of mankind's greatest religious ideals, but these are not to be found in the interpretations given by his critics. His great religious ideal was *chih* or wisdom. This ideal received such scant attention among his critics that many accounts omit it entirely. It was the chief task and achievement of Mencius to defend and expand this great ideal.

Before we show how Mencius did this, let us show how he defended the position of Lao-tzu and Confucius that human nature is basically good. Such a view seemed so obvious to Confucius that he never felt called upon to discuss it. The Taoistic view that whatever is natural is good was so much a matter of common sense that it did not need questioning. Evil consists in deviation from one's own nature. Save a man from deviation and good automatically ensues. But after the bitter criticisms of Mo Ti, who believed that men naturally remain selfish rather than social, Mencius was called upon to defend the goodness of man in a way Confucius had never done. Mencius argued his case by citing evidence available to everyone. We find, for example, an unwillingness in men to see other men suffer. To illustrate this, Mencius recalled how, when you happen to see a child about to fall in a well, you suddenly feel alarmed and distressed. The universality of such feelings of alarm stands witness that men are instinctively concerned with the welfare of others. That is, men are by nature social and not, as Mo Ti, Hsun tzu, and Han Fei-tzu claimed, merely selfish beings.

Further details of his argument include pointing out that we feel such distress regardless of whether the child is our own or that of a stranger. One tries, if he can, to rescue the child, not because he desires praise or reward, and not because he fears being blamed and shamed if he refuses. His response and efforts occur so spontaneously that he has no time to think of these possibilities. The sense of shame itself, also something universal in men, implies concern for one's reputation in the eyes of others and presupposes some inherently social nature. A person lacking in instinctive compassion and shame is not really human.

Our instinctive feelings of compassion are the source of our adult good will (*jen*). Our instinctive feelings of shame are the source of our interest in the best way of doing things, *i.e.,* the principles of morality such as reciprocity and sincerity (*yi*). Our instinctive feelings of modesty are the source of our desire for appropriate modes of social interaction (*li*). Our intuitive sense of what is so and what is not so, or of genuineness and artificiality, is the source of our religious ideal of yea-saying or wisdom (*chih*). (See *Mencius,* II, A. 6.)

Mencius elaborated upon Confucius' ideal of *chih,* not for the purpose of modifying it but to explain it. The simple *chih* of Confucius becomes the complex *hao jan chih ch'i,* sometimes rendered into English as "The Great Morale." (*See* Fung Yu-lan, *The Spirit of Chinese Philosophy,* pp. 24–28.) Confucius' *chih* is that ideal condition of life in which we have perfected our knowledge of *yi,* fully achieved *jen,* intuitively know and habitually practice *li,* and no longer act with any doubt, mistrust, or hesitation inhibiting the perfection of our yea-saying to whatever life offers.

To explain Confucius' *chih,* Mencius seems to have added first the concept of *ch'i,* morale. Now one might have morale in isolation from others in the sense that when alone on a journey he maintains his hope that he will complete the journey successfully. But what Mencius means is that kind of morale which people have together when their joint confidence serves as a mutually sustaining force. His description calls to mind Jesus' ideal of that "Kingdom of Heaven," which is at once within you and among you and is pervaded by that love "which casteth out fear." *Chih ch'i* is no momentary festival of convivial togetherness in which usual animosities have been temporarily forgotten. It can be attained only by the gradual growth of profound respect for the common interests of people who have lived together for long periods of time. It manifests itself as an habitual response to both the present and continuing needs of others as if fulfillment of them were as much to be expected as of one's own needs. That Confucius' *chih* was essentially a social morale is something that Mencius explicitly reemphasized.

But a second, possibly more significant, addition for those seeing religion as cosmic at-homeness appears in the terms *"hao jan,"* meaning "great to a supreme degree." *Chih* is the affirmation not merely of self and of society but of the cosmic universe, of Tao, of *yang* and *yin,* of *T'ien* (that Nature which is above man), of the Five Elements, and of the cyclical processes that brought mankind into being and that conduct each man into and out of existence in due course. Hence *hao jan chih ch'i* consists in the perfect embodiment in men of an unquestioning confidence in the natural course of cosmic as well as human events. After Mencius, no doubt should have remained that *chih* as an ideal epitomizes, perhaps, mankind's greatest religious idealism. Yet, to people troubled with animosities, hunger, or doubts, and especially to those who hope for more than they deserve, this supreme ideal is, as Mencius admits, "difficult to explain."

Later defenders of Confucius, throughout more than two millennia of Chinese history, were numerous. "The Four Books," expressing ideas attributed primarily to him, and "The Five Classics," commonly associated with him, became required subjects for official examinations for civil service positions in 125 B.C. His supporters prompted various special Imperial honors from time to time. In 1 A.D., he was given the title "Duke." In 59 A.D., sacrifice in his honor in all schools in larger cities was decreed. In 422, a temple honoring him was erected at his place of birth. Successively, he was entitled "Foremost Teacher" (609), "Foremost Sage" (628), "Prince" (739), and "Grand Perfection and Ultimate Sage" (1308). Thus a gradually growing tendency to deify Confucius gained momentum until he was finally accorded the same ceremonious sacrifice by the Emperor as was made to *T'ien* or Heaven. Confucianism became a kind of state cult. Yet reverence for his greatness never went so far as to interpret him as a god, a creator, a savior, or a transcendental power. Not only did acceptance of Confucian doctrines by ruling dynasties help to spread his fame and influence, but too close identification of his teachings with the status quo led many to reject his tenets as not only conservative but as reactionary when times were ripe for revolutions inspired in part by Western scientific, political, and economic ideals.

"Confucianism" has come to mean a whole long complex history of cultural developments. Confucian philosophy was modified again and again by later interpreters, both under the increasingly intricate criticisms of Buddhist and Taoist thinkers, who themselves held modified views, and under the attempts of supporters—such as the famous Neo-Confucianist, Chu Hsi (1130–1200 A.D.)—to transform the Confucian *li* (meaning "form" as well as "propriety") into a Platonic "Idea" or essence. Speculations about cosmic "Reason" and about transcendental realities added new dimensions of thought to the broadening stream of Confucianism. The practices of political etiquette growing from modifications dictated by changing times continue to be called "Confucian." The misunderstandings of critics, which find their place in literature and history, also bear the name "Confucian." Present perspective suggests a double fate now in store for Confucius: a deliberate annihilation of such evidences of his influence in China as seem "imperialistic" and "reactionary" to Communist rulers and a growing absorption of his ideals as part of the wisdom of mankind. Will the teachings of Confucius, like those of Gotama, the Buddha, in India, and those of Jesus Christ, in Judea, suffer a declining in interest in his homeland while it grows in magnitude throughout the world?

END OF UNIT QUESTIONS

Directions: Use what you have learned in Unit III to respond to the questions below.

1. How has China's history effected the development of religious traditions in its country?

2. Describe the complexity of Daoism. Consider how it incorporates many different elements into its practice.

3. What are the important social relationships in Confucianism?

4. How do Daoism and Confucianism accept other practices in their religious tradition?

FOR FURTHER READING

Goodrich, L. Carrington. *A Short History of the Chinese People*. Mineola, NY: Dover Publications, 2002.

Hinton, David. *The Analects: Confucius*. Washington, DC: Counterpoint, 1998.

Kohn, Livia. *Introducing Daoism*. London: Routledge, 2009.

Komjathy, Louis. *The Daoist Tradition: An Introduction*. London: Bloomsbury, 2013.

Wong, Eva. *Taoism: An Essential Guide*. Boston: Shambhala, 2011.

Yao, Xinzhong. *An Introduction to Confucianism*. Cambridge, UK: Cambridge University Press, 2000.

The Abrahamic Religious Traditions

The Abrahamic Religious Traditions

Editor's Introduction

Abrahamic traditions is the last section. The following religious traditions—Judaism, Christianity, and Islam—all claim Abraham as the patriarch of their respective tradition. But their historical development and growth have taken different paths. The readings are organized similar to the previous sections, with added readings on Jewish daily life, Christian ethics, and the holy book of Islam. The land area of the Middle East contains the people, cultures, and religions that influenced the Abrahamic traditions. This vast region has some of the oldest surviving cultures and religions of the world. It now includes seventeen different countries that share some similar cultural and religious characteristics.

The readings "Reform, Orthodox, and Conservative Judaism, Zionism" by Jacob Neusner and "Judaism and Daily Life" by Eliezer Segal provide an introduction to Judaism. It is an Abrahamic tradition that has developed over many centuries and continues to be transformed today. At the heart of its tradition is the Torah (the Law), which has been written and orally transmitted. It is the Torah that continues to define many Jewish practices today. The Jewish bible, called the Tanakh, contains the Torah and provides also the history, traditions, and practices for the people. Judaism traces its origins to the covenant between God and Abraham. Faithful Jews profess faith in one God who created the universe. Judaism believes humans are created in the image of God and to continue to keep God's law on earth. The Sabbath is a holy day set aside for strict rest.

The reading "Christianity" by Christopher D. Martinez examines the second of the three Abrahamic traditions, Christianity. It developed out of Judaism and was founded on the life and teachings of Jesus Christ. It is the largest organized religion in the world, with over two billion followers. Attention will be given to its history, beliefs, and practices, but also some contemporary influences and developments will be considered.

Traditional Christian beliefs include the belief in the one and only true God, who is one and exists as Father, Son, and Holy Spirit, and the belief that Jesus is the divine and human Messiah sent to save the world. Christianity is also noted for its emphasis on faith in Jesus Christ. The sacred text of Christianity is the Bible, including both the Hebrew Scriptures (also known as the Old Testament) and the New Testament. Central to Christian practice is the gathering at churches for worship, fellowship, and study and engagement with the world through evangelism and social action.

The reading "Christian Ethics and Politics" by James R. Adair takes up further the idea that Christians have been influential in justice and social issues in their respective societies. It is important to understand that Christianity is not just about worship but about how Christians treat one another in the wider world. This reading takes into consideration the importance of the Christian influence on society and politics.

The reading "The Qur'an: God Speaks" by William E. Shepard turns to Islam. It is the third of the Abrahamic traditions. Islam is a monotheistic religious tradition that developed in the Middle East in the seventh century CE. Islam, which literally means "surrender" or "submission," was founded on the teachings of the Prophet Muhammad as an expression of surrender to the will of Allah, the creator and sustainer of the world. The Qur'an, the sacred text of Islam, contains the teachings of the Prophet that were revealed to him from Allah. Essential to Islam is the belief that Allah is the one and true God, with no partner or equal.

Islam has several branches and much variety within those branches. The two divisions within the tradition are the Sunni and Shi'a, each of which claims different means of maintaining religious authority. One of the unifying characteristics of Islam is the Five Pillars, the fundamental practices of Islam. One of the defining characteristics of Islam is the primacy of sacred places, including Mecca, Medina, and Jerusalem. Muslims gather at mosques to worship Allah, pray, and study scripture. There is not a sharp distinction between the religious and secular aspects of life in Islam; all aspects of a Muslim's life are to be oriented to serving Allah. Islam expanded almost immediately beyond its birthplace in the Arabian Peninsula and now has significant influences in Africa and throughout Asia, Europe, and the Americas.

Reading 9 Middle East: History, Beliefs, Practices

By J. Andrew Dearman

History

Religion in the Middle East casts a long shadow, with material cultural remains providing evidence of religious practices millennia before writing developed. With the advent of writing in the great civilizations of Egypt and Mesopotamia (ca. 3000 BCE), there is documented evidence of complex religious systems, central to their societies, and complete with institutions such as temples, specialized personnel, and sacrificial cults to serve the gods. In addition to matters common to religious development, the region has experienced several fundamental shifts in political hegemony, cultural profile, and language usage, all of which also affected the practice of religion. The religious heritage of Egypt, Canaan, Syria, Asia Minor, and Mesopotamia, as known from the third and second millennia BCE, is now difficult to identify in the current religions of Judaism, Christianity, and Islam, each of which essentially assimilated their older counterparts and succeeded them. Judaism, which emerged from the Iron Age states of Israel and Judah during the Persian period, has its heirs in the small, modern state of Israel. Christianity, which emerged from Greco-Roman Judaism, has its heirs in most modern Middle Eastern states, but is now the majority in none of them. Islam, which emerged from the Arabian Peninsula in the seventh century CE to control the whole region, remains the majority religion in every modern Middle Eastern state with the exception of Israel. It is also the reason for the centrality of Arabic as the lingua franca, the most widely used language in the region.

The end of the second millennium BCE saw the collapse of traditional centers of power in much of the region, and in the aftermath a number of new entities emerged into recorded history. Among these newly emerged states was Israel, whose constituent tribes and cities were heirs to the Bronze Age traditions of Canaan and Syria. In the centuries that followed, Israel and Judah produced a collection of authoritative writings now known to Jews as the Hebrew Bible and to Christians as the Old Testament. In the ninth through seventh centuries BCE, Neo-Assyrian forces expanded

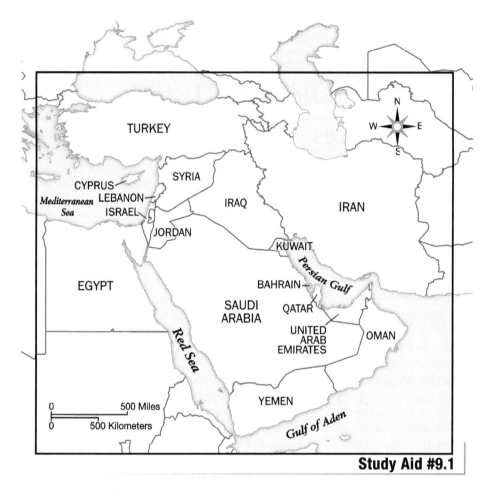

Study Aid #9.1

from their center in northern Mesopotamia, moving west into Syria-Palestine and eventually for a time into Lower (northern) Egypt. When the Neo-Assyrian Empire crumbled, it was succeeded by the Neo-Babylonian Empire and the vigorous King Nebuchadnezzar (ca. 605–539 BCE). Next came the Persian Empire under Cyrus the Great and a series of successors (ca. 539–330 BCE). As with the Assyrians, the Babylonians and Persians eventually ruled much of the ancient Near East and briefly parts of Egypt. These immense political changes brought with them cultural diffusion as well; so, for example, Assyrian astral cults and Persian dualism interacted with the religions of Syria-Palestine and Egypt.

Another immense cultural change came to the region with the military campaigns of Alexander the Great (334–323 BCE). Through military prowess he brought about a reordering of the political map of the ancient Near East. After his death in 323, his successors carved out spheres of influence and dominated the Mediterranean and Near Eastern regions for the next 175 years. Even more influential and much longer lasting was the change brought in by the Greek language and culture of the time, known today as Hellenism. Eventually a form of Greek became the common language of the region. Egyptian and Semitic deities were identified with Greek counterparts, even as new temples were built.

The arrival of Roman imperialism in Egypt and the eastern Mediterranean brought yet more change and eventually a broader cultural mix between Greco-Roman institutions and those of longer duration in the region. Christianity began as a Jewish messianic sect during Roman hegemony in Palestine. With the so-called conversion of Constantine, the Roman ruler of the eastern empire, Christianity emerged as a favored religion in the first quarter of the fourth century CE and as the official religion of the empire by the end of that century. Political power was centered in Byzantium, renamed Constantinople and located on the former land bridge between Asia and Europe at the Bosporus Strait.

The Byzantine Christian Empire lasted until the arrival of Muslim forces from Arabia, just a few years after Muhammad's death in Medina in 632. Egypt, Palestine, Syria, and Iraq were all incorporated into the Islamic sphere, and the process of creating an Islamic culture began. Two primary forms of Islam developed, the Sunni and the Shi'a. The latter looked to the male descendants of Muhammad as the rightful leaders of the community, while the Sunnis saw continuity in leadership based on maintaining the pattern of the prophet's leadership. The political center of the Islamic world varied in the following centuries. It would be located in places such as Damascus, Baghdad (a city formed initially as a capital for Muslim rulers), Cairo, and eventually Constantinople, which was captured by Muslim forces in 1453 and renamed Istanbul. The Ottoman Empire had its capital in Istanbul and ruled the Middle Eastern region from around 1520 until 1918.

The middle decades of the twentieth century saw much of the Middle Eastern political map redrawn by the British and French governments, the victors over the Ottoman Empire in World War I. In 1948, Jewish immigrants to the region declared a modern state of Israel and made Modern Hebrew one of its official languages. In the latter half of the twentieth century, other states in the region emerged from colonial influence to form national governments and identities. A Muslim identity is common to these other states, although Christianity, Druze, and Baha'i are also present.

Beliefs

The primary structure of ancient Near Eastern religions was that of polytheism. This is the case even with the diversity of regional cultures, the long history of development, and the massive syncretistic

---

Study Aid #9.2

Countries of the Middle East

Bahrain	Israel	Palestine	Turkey
Cyprus	Jordan	(territories)	United Arab
Egypt	Kuwait	Qatar	Emirates
Iran	Lebanon	Saudi Arabia	Yemen
Iraq	Oman	Syria	

and assimilating shifts that came with the advent of Greco-Roman cultures. The deities were understood as a hierarchical interactive community, in some sense like a state or urban bureaucracy, where their tasks with weather, fertility, trade protection, crafts, and health were carried out. Indeed, the language of king and queen could be used of chief deities, as could terms like "father" or "creator of the gods." The deity Assur, for example, was the patron of the Assyrian city of the same name and was proclaimed as the divine king in the Assyrian realm. Ishtar was the Queen of Heaven among the Assyrians. In a pantheon, other deities might be understood as members of a lower rank, though important in their own sphere, and perhaps as offspring of a high or primordial deity. The creation of the world could be associated with primordial deities (as in Mesopotamia), or with a high deity such as El in parts of Bronze Age Canaan, or with a variety of deities in Egypt. The abode of the gods was understood to be heaven, even when they were associated with mountains, seas, or other earthly terrain such as particular cities or regions. Thus some deities were associated with astronomical phenomena. Shamash was the sun deity in Mesopotamia; Re was the sun deity in Egypt. In Syria-Palestine the vigorous storm deity was known as master (Baal) and rider of the clouds. With the advent of Hellenism, some new deities were added to the region and some indigenous deities were identified with Greco-Roman counterparts. Ishtar, for example, was identified with Venus, and Melqart, the patron deity of Tyre, was identified with Heracles.

There is evidence that several of the tribal societies of Syria-Palestine understood their collective identity in light of a chief or patron deity. This is not monotheism per se, which entails the denial of the existence of any other deity, but can be defined as monolatry, at least at the level of the ruling dynasty and/or the sponsored cult of a capital city. In Egypt, Pharaoh Akhenaten (fourteenth century BCE) sought to reform Egyptian religion similarly to the primary worship of Aten, although he did not deny the existence of other Egyptian deities. His reforming efforts were resisted and died with him. Israelite religious beliefs were forged in these circumstances. Israel's deity (YHWH), often pronounced Yahweh, was proclaimed Israel's sole deity. The strong prohibition in the Hebrew Bible against the worship of other deities (Exod. 20:3) assumes their potential appeal, but also that Yahweh (typically translated as "Lord") was sufficient for the needs of his people. Yahweh as Lord is carefully differentiated from the Canaanite Baal, though he wielded similar powers. Yahweh is also called (the)

Study Aid #9.3
Middle East Empires, Eras, Ages

Neo-Assyrian: 9th–7th centuries BCE	Byzantium: 5th–7th centuries
Neo-Babylonian: 6th century	Islam: 8th–15th centuries
Persian: 5th–4th centuries	Ottoman: 16th–19th centuries
Hellenism: 3rd–1st centuries	Colonial: 20th century
Roman: 1st–4th centuries CE	

"God," using the common terminology for the high god El, recognized as the creator in the Canaanite realm, and he is addressed as the cosmic king.

It is ironic, historically speaking, that the three monotheistic religions either emerge from or take strong root in the region. Judaism is an outgrowth of the religious traditions of Israel and dependent on the Hebrew Bible and authoritative postbiblical texts such as the Mishnah, the Jerusalem and Babylonian Talmuds, and various Midrashic compositions. In the formative years of classical Judaism, Jerusalem and the Jewish temple located there were central to Jewish identity. The second temple was destroyed in 70 CE, and Jews were expelled from Jerusalem after a subsequent revolt against Roman rule. While there remained a strong Jewish presence in the region, there was no Jewish state until 1948 and the formation of the modern state of Israel.

Islam was birthed in the Arabian Peninsula and understood itself as the final and complete revelation that the only true God (Allah in Arabic) conveyed to Muhammad, having raised up prophets in previous generations beforehand. Both Christians and Jews are understood as People of the Book, with Moses understood as giver of the Torah and Jesus as giver of the gospel. Neither Torah nor gospel, however, is identified with the text by that name as preserved in Judaism and Christianity. The written revelation of Allah, given to Muhammad, is the Qur'an. "Islam" is the Arabic term for submission and characterizes the posture of a Muslim who submits his or her life to the revealed will of Allah. Abraham, known from the Hebrew Bible (the Christian Old Testament) and the New Testament, is not reckoned as a Jew, but as a prophet and one who submitted his life to Allah.

Practices

One may summarize the primary practice of ancient Near Eastern religions as the care for and service of the gods. Devotion or piety is actualized through prayer, sacrifice, testimony, and fidelity to the teaching of priests and the wisdom of sages. Temples for seasonal sacrifice and votive offerings were central institutions of society. The gods governed the affairs of the regions in which they were worshiped, and they were petitioned to bless their patron cities and lands with fertility and peace and to ward off the powers of pestilence.

Jewish monotheistic worship at the temple in Jerusalem had the basic characteristics of an ancient Near Eastern sacrificial cult and followed a calendar of festivals based on the history of God's actions on behalf of Israel. Three in particular were pilgrimage festivals. In early spring was Passover, celebrating the deliverance of Israel's ancestors from Egyptian slavery. In late spring was the Festival of Weeks, which celebrated the firstfruits of agricultural harvest and the giving of the covenant and God's instructional code at Mount Sinai. In the fall came a New Year's celebration, the Day of Atonement, and the festival known as Ingatherings or Booths. This last celebration commemorated God's care of Israel's ancestors, who wandered in the wilderness on the way from Egypt to the promised land in Canaan, and provided an occasion to give thanks for a fall agricultural harvest. Jews in dispersion from the land of Israel had also developed patterns of nonsacrificial worship on the Sabbath day (seventh day of the week), when they gathered at synagogues (= place of assembly) to read from the Law and the Prophets, to hear their significance expounded for the life of faith, and to pray. With the destruction of the temple, this pattern of worship became the norm for Jews. Classical Jewish practices include a dietary code, cessation of work and corporate worship on the Sabbath, confession that the Lord is "one" (Deut. 6:4), study of the law, circumcision of males as a sign of God's covenant with them, ritual practices designed to reflect the holiness of service to God, and acts of charity.

Classical Islamic practices are conveniently arranged as Five Pillars of the faith. They are as follows: the confession that there is no god except Allah and Muhammad is his prophet; daily prayer (a "call" to prayer is issued five times a day); pilgrimage to Mecca, the holiest city in Islam; fasting in the daylight hours during the month of Ramadan; and the giving of alms to the poor. The Muslim house of worship is known as a mosque. Daily prayers may be said in the mosque or elsewhere. Friday-noon prayers are accompanied by a sermon expounding a text from the Qur'an, delivered by a community leader. Believers prostrate themselves in the direction of Mecca, where Muhammad first received revelation from Allah.

From the time of Muhammad, there has traditionally been no distinction made between the political governance of an Islamic society and the practices of the faith. At the same time, Islam has traditionally held that there should be no compulsion in religion. Historically, Muslim rulers in the Middle East have protected the right of minority religions (e.g., Judaism, Christianity) to assemble and worship but have forbidden their proselytizing activities and reckoned conversion as apostasy to Islam and a criminal offense.

Sources

John L. Esposito, ed. *The Oxford Encyclopedia of the Islamic World*. Oxford University Press, 2005.

Richard C. Martin, ed. *Encyclopedia of Islam and the Muslim World*. Macmillan, 2004.

Jacob Neusner, Alan J. Avery-Peck, and William Scott Green, eds. *The Encyclopedia of Judaism*. Brill, 2005.

F. E. Peters. *The Monotheists: Jews, Christians, and Muslims in Conflict and Competition*. Princeton University Press, 2003.

Donald B. Redford, ed. *The Oxford Encyclopedia of Egypt*. Oxford University Press, 2001.

Jack M. Sasson, ed. *Civilizations of the Ancient Near East*. Hendrickson, 2000.

Antoine Sfeir, ed. *The Columbia World Dictionary of Islamism*. Columbia University Press, 2007.

Fred Skolnik, ed. *Encyclopedia Judaica*. Macmillan Reference, 2007.

Reading 10   Reform, Orthodox, and Conservative Judaisms, Zionism

By Jacob Neusner

T he urgent question that was deemed by many Jews to require an answer shifted in modern times, the eighteenth century to the present. The question "Why is Israel subordinated to the gentiles?" had found its answer in Israel's sanctification and God's judgment for Israel's failures. With the political changes represented by the emancipation of the Jews and their gaining citizenship, a new urgent question arose: How is it possible to be both an Israelite and something else—a French, German, British, or American citizen, for example?

Reform Judaism responded and fixed the pattern of all modern Judaism. It redefined "Israel" to stand for a religious community with a universal mission. It affirmed changes in the way of life and worldview of the received, rabbinic system. These were meant to affirm that the Israelite could integrate and be in addition loyal to France, Britain, Germany, or the U.S.A. Practices that separated the Israelite from the rest of humanity—dietary laws, for example—were to be dropped. Responding to the advent of Reform Judaism, Orthodox Judaism in Germany and the other Western countries rejected the changes Reform made. But Orthodoxy in its integrationist model held that while Judaism endured unchanging, the Israelite should combine study of the Torah with study of secular sciences. So one could both practice Judaism and integrate one's life within the national culture. Conservative Judaism mediated between the two positions, affirming that tradition could change, but only in accord with the historical processes of Judaism over the centuries.

A political, not a religious system, Zionism did not trust the promise of emancipation. It rejected the hope that the Jews could ever be secure in the gentile nations and proposed the creation of a Jewish state in Palestine, where Jews in security could be Jewish and nothing else, for example, speaking Hebrew as their everyday language.

Jacob Neusner, "Reform, Orthodox, and Conservative Judaisms, Zionism," *Judiasm: The Basics*, pp. 148-167, 191-193.

Competition in Defining Judaism in Modern Times

Basic to Judaism from the nineteenth century to the present day has been the division, into distinct movements, of the received Rabbinic Judaism. Of these in the English-speaking world, in the U.S.A., Canada, Britain, and elsewhere, three sizable denominations or movements predominate: Orthodox, Reform, and Conservative Judaism. In North America, approximately half of all Jews affiliated with synagogues identify as Reform, about a third are Conservative, and most of the rest are Orthodox.

To the same circle of new versions of Scripture and tradition belongs Zionism, a political movement aimed at restoring the Jewish people to the Land of Israel, founding the Jewish state, and realizing the nationalism of the Jewish people. Zionism came to fruition in the middle of the twentieth century in the creation of the State of Israel in 1948. These four systems—three religious and Judaic, one political and Jewish—competed productively and continue to thrive. All form mass movements, not just celebrations of particular theologians and their doctrines. All have endured for more than a century.

Why Did the Rabbinic System Meet Competition?

In the late eighteenth and nineteenth centuries, sweeping changes made urgent political issues that formerly had drawn slight attention. The Jews had formerly constituted a distinct group. They segregated themselves in culture and ethnic identity and in politics as well. Now in the West they were expected—and aspired—to integrate and form part of an undifferentiated mass of citizens, all of them equal before the law. Jews wanted civil rights and accepted civil obligations of citizenship.

The received Judaism did not address that circumstance. It fostered the self-segregation of the Jews as Holy Israel, their separation from the gentiles in politics and culture, not only in religion. The received system rested on the political premise that God's law formed God's people and governed the Jews. And that sufficed to identify what was meant by "Israel," "a people that dwells apart," in the language of Scripture. The received system did not answer the question, "How can Jews both practice Judaism and also participate in secular society and culture?" None aspired to a dual role. The two political premises—the one of the nation-state, the other of the Torah—scarcely permitted reconciliation.

The consequent Judaic systems, Reform Judaism, a Westernized Orthodoxy that is called integrationist Orthodox Judaism, positive Historical Judaism (in the U.S.A. "Conservative Judaism"), each addressed issues of politics and culture that were regarded as acute and not merely chronic. Reform favored total integration of the Jews into Western culture. Integrationist Orthodoxy concurred but reaffirmed the separateness of Israel, the Holy People, in religious matters. Positive Historical Judaism/Conservative Judaism took the middle position.

The three systems met the political challenge and mediated the cultural ones. All repudiated Judaic self-segregation. Each maintained that Jews could both practice Judaism and serve as good citizens of the nation and participants in the culture of the countries where they found themselves. All alleged that they formed the natural next step in the unfolding of "the tradition," meaning the Judaic system of the dual Torah. Where politics precipitated a new problem, the Judaic systems that emerged responded. In the Russian Empire before Communism (1917), in Russian Poland, White Russia, and Ukraine, Reform, integrationist Orthodox, and Conservative Judaism never registered; the received system continued to answer the urgent questions of the age. No political revolution required change.

Reform Judaism

Reform Judaism (a.k.a. liberal or progressive Judaism) responded to the new questions Jews faced in political emancipation. These changes, particularly in western Europe and the U.S.A., accorded to Jews the status of citizens like other citizens of the nations in which they lived. But they denied the Jews the status of a separate, holy people, living under its own laws and awaiting the Messiah to lead it back to the Holy Land at the end of history. Rather, Reform Judaism looked forward to a messianic age, when the social order would be perfected in justice and humanity, and defined for its "Israel" a mission to hasten the coming of the messianic age. Meanwhile Jews would integrate themselves into the common cultures of the nations where they lived.

Reform Judaism insisted that change in the religion, Judaism, in response to new challenges represented a valid continuation of that religion's long-term capacity to evolve. Reform Judaism denied that any version of the Torah enjoyed eternal validity. All responded to the changes that history brought. Accordingly, Jews should adopt the politics and culture of the countries where they lived, preserving differences of only a religious character, with religion narrowly construed.

Changes in Synagogue Worship

Reform Judaism finds its beginnings to the nineteenth century in changes, called reforms and regarded as the antecedents of Reform, in trivial aspects of public worship in the synagogue (Petuchowski 1971). The motive for these changes derived from the simple fact that many Jews rejected the received theological system and its liturgical expression. People were defecting from the synagogue. Since it was then taken for granted that there was no secular option, giving up the faith meant surrendering all ties to the group. (Secular Jewish systems, Jewish but not religious, typified by Zionism, emerged only at the beginning of the twentieth century.) The beginning of change addressed two issues at one time: (1) Making the synagogue more attractive so that (2) defectors would return, and others would not leave. The reform of Judaism in its manifestation in synagogue worship—the cutting edge of the faith—therefore took cognizance of something that had already taken place. And for a sizable sector of Jewry that was the loss for the received system—way of life, worldview, addressed to a defined Israel—of its standing as self-evident truth.

To begin with, the issue involved not politics but merely justification for changing anything at all. The reformers maintained that change was all right because historical precedent proved that change was all right. But change long had defined the constant in the ongoing life of the received

Judaism. The normative Judaism endured, never intact but always unimpaired because of its power to absorb and make its own the diverse happenings of culture and society. [...] Implacable opposition to change represented a change. That was not the real issue. The integration of Israel among the gentiles was.

Box 10.1   The Pittsburgh Platform of Reform Judaism

For Reform Judaism in the nineteenth century, the full and authoritative statement of the system—its worldview, with profound implications on its way of life, and its theory of who is Israel—came to expression in America, in an assembly in Pittsburgh in 1885 of Reform rabbis. At that meeting of the Central Conference of American Rabbis, the Reform Judaism of the age, by now nearly a century old, took up the issues that divided the Judaism and made an authoritative statement on them, one that most Reform Jews could accept. What is important is its formulation of the issue of Israel as political circumstances defined it. Critical to normative Judaism was its view of Israel as God's people, a supernatural polity, living out its social existence under God's Torah. The way of life, one of sanctification, and the worldview, one of persistent reference to the Torah for rules of conduct, on the one side, and of the explanation of conduct, on the other, began in the basic conception of who is Israel. Here too we find emphasis on who is Israel, with that doctrine exposing for all to see the foundations of the way of life and worldview that these rabbis had formed for the Israel they conceived:

> We recognize in the Mosaic legislation a system of training the Jewish people for its mission during its national life in Palestine, and today we accept as binding only its moral laws and maintain only such ceremonies as elevate and sanctify our lives, but reject all such as are not adapted to the views and habits of modern civilization ... We hold that all such Mosaic and rabbinical laws as regular diet, priestly purity, and dress originated in ages and under the influence of ideas entirely foreign to our present mental and spiritual state ... Their observance in our days is apt rather to obstruct than to further modern spiritual elevation ... We recognize in the modern era of universal culture of heart and intellect the approaching of the realization of Israel's great messianic hope for the establishment of the kingdom of truth, justice, and peace among all men. We consider ourselves no longer a nation but a religious community and therefore expect neither a return to Palestine nor a sacrificial worship under the sons of Aaron nor the restoration of any of the laws concerning the Jewish state ...

Reform Judaism affirmed integration and made important changes in the law and theology of Judaism to accommodate it. It did this when the Reform rabbis in the U.S.A. adopted the Pittsburgh Platform of 1885, which stated the Reform system in a clear way (see Box 10.1). The Platform takes up each component of the Reform system in turn. Who is Israel? What is its way of life? How does it account for its existence as a distinct, and distinctive, group?

Israel once was a nation ("during its national life") but today is not a nation. It once had a set of laws that regulate diet, clothing, and the like. These no longer apply, because Israel now is not what it was then. Israel forms an integral part of Western civilization. The reason to persist as a distinctive group was that the group has its work to do, a mission—to serve as a light to the nations. That meant, namely, to realize the messianic hope for the establishment of a kingdom of truth, justice, and peace. For that purpose Israel no longer constitutes a nation. It now forms a religious community.

What that means is that individual Jews do live as citizens in other nations. Difference is acceptable at the level of religion, not nationality, a position that accords fully with the definition of citizenship of the Western democracies. The Reform worldview then lays heavy emphasis on an as-yet-unrealized, but coming, perfect age. Its way of life admits to no important traits that distinguish Jews from others, since morality, in the nature of things, forms a universal category, applicable in the same way to everyone. The theory of Israel then forms the heart of matters, and what we learn is that Israel constitutes a "we," that is, that the Jews continue to form a group that, by its own indicators, holds together and constitutes a cogent social entity. All this, in a simple statement of a handful of rabbis, forms a full and encompassing Judaism, one that, to its communicants, presented truth of a self-evident order.

Reform Judaism would evolve beyond the Pittsburgh Platform in the mid-twentieth century, affirming the peoplehood of Israel and renewing received rites. When in 1897 Zionism made its appearance, Reform Judaism rejected it: "Germany is our promised land, and Berlin is our Jerusalem." But by the later 1930s, Reform Rabbis affirmed Zionism. By the twenty-first century, its principles had defined the norm for all communities of Judaism outside the Orthodox framework. It was and remains the most successful Judaic system of modernity. One cannot help admiring the nineteenth-century framers of Reform Judaism for their optimism and their adaptability, their affirmation of progress and their invention of a mission of Israel to help God perfect creation.

But the hopeful version of Reform Judaism would meet its challenge in the Holocaust, and Reform Judaism from World War II onward parted company from its classical formulation in Pittsburgh. Today, Reform Judaism makes provision for religious practices that differentiate Jews from gentiles. It stresses Jewish peoplehood, the ethnic side to things that the founding generations of Reform Judaism relinquished.

Integrationist Orthodox Judaism

The broad category, Orthodox Judaism, requires definition and differentiation. The point of distinction is attitude toward gentile culture. "Integrationist Orthodoxy" differs from "self-segregationist Orthodox."

By "integrationist Orthodox Judaism" in the context of modernizing Judaic systems is meant a very particular approach. It is one that affirms the divine revelation and eternal authority of the Torah, oral and written, *but* that favors the integration of the Jews ("holy Israel") into the national life of the countries of their birth. In cultural terms, this meant study of the Torah and also study of philosophy. I call it "integrationist" for its cultural policy. It also is known as "modern Orthodoxy" or "Western Orthodoxy" or "neo-Orthodoxy."

Other Orthodox communities of Judaism—and they are diverse and many—in common favor the segregation of the holy Israel from other people in the countries where they live, including the State of Israel. Indicators such as clothing, language, above all, education differentiate integrationist from self-segregationist Judaisms. For example, integrationist Orthodoxy holds that secular studies are legitimate, indeed essential, so that Yeshiva University in the U.S.A. and Bar Ilan University in the State of Israel, both successful institutions of integrationist Orthodoxy, offer full academic programs in all sciences and humanities. In them, Judaic religious sciences take cognizance of the challenges of reason and history.

Self-segregated communities of Judaism bear a variety of names, such as traditional, authentic, Haredi (a Hebrew word referring to those that tremble before the Lord), and the like. Self-segregationist Orthodox centers of learning, called *yeshivot*, teach only the sacred sciences, for instance the Talmud and its commentaries. One indicator of the difference between integrationist- and self-segregationist Orthodox Judaisms is the matter of language. The self-segregationists reject the use of Hebrew and preserve Yiddish as the everyday language of the community. Integrationist Orthodoxy in the State of Israel is Hebrew-speaking, like other Israelis. A wide variety of communities of Orthodox Judaism fall into the category of self-segregation. Some are Hasidic, [...] some reject Hasidism and adhere to the classical tradition in all its depth of reason and rationality. But all self-segregated communities of Judaism concur that Holy Israel is not to mix with the gentiles.

Integrationist Jews kept the law of the Torah, for example as it dictated food choices and use of leisure time (to speak of the Sabbath and festivals in secular terms). They sent their children to secular schools, in addition to or instead of solely Jewish ones, or in Jewish schools, they included in the curriculum subjects outside of the sciences of the Torah. In these ways, they marked themselves as integrationist. For the notion that science or German or Latin or philosophy deserved serious study in the nineteenth century struck as wrong those for whom the received system remained self-evidently right. Those Jews did not send their children to gentile schools, and in Jewish schools did not include in the curriculum other than Torah study.

Exactly where and when did integrationist Orthodox Judaism come into being? It was in Germany, in the middle of the nineteenth century, a generation after Reform got going in the same country. Integrationist Orthodoxy responded to the advent of Reform Judaism, which defined the issues of debate. The issues addressed by all parties concerned change and history. The reformers held that Judaism could legitimately change. Judaism was a product of history. The integrationist Orthodox opponents (not to mention the self-segregationist communities of Judaism) denied that Judaism could change. They insisted that Judaism derived from God's will at Sinai and was eternal and supernatural, not historical and man-made. In these two convictions, of course, the integrationist Orthodox recapitulated the convictions of the received system and no one in the self-segregationist Orthodox world would take exception to this position.

Accordingly, the integrationist Orthodox Judaism dealt with the same urgent questions as did Reform Judaism, questions raised by political emancipation. But it gave different answers to them, even though both Reform and integrationist Orthodoxy set forth equally reasoned, coherent theological answers to questions of history and ambient culture. That Orthodoxy maintained the worldview of the received dual Torah, constantly citing its sayings and adhering with only trivial variations to the bulk of its norms for the everyday life. At the same time, integrationist Orthodoxy held, and today holds, that Jews adhering to the dual Torah may wear clothing similar to that which non-Jews wear. The sole exceptions were religious duties not to mix flax and wool (vegetable and animal products woven into cloth), obligatory by the law of the Torah (Lev. 19:19 and Deut. 22:9–11) and to wear show-fringes. They live within a common economy and do not practice distinctively Jewish professions. Many shave and do not grow beards. They take up a life not readily distinguished in important characteristics from the life lived by ordinary people in general.

So for integrationist Orthodoxy, a portion of an Israelite's life may prove secular. The Torah does not dictate and so sanctify all of life's details under all circumstances. The difference between integrationist Orthodoxy and the normative, received system, such as persisted in self-segregationist Judaic circles, therefore comes to expression in social policy: Integration, however circumscribed, versus the total separation of the Holy People from the nations among whom they lived.

Integrationist Judaism thus faced critics in two directions, inside and outside. But it was Reform that precipitated the organization of the integrationist communities of Judaism. Just as the reformers justified change, the integrationist Orthodox theologians denied that change was ever possible. As Walter Wurzburger wrote, "Orthodoxy looks upon attempts to adjust Judaism to the 'spirit of the time' as utterly incompatible with the entire thrust of normative Judaism which holds that the revealed will of God rather than the values of any given age are the ultimate standard" (Wurzburger 1971). To begin with the issue important to the reformers, the value of what was called "emancipation," meaning, the provision to Jews of civil rights, defined the debate. If the Reform made minor changes in liturgy and its conduct, the Orthodox rejected even those that, under other circumstances, might have found acceptance.

Saying prayers in the vernacular, for example, provoked strong opposition. But everyone knew that some of the prayers were said in Aramaic, the vernacular of the ancient Near East. The Orthodox thought that these changes, not reforms at all, represented only the first step of a process leading Jews out of the Judaic world altogether, so, as Walter Wurzburger says, "The slightest tampering with tradition was condemned."

Conservative Judaism

We treat the German Historical School and Canadian and U.S. Conservative Judaism as a single Judaism, because they share a single viewpoint: Moderation in making change, accommodation between "the tradition" and the requirements of modern life, above all, adaptation to circumstance all validated by historical research and precedent. The emphasis on historical research in settling theological debates clearly explains the name of the group of German professors who organized the system.

Arguing that its positions represent matters of historical fact rather than theological conviction, the Historical School and Conservative Judaism maintained an essentially secular position. It was that "positive historical scholarship" would prove capable, on the basis of historical facts, of purifying and clarifying the faith, joined to far stricter observance of the law than the reformers required. Questions of theology found their answers in history. Representing in practice a middle position, between integrationist Orthodoxy and Reform, it was in fact an extreme proposition, since it abdicated the throne of theology altogether and established a regency of secular learning. Reform Judaism appealed in the end to systematic religious thinking, while Conservative Judaism accorded an at-best-perfunctory hearing to theological argument and system-building.

The fundamental premise of the Conservatives' emphasis on history rested on the conviction that history and verifiable fact demonstrated the truth or falsity of theological propositions. We should look in vain in all of the prior writings of Judaic systems for precedent for that insistence on critical fact, self-evident to the nineteenth- and twentieth-century system-builders. The appeal to historical facts was meant to lay upon firm, factual foundations whatever change was to take place. In finding precedent for change, the Conservatives sought reassurance that some change—if not a great deal of change—would not endanger the enduring faith they wished to preserve. But there was a second factor. The laws and lessons of history would then settle questions of public policy near at hand.

Both in Germany in the middle of the nineteenth century and in America at the end of the nineteenth century, the emphasis throughout lay on "knowledge and practice of historical Judaism as ordained in the law of Moses expounded by the prophets and sages in Israel in Biblical and Talmudic writings," so the articles of Incorporation of the Jewish Theological Seminary of America Association stated in 1887. Calling themselves "traditionalists" rather than "Orthodox," the conservative adherents accepted for most Judaic subjects the principles of modern critical scholarship. Conservative Judaism therefore exhibited traits that linked it to Reform but also to Orthodoxy, a movement very much in the middle. Precisely how the Historical School related to the other systems of its day—the mid- and later nineteenth century requires attention to that scholarship that, apologists insisted, marked the Historical School off from Orthodoxy.

Not surprisingly, Conservative Judaism derived from professors and relied for its institutions upon academic authority. In the U.S.A., the head of the organization of Conservative Judaism is the academic chancellor of the Jewish Theological Seminary of America. Maintaining the law and theology of the received Judaism alongside integrationist Orthodoxy, the Historical School, a group of nineteenth-century German scholars, and Conservative Judaism, a twentieth-century mass movement of Judaism in America and Canada, like Reform Judaism, affirmed through secular historical fact the religious legitimacy of change.

The Historical School began among German Jewish theologians who advocated change but found Reform extreme. They parted company with Reform on some specific issues of practice and doctrine, observance of the dietary laws and belief in the coming of the Messiah for example. But they also found the ambient Orthodoxy immobile. Conservative Judaism in America in the twentieth century carried forward this same centrist position and turned a viewpoint of intellectuals into a way of life, worldview, addressed to an Israel. The Historical School, accordingly, shaped the worldview, and Conservative Judaism later on brought that view into full realization as a way of life characteristic of a large group of Jews, nearly half of all American Jews in the middle of the twentieth century, but only a third of American Jewry by the early twenty-first century.

The Historical School in Germany and Conservative Judaism in America affirmed a far broader part of the received way of life than Reform, while rejecting a much larger part than did Orthodoxy of the worldview of the received system. The Historical School concurred with the reformers concerning the norm-setting power of history (Hertzberg 1971). That meant that questions of theology and law could be referred to historians, who would settle matters by appeal to historical precedent. Thus, for example, if one could show that a given law was not practiced prior to a specified period of time, that law could be set aside or modified. If it could be shown, by contrast, that that law goes "way back," then it was treated as sacrosanct. The reformers had held that change was permissible and claimed that historical scholarship would show what change was acceptable and what was not. Concurring in principle, the proponents of the Historical School differed in matters of detail.

Toward the end of the nineteenth century, rabbis of this same centrist persuasion in the U.S.A. organized the Jewish Theological Seminary of America, in 1886–7, and from that rabbinical school, the Conservative Movement developed. The order of the formation of the several Judaisms of the nineteenth century therefore is, first, Reform, then Orthodoxy, finally, Conservatism—the two extremes, then the middle. Reform defined the tasks of the next two Judaisms to come into being. Orthodoxy framed the clearer of the two positions in reaction to Reform, but, in intellectual terms, the Historical School in Germany met the issues of Reform in a more direct way.

The stress of the Historical School in Europe and Conservative Judaism in America lay on two matters. First, critical scholarship, such as yielded the secular account of the history of Judaism [...], was assigned the task of discovering those facts of which the faith would be composed. Second, Conservative Judaism emphasized the practical observance of the rules of the received Judaism. A fissure opened, then, between scholarship and belief and practice. A professedly free approach to the study of the Torah, specifically through what was called "critical scholarship," would yield an accurate account of the essentials of the faith. But what if that did not emerge? Then the scholars and lay people alike would keep and practice nearly the whole of the tradition just as the Orthodox did.

The ambivalence of Conservative Judaism, speaking in part for intellectuals deeply loyal to the received way of life, but profoundly dubious of the inherited worldview, came to full expression in the odd slogan of its intellectuals and scholars: "Eat kosher and think *traif*." "Traif" refers to meat that is not acceptable under Judaic law, and the slogan announced a religion of orthopraxy: Do the right thing and it doesn't matter what you believe. That statement meant people should keep the rules of the holy way of life but ignore the convictions that made sense of them. Orthopraxy is the word that refers to correct action and unfettered belief, as against Orthodoxy, right action, and right doctrine. Some would then classify Conservative Judaism in America as an orthoprax Judaism defined through works, not doctrine. Some of its leading voices even denied Judaism set forth doctrine at all; this is called "the dogma of dogmaless Judaism."

What separated Conservative Judaism from Reform was the matter of observance. Fundamental loyalty to the received way of life in the nineteenth and earlier twentieth centuries distinguished the Historical School in Germany and Conservative Judaism in America from Reform Judaism in both countries. When considering the continued validity of a traditional religious practice, the Reform asked "Why?", the Conservatives, "Why not?" The Orthodox, of course, would ask no questions to begin with. The fundamental principle, that the worldview of the Judaism under construction would rest upon (mere) historical facts, came from Reform Judaism. Orthodoxy could never have concurred. The contrast to the powerful faith despite the world, exhibited by integrationist Orthodoxy's stress on the utter facticity of the Torah, presents in a clear light the positivism of the Conservatives, who, indeed, adopted the name "the *positive* Historical School."

But orthopraxy did not yield a stable social order. In America, a pattern developed in which essentially nonobservant congregations of Jews called upon rabbis whom they expected to be observant of the rules of the religion. As a result, many of the intellectual problems that occupied public debate concerned rabbis more than lay people, since the rabbis bore responsibility—so the community maintained—for not only teaching the faith but, on their own, embodying it. An observer described this Judaism as "Orthodox rabbis serving Conservative synagogues made up of Reform Jews."

How do the Reform, integrationist Orthodox, and Conservative systems then compare? Reform identified its Judaism as the linear and incremental next step in the unfolding of the Torah. The Historical School and Conservative Judaism later on regarded its Judaism as the reversion to the authentic Judaism that in time had been lost. Change was legitimate, as the Reform said, but only that kind of change that restored things to the condition of the original and correct Judaism. That position formed a powerful apologetic, because it addressed the Orthodox view that Orthodoxy constituted the linear and incremental outgrowth of "the Torah" or "the tradition," hence, the sole legitimate Judaism. It also addressed the Reform view that change was all right. Conservative Judaism established a firm criterion for what change was all right: The kind that was, really, no change at all. For the premise of the Conservative position was that things should become the way they had always been.

Here we revert to the strikingly secular character of the Reform and Conservative systems: Their insistence that religious belief could be established upon a foundation of historical fact. The category of faith, belief in transcendent things, matters not seen or tangible but nonetheless deeply felt and vigorously affirmed—these traits of religiosity hardly played a role. Rather, fact, ascertained by secular media of learning, would define truth. And truth corresponded to here-and-now reality: How things were. Scholarship would tell how things had always been and dictate those changes that would restore the correct way of life, the true worldview, for the Israel composed of pretty much all the Jews—the center. Historical research therefore provided a powerful apologetic against both sides. Like Orthodoxy, Conservative Judaism defined itself as Judaism, pure and simple. But it did claim to mark the natural next step in the slow evolution of "the tradition," an evolution within the lines and rules set forth by "the tradition" itself.

Zionism

Another response to the question of political emancipation, Zionism, founded in Basel, Switzerland, in 1897, constituted the Jews' nationalist movement. Its "Israel" was a nation ("the Jewish people") in quest of a state. It was a secular political movement utilizing the story of Scripture concerning the restoration of Israel, defined as "a People, One People," to the Land of Israel in the end of days. It achieved its goal in the creation of the State of Israel in 1948.

Zionism dismissed the questions answered by Reform and integrationist Orthodox and Conservative Judaisms. Reform Judaism had begun in the premise that the Jews could find a place for themselves in the European nation-states, if they adapted themselves to the duties of shared humanity and a common politics. Integrationist Orthodoxy addressed the same issue. But political anti-Semitism at the end of the nineteenth century—the organization of political parties on a platform of exclusion and repression of the Jews in the European nations—called into question the premises of the Reform and integrationist Orthodox theologians.

It became clear that the Jews, now resident in Europe for more than fifteen centuries, could not hope for the integration they had anticipated at the beginning of the century and for which they had prepared themselves. The urgent question became, "What is to be done to solve what the gentile Europeans called 'the Jewish question'?" Foreseeing exterminationist anti-Semitism, Zionism thus responded to a political crisis, the failure, by the end of the nineteenth century, of emancipation, meaning the promises of political improvement in the Jews' status and condition.

Once more, history defined the arena of contention. To formulate its worldview, Zionism, like Reform Judaism, invented a usable past. Zionism, furthermore, called to the Jews to emancipate themselves by facing the fact that gentiles hated Jews. As to its way of life, Zionism defined itself as the political movement aimed at founding a Jewish state where Jews could free themselves of

---

Box 10.2   Zionism and Judaism: Competing Worldviews

The Zionist worldview explicitly competed with the religious one. The formidable statement of Jacob Klatzkin (1882–1948) provides the solid basis for comparison:

> In the past there have been two criteria of Judaism: The criterion of religion, according to which Judaism is a system of positive and negative commandments, and the criterion of the spirit, which saw Judaism as a complex of ideas, like monotheism, Messianism, absolute justice, etc. According to both these criteria, therefore, Judaism rests on a subjective basis, on the acceptance of a creed ... a religious denomination ... or a community of individuals who share in a *Weltanschauung* ... In opposition to these two criteria, which make of Judaism a matter of creed, a third has now arisen, the criterion of a consistent nationalism. According to it, Judaism rests on an objective basis: To be a Jew means the acceptance of neither a religious nor an ethical creed. We are neither a denomination nor a school of thought, but members of one family, bearers of a common history ... The national definition too requires an act of will. It defines our nationalism by two criteria: Partnership in the past and the conscious desire to continue such partnership in the future. There are, therefore, two bases for Jewish nationalism – the compulsion of history and a will expressed in that history.
>
> (Hertzberg 1971)

anti-Semitism and build their own destiny. Activities to secure political support and also persuade the Jewish communities of the need to found a Jewish state formed the way of life.

The Zionist system corresponds in its components to those of Reform and integrationist Orthodoxy: A definition of Israel, a worldview, a way of life (see Box 10.2). Let us therefore turn to the analysis of Zionism viewed within the categories we have used to describe any Judaic system.

For one thing, Zionism enunciated a powerful and original doctrine of Israel. Jews form a people, one people, and should build a nation-state. Given Jews' secular diversity, people could more easily concede the supernatural reading of Judaic existence than the national construction given to it. For, scattered across the European countries as well as in the Muslim world, Jews did not speak a common language, follow a single way of life, or adhere in common to a single code of belief and behavior. What made them a people, one people, and further validated their claim and right to a state, a nation, of their own, constituted the central theme of the Zionist worldview. No facts of perceived society validated that view. In no way, except for a common fate, did Jews form a people, one people. True, in Judaic systems they commonly did. But the received system and its continuators in Reform and integrationist Orthodox Judaisms imputed to Israel, the Jewish people, a supernatural status, a mission, a calling, a purpose. Zionism did not: A people, one people—that is all.

What about its worldview? Zionist theory sought roots for its principal ideas in the documents of the received Judaism, Scripture for example. Zionist theory had the task of explaining how the Jews formed a people, one people, and in the study of "Jewish history," read as a single, continuous and unitary story, Zionist theory solved that problem. The Jews all came from some one place, traveled together, and were going back to that same one place: One people. Zionist theory therefore derived strength from the study of history, much as had Reform Judaism in its quest to validate change, and in time generated a great renaissance of Judaic studies as the scholarly community of the nascent Jewish state took up the task at hand.

The sort of history that emerged took the form of factual and descriptive narrative. But its selection of facts, its recognition of problems requiring explanation, its choice of what mattered and what did not—all of these definitive questions found answers in the larger program of nationalist ideology. The form was secular and descriptive, but the substance ideological.

At the same time, Zionist theory explicitly rejected the precedent formed by the Torah, selecting as its history not the history of the faith, of the Torah, but the history of the nation, Israel construed as a secular entity. So we find a distinctive worldview that explains a very particular way of life and defines for itself that Israel to which it wishes to speak.

Like Reform Judaism, Zionism found more interesting the written component of the Torah than the Oral; Scripture outweighed the Talmud. And in its search for a usable past, it turned to documents formerly neglected or treated as not authoritative—for instance, the book of Maccabees, a Jewish dynasty that exhibited military prowess. Zionism went in search of heroes unlike those of the present, warriors, political figures, and others who might provide a model for the movement's future, and for the projected state beyond. So instead of rabbis or sages, Zionism chose figures such as David or Judah Maccabee or Samson—David the warrior king; Judah Maccabee, who had led the revolt against the Syrian Hellenists; Samson the powerful fighter.

These provided the appropriate heroes for a political Zionism. The secular system thus proposed to redefine Jewish consciousness, to turn storekeepers into soldiers, lawyers into farmers, corner grocers into builders and administrators of great institutions of state and government. The Rabbinic Judaism had treated David as a rabbi. The Zionist system saw David as a hero in a more worldly sense: A courageous nation-builder.

In its eagerness to appropriate a usable past, Zionism and Israeli nationalism, its successor, dug in the sand to find a deed to the Land. That stress in archaeology on Jewish links to the past extended to even proofs for the biblical record to which, in claiming the Land of Israel, Zionism pointed. So in pre-state times and after the creation of the State of Israel in 1948, Zionist scholars and institutions devoted great effort to digging up the ancient monuments of the Land of Israel, finding in archaeological work the link to the past that the people, one people, so desperately sought.

Archaeology uncovered the Jews' roots in the Land of Israel and became a principal instrument of national expression. Zionism was not alone, for contemporary believers in Scripture archaeology would prove the truths of the biblical narrative. It was not surprising, therefore, that in the Israeli War of Independence, 1948–9, and in later times as well, Israeli generals explained to the world that by following the biblical record of the nation in times past, they had found hidden roads, appropriate strategies—in all, the key to victory.

Why did Zionism succeed where nineteenth-century Reform Judaism gave way? Its advocates claimed that history validated its worldview, way of life, and definition of Israel. From the end of the nineteenth century, Zionism faced political reality and explained it and offered a program, inclusive of a worldview and a way of life, that worked. At the end of World War II, with millions murdered, as Zionism had predicted they would be, Zionism offered Jewry the sole meaningful explanation of how to endure. Zionism had led at least some Zionists to realize as early as 1940 what Hitler's Germany was going to do. At a meeting in December 1940, Berl Katznelson, an architect of Socialist Zionism in the Jewish community of Palestine before the creation of the State of Israel, announced that European Jewry was finished:

> The essence of Zionist awareness must be that what existed in Vienna will never return, what existed in Berlin will never return, nor in Prague, and what we had in Warsaw and Lodz is finished, and we must realize this! Why don't we understand that what Hitler has done, and this war is a kind of Rubicon, an outer limit, and what existed before will never exist again ... And I declare that the fate of European Jewry is sealed.
>
> (Shapira 1974).

Zionism, in the person of Katznelson, even before the systematic mass murder got fully underway, grasped that, after World War II, Jews would not return to Europe, certainly not to those places in which they had flourished for 1,000 years, and Zionism offered the alternative: The building, outside of Europe, of the Jewish state. So Zionism took a position of prophecy and found its prophecy fulfilled. Its fundamental dogma about the character of the diaspora as exile found verification in the destruction of European Jewry. And Zionism's further claim to point the way forward proved to be Israel's salvation in the formation of the State of Israel on the other side of the Holocaust. So Katznelson maintained: "If Zionism wanted to be the future force of the Jewish people, it must prepare to solve the Jewish question in all its scope" (Shapira 1974: 290).

The secret of the power of Zionism lay in its power to make sense of the world and to propose a program to solve the problems of the age. That same power animated Reform, integrationist Orthodox, and Conservative Judaisms.

References

Hertzberg, Arthur (1971) "Conservative Judaism," *Encyclopaedia Judaica*, Vol. V. Jerusalem: Keter, pp. 901–6.

Petuchowski, Jakob J. (1971) "Reform Judaism," *Encyclopaedia Judaica*, Vol. XIV. Jerusalem: Keter, pp. 23–8.

Shapira, Anita (1974) *Berl: The Biography of a Socialist Zionist. Berl Katznelson 1887–1944*. Cambridge: Cambridge University Press.

Wurzburger, Walter (1971) "Orthodox Judaism," *Encyclopaedia Judaica*. Jerusalem: Keter.

Reading 11   Judaism and Daily Life

By Eliezer Segal

In This [Reading]

The diversity of Jewish law and ritual affects all aspects of life. As regards women, traditional Jewish law usually assumes that they are primarily occupied as wives and mothers. Various consequences emerge from that premise that limit their responsibilities in the public sphere. This [reading] describes the legal structures of Jewish marriage and divorce as regulated in the halakhah. In the realm of ritual, talmudic law generally exempted women from time-bound ritual performance, but later generations were inconsistent about how strictly to maintain the exemption, or to increase or lessen women's participation in ritual activities. Some central precepts observed in the home were considered the special domain of women. Modern Jewish movements have generally supported equal treatment of women in religious matters.

The daily regimen of traditional Jews is guided by formal prayers that are recited at fixed times of the day, preferably in a congregational setting. The most prominent prayers are the *Shema'*, a declaration of God's oneness; and the *Tefillah*, a composition of blessings on various themes involving praise, pleas and thanks addressed to God. These are organized into three services, in the morning, afternoon and evening. Jewish rationalists, who stressed their belief in an impersonal and unchanging deity, had to reinterpret the function of prayer. Hasidism instilled in its followers a simple faith in God as a loving father figure, and turned prayer into a mystical experience through its teachings about cleaving to God (*devekut*) and ecstatic experience (*hitlahavut*).

Jewish tradition ordains a complex system of restrictions that determine which foodstuffs may be eaten. As with much Jewish ritual, no definitive rationale was provided, and commentators have proposed different medical, moral or symbolic explanations for the laws. The "kosher" laws relate to the nature of the species, the manner in which creatures are killed, the separation of milk and meat, and other factors. The religious status and social context of these laws have undergone much change in modern times.

Main Topics Covered

- Religion in the daily lives of Jews
- Jewish Women
- Daily prayer
- The *Shema'*
- The *Tefillah* ("Eighteen Blessings")
- Philosophical attitudes to prayer
- Hasidic prayer
- The significance and purpose of the Jewish dietary laws
- Definitions of permissible and forbidden species
- Ritual slaughter (*sheḥitah*)
- Separation of milk and meat
- Tithing
- Modern developments in the Jewish dietary laws

Religion In the Daily Lives of Jews

Most of the [readings] in this book deal with, and derive from, formal works of religious literature. For the most part, these compendia of biblical exegesis, talmudic law and theology constitute the only source that we have for information about the Jewish religion at the time. Though such writings do reveal to us a wealth of information, the picture that they paint will inevitably be an incomplete one. The compilations in question belong to a limited range of literary genres, and only matters that are relevant to those genres are likely to get mentioned. The common occurrences of day-to-day life, the ones that undoubtedly affected the lives of most ordinary Jews, are precisely the ones that tend to be omitted from the standard works of advanced religious scholarship. Furthermore, those works were composed by relatively small circles of male scholars and authors, and deal with academic or institutional topics. Consequently, the religious lives of women, who did not play an active role in the synagogues, academies or institutions of religious leadership, were not described in a systematic manner, leaving major gaps in the information that was preserved about them. Jews in those days did not write memoirs, novels or other genres of personal expression that would provide us with a basis for reconstructing their actions and religious feelings. Legal discussions, in particular, are far more likely to deal with crises and anomalies, rather than with normal situations.

This is not to say that we are completely in the dark about the ordinary religious lives of Jewish men, women and children in former times. The scope of subjects that found their way into the standard literary genres could be surprisingly flexible, so that glimpses of such phenomena occasionally peek through. Particularly valuable from this perspective is the literature of the Responsa that responded to concerns of a living society. Much valuable information of this kind is also preserved in works devoted to the recording of ritual customs.

It is also crucial to keep in mind that the classification of "religious" phenomena is much more extensive in pre-modern Judaism than it is in modern western liberal society. So extensive is the range of human activities that fall within the compass of the *halakhah* that it is hard to identify an activity that a person performs during the day that would be religiously neutral. Thus, for traditional Judaism, the preparation of food according to the complex Jewish dietary laws, or the rhythms of menstruation and sexual relations, constitute religious activities of no less importance than participation in communal prayer or the authoring of learned Talmud commentaries.

Unfortunately, none of this alters the basic fact that the literature in our possession was (with a few interesting exceptions) composed by an intellectual elite, and reflects their own perspectives. The present [reading] will not strive for completeness, but merely to present a selection of characteristic phenomena.

Jewish Women

The religion of Jewish women did not get recorded in any consistent manner, and we are compelled to extrapolate it from standard works of Jewish law and exegesis and similar documents. Nevertheless, the diversity of the literature touches on many relevant aspects of female religious activity and spirituality. It is typical of Judaism that most of the issues that we think of as defining the "status" of women were carefully demarcated in Jewish religious law. Based on the principles set down in talmudic literature, women were considered to be obligated in the performance of the great majority of the biblical commandments and laws. However, the small number of precepts from which they were exempted included the most visible communal rituals, the ones that western society regards as more definitively "religious." The Talmud's determination of which laws were incumbent upon women and which were not was justified by the rabbis' exegetical reading of various biblical texts, in accordance with the technical methods of midrashic hermeneutics. The ancient sources did not normally justify such rules by ideological or sociological principles. Nevertheless, historians usually presume that, underlying the specific rules was a general, and realistic, assumption that the woman's domestic responsibilities, especially those related to child-rearing, made it unreasonable to impose excessive ritual demands on her time. When examining these phenomena from a modern perspective, it is important to recognize that the assignment of gender roles was, on the whole, not a function of the religious traditions. Rather, the major patterns were determined by basic realities of biology and economics; and religious law merely regulated people's behavior within those parameters.

For the duration of their reproductive years, women would usually be involved in a cycle of pregnancy, childbirth and nursing, a fact that minimized their usefulness as physical laborers, or in other types of work that would take them outside the home. Although Jewish law declared that to "be fruitful and multiply," was an important religious commandment—in fact, the very first commandment to be recorded in the Torah—in practical terms this was not something that was really under people's control prior to the recent introduction of effective contraception. Conversely, men were at a disadvantage as child-rearers if only because of their inability to breast-feed. Therefore, the traditional "patriarchal" model of women working in the home and men outside it was not the result of religious doctrines or edicts.

The society that emerges from ancient Jewish texts is based on heterosexual, polygamous families. The Torah outlawed homosexual relations as an "abomination" and this perspective was not challenged in the classical sources. Jews were aware that their view differed radically from much of Greek thought, where a man's marriage to a wife was dismissed as an unpleasant social obligation while true erotic devotion was directed towards adolescent boys. Notwithstanding the rare case of the Essenes, who eschewed marriage out of misogynistic motives, we find almost no disparagement of sexuality or celebration of celibacy. A Jew was to aspire to marriage and children, if at all possible.

Marriage was regarded primarily as a way to protect women. Much stress was placed on the need for a *ketubbah*, a prenuptial contract that guaranteed the rights of the parties during the marriage, and especially those of the wife after its dissolution. The Torah mentions a procedure for divorce, and though early rabbinic traditions disagreed about the religious desirability of the institution, the view that prevailed was that divorce was a legitimate option with no stigma attached to either party. Arguably, most of the relevant discussions in talmudic literature are concerned with deathbed situations where divorce is to the woman's legal advantage, as a means of exempting her from ritual complications that would ensue if she were left a widow. Although complications resulting from polygynous families were discussed at length in talmudic literature, it appears that most actual marriages were monogamous, if only for economic reasons.

Several of the above assumptions became subject to modification in the Middle Ages, and it is interesting to note how Judaism dealt with those instances. To take one straightforward example, we note that in Christian society several women were able to pursue spiritual and mystical callings by adopting monastic discipline, which freed them from commitments to home-making and child-rearing. This was not an option for Jewish women, because Judaism had a deep-rooted antipathy to voluntary celibacy, which it regarded as a tragic violation of the natural order.

Developments in medieval Jewish society did create limited opportunities for redefining certain aspects of gender roles. For example, the affluence of certain Jewish communities allowed many women to delegate their domestic chores to servants, thereby removing some of the traditional obstacles to participation in religious rituals. Similarly, the fact that many medieval Jews were occupied in commerce rather than in agriculture meant that housewives would frequently take care of a family business, and take on other economic roles that their talmudic ancestors had not anticipated. Their enhanced social status inspired some women to be more assertive in claiming an increased role in religious observance. Furthermore, during talmudic times, when it was forbidden to study oral traditions from written books, it was necessary for scholars to wander from their

> The leadership role of males in the traditional Jewish community was closely bound to their access to the authoritative texts. Under the threat of the Spanish Inquisition, when communities of "Conversos" attempted to maintain their Judaism in secret while outwardly accepting Christianity, the textual basis of the religion was removed, because Jews were denied access to all works of Jewish literature. Under these circumstances, women, with their experience in maintaining unwritten customs and traditions, emerged as figures of spiritual or charismatic leadership in several crypto-Jewish communities.

homes in order to study with their masters, a possibility which effectively ruled out women's participation in religious learning. In the Middle Ages, on the other hand, the Talmud and other works were available in written form, facilitating somewhat women's access to religious education and scholarship.

The responses of the Jewish religious authorities, and of the women themselves, to these developments varied widely. The rule of thumb that was set down in the Talmud (a rule that admitted of several exceptions) stated that women were exempted from "positive commandments that are time-defined." While this served to include virtually all the ethical and civil laws, it exempted them from many of the rituals associated with the various calendrical cycles. As we shall see, much depended on whether or not the exemption was perceived as precluding or discouraging voluntary performance of the rituals. This issue was discussed by the rabbinical authorities of the eleventh and twelfth centuries, including such eminent figures as Rashi and his grandson Rabbi Jacob Tam; and the scholars responded in different ways. Some permitted the women to perform such rituals as the taking of the "four species" on the Feast of Tabernacles, and to recite the accompanying blessing even though it contained the formula "Blessed are you, O Lord ... who has sanctified us through your commandments and commanded us to ..."—which was not, strictly speaking, true according to the premise that women are exempt from time-bound precepts. Other authorities regarded this as an unjustified transgression of the Torah's prohibition "Ye shall not add unto the word which I command you" (Deuteronomy 4:2). Even where women were permitted or encouraged to voluntarily adopt time-limited religious practices, the logic of the talmudic reasoning led to the corollary that they could not vicariously represent or lead the community in the performance of those rituals because they would then be performing the precepts on behalf of people who had a more solid, biblically based, obligation.

In several areas of Jewish observance it is possible to discern a lessening of women's roles *vis à vis* the talmudic era. For example, they were removed from the synagogues into separate sanctuaries or women's galleries. Some other instances that come to mind are:

- Talmudic law places women on an equal footing with men with regards to several prayers and blessings, especially those that were believed to be of rabbinic origin, rather than from the Bible. By the Middle Ages, it was considered unimaginable in some circles that women could participate so actively in organized worship; so the ancient sources were reinterpreted in order to justify the prevailing situation. The most influential rationale was that of Maimonides who ruled that women share the obligation of prayer in a generic sense, but are not required to participate in specific congregational services, or to worship at fixed times.
- Talmudic law gave women an equal status in the public reading of the scroll of Esther, the principal observance associated with the festival of Purim. Because Purim originated in a later book of the Bible rather than in the Torah, it was not necessarily subject to the rule that exempted women from time-defined precepts. The Talmud even ruled that women should be allowed to read the Scroll of Esther on behalf of the congregation. However, the early medieval authorities reformulated the relevant Talmudic passage so as to grant women an equal obligation only in *hearing* the recitation, not in *performing* it.
- The wearing of fringes or tassels (*ẓiẓit*) on the corners of garments, in accordance with Numbers 15:38, is not a time-defined precept in the normal sense of the concept. Nevertheless, because the prevalent position of talmudic law was that nightgowns were not subject to the obligation of fringes, the rabbis debated whether this limitation constituted a sufficient reason to classify the precept as time-defined. Evidently, the dominant view in ancient times was that women were obligated to wear the fringes. Medieval Jewish law unanimously assumed that women were exempt from the practice, and generally discouraged women from taking it on even as an expression of voluntary piety. Nevertheless, there were women who insisted on wearing fringes. Thus, it was reported concerning Rabbi Jacob Moellin (known as "Maharil"), the influential fifteenth-century authority on Ashkenazic customs, that

> he could not fathom why women would want to take upon themselves the obligation of fringes. They asked him why he did not protest against the rabbi's wife known as Bruna who lived in his city [of Mainz], who always wore the ritually fringed undergarment. He replied: Perhaps she will not heed me; and regarding such situations it says [in the Talmud]: It is preferable that they transgress unintentionally than deliberately.

- The Talmudic sources are unmistakable in stating that the obligation of Torah study applies to males and not to females. As with other such exemptions, it is not as clear whether women are nevertheless permitted, or even encouraged, to pursue religious studies. In a passage from the Talmud that was not necessarily intended to be grasped as a normative legal discussion, Rabbi Eliezer ben Hyrcanus commented that "if one teaches his daughter Torah, it is as if he is teaching her lewdness." Maimonides ruled that women are forbidden to study Torah except for those topics that are necessary for their practical religious lives. Maimonides's view, which is consistent with his own negative assessment of the intellectual abilities of women (and with the attitudes prevalent in the surrounding society), became normative for subsequent legal rulings on the topic, and a large body of literature evolved to define what areas of Torah it is permitted to teach to women.

- The prevailing opinion in the Talmud permitted women to perform circumcisions, and this position was codified in several early compendia of Jewish law. It appears that the original practice in Ashkenazic communities was that the mother took an active and visible role in the circumcision ceremonies of her sons, including holding the baby in her lap during the operation. The Tosafot forbade women to perform the circumcision, claiming that this case constituted an exception to the normal rules governing decisions in talmudic arguments. In the thirteenth century, Rabbi Meir of Rothenburg objected strongly to the mother's holding the child during the circumcision, "because it is not seemly for a lavishly dressed woman to be among the men and before the divine presence." Rabbi Meir's approach, which reflected the contemporary social norms regarding the separation of the sexes, was almost universally adopted by subsequent authorities.

Although the matter requires extensive study, there seems to be a general pattern of women's ritual obligations being diminished as part of the transition to medieval society. The phenomenon was most pronounced in Islamic countries.

There were nevertheless areas of Jewish ritual in which Jewish women were specially subject to certain religious duties. A passage in the Mishnah listed three precepts that were associated most closely with women. In the Middle Ages, these were viewed as prototypes for distinctively female commandments:

The list includes:

- *The kindling of sabbath lamps.* The nature and origin of this practice, which is not technically limited to women, will be discussed in connection with the Jewish ritual calendar. It will suffice for our present purposes to note that rabbis stated that it has a special relevance to women, either because they were most likely to be in the home when the time came to light the lamps, or because of an allegorical association with the sin of the first woman, Eve, when she "extinguished the light of the world" by bringing death to humanity through her disobedience.

- *The dough offering* (*hallah*). According to Biblical law, during the process of baking bread a portion must be set aside from the dough to be assigned to the priests for their upkeep. Although this ritual was not assigned specifically to women, women were normally the persons involved in baking bread for their household. The concept of *hallah* came to symbolize the full range of religious laws that dealt with the preparation of food and the application of the Jewish dietary laws. In the vast majority of cases, the observance and enforcement of these rules were entrusted to women.

- *Menstrual impurity* (*niddah*). Biblical law decreed that women are impure and sexually unavailable for one week after the onset of menstruation. A talmudic tradition relates that the "daughters of Israel" were so meticulous in their observance of these rules that, in order to avoid violating the more stringent prohibitions that relate to bleeding outside their normal periods, they took it upon themselves to extend the restrictions through the week following the cessation of their uterine bleeding. At the conclusion of the term of impurity they would bathe in a *mikveh*, a special purification bath, before being allowed to resume marital relations. The *niddah* prohibitions were among the few areas of the biblical purity system to survive the destruction of the Temple; though, strictly speaking, what was being observed was not the purity aspect, but separate prohibitions governing sexual relations. The observance of these rules would obviously have far-reaching effects on the relationships within the family. Although the Torah's concern with menstruation seemed to focus on its effects on the males, the application of the laws rested solidly on the women.

The language of the Biblical purity code normally suggests an association between ritual defilement and physical or moral "uncleanness," conjuring up images of filth and ugliness. The talmudic texts, on the other hand, tend to minimize such imagery, and generally deal with the rules as technical issues that carry no moral stigma, but are a component of the full Jewish religious regimen. Notwithstanding that some talmudic texts ascribe the imposition of these blood-related rules on women as a penalty or atonement for Eve's having "shed blood" and introduced death in the Garden of Eden, menstruation was typically accepted as a natural and healthy part of the biological rhythm, rather than as a demonic taboo. An oft-quoted talmudic tradition explained the menstrual prohibitions as designed to enhance a wife's desirability to her husband. Maimonides pointed out that in all the purity laws, the activities and biological processes that the Torah designated as sources of defilement were not unnatural or immoral ones, but on the contrary, they were the most natural and recurrent stages of the life cycle. For Maimonides, the purpose of these laws was not to discourage or stigmatize those actions or processes, but rather to enhance the sanctity of the Temple and sacred objects by restricting access to them.

We must keep in mind that the average woman prior to modern times probably did not have occasion to menstruate very often during her lifetime. Women would marry shortly after reaching puberty, and most of their childbearing years would be spent pregnant or nursing. Nevertheless, the observance of the rules made considerable demands on a woman. They required periodic self-examination, which included checking for bloodstains on their undergarments. The immersion in the *mikveh* at the conclusion of the term of impurity was governed by diverse regulations, including some that were designed to make sure that her entire body came into direct contact with the water. This involved carefully washing one's hair and unraveling any knots, removing jewelry, rubbing off scabs, and so forth.

The cleansing in the *mikveh*, in the awareness that it would lead to a resumption of marital relations, possesses a powerful erotic as well as a spiritual dimension. Depending on the physical cleanness and comfort of the *mikveh*, the immersion might also be an unpleasant ordeal in settings that do not possess efficient means for heating water or buildings. In small communities, the awareness of who was and was not going to the *mikveh* can provide women with intimate knowledge of each other's sexual lives, pregnancies and the like.

The varied changes that affected the lives of modern women also had an impact on Jewish women, and these changes often defined the borders between liberal and traditionalist communities. Among the earliest enactments of the Reform movements were measures intended to remove the limitations on the participation of women in religious life. Because the Reformers did not subscribe to the doctrine of divinely commanded laws, and did not acknowledge the obligatory status of rituals, they did not normally have to deal with concepts of obligation or exemption from commandments, or with women's status in the civil and criminal law systems. At any rate, the movement, virtually from its beginnings, did support the ordination of female rabbis, though only one woman actually received ordination in Europe before the Holocaust. The ordination of a female Reform rabbi in 1972 initiated a trend that became commonplace in the ensuing decades. Similar developments occurred shortly afterwards in the Reconstructionist movement and, in a decision that proved very controversial and divisive, in the Conservative movement, where women were counted in the required quorum of ten for congregational worship in 1974, and in 1983 were allowed rabbinical ordination. In recent years, even some strands of Orthodoxy in the United States and in Israel have come close to allowing women rabbinic status, in such areas as the training of "rabbinic pleaders" to represent women's interests before religious courts, or in the increasing opportunities available for study of the Talmud and other subjects from which they were previously excluded.

Daily Prayer

Underlying the formal institution of prayer is the simple belief that God listens to prayers and responds. The most common Hebrew term for prayer is the root *PLL*, meaning "to judge," suggesting that self-evaluation is an important element in the prayer experience.

While the Bible preserves a rich literature of prayers, texts addressed to God in praise, petition or thanksgiving (including the entire book of Psalms), there is scarcely any mention of a "liturgy" in the sense of standardized texts, prayer times or practices. On the whole, the offering of sacrifices in the Jerusalem Temple was assumed to be the preferred vehicle of worship. The Qumran library preserves numerous prayers and liturgical documents from the late Second Temple era, but scholarship has not had an easy time correlating those texts with the talmudic evidence about the origins of the rabbinic liturgy. The Talmud discusses many details about how to conduct worship, but does not include a full text of the liturgy. It was not until well into the Middle Ages that the words and regulations of the liturgy were systematically set forth in prayer books.

Although there is much debate over the details of the process, scholars generally confirm the talmudic tradition that the main foundations of Jewish prayer as we know it were established by the rabbis at Yavneh following the destruction of the second Temple. There is no agreement as to whether that original liturgy had a precisely defined text, or merely a set of thematic guidelines that left the wording to the individual worshipper or prayer leader.

The standardized prayers deal with the needs and concerns of the entire community. Individual prayer, often characterized as petitions for divine mercy, existed but was not discussed extensively in the literature. Though it is considered preferable to participate in communal worship, the prayers are deemed obligatory even when the person is not in a congregational setting. When recited in a community, one individual leads the prayers on behalf of the others. At appropriate points, the participants respond "amen" to indicate their consent to the leader's words. Certain passages, notably those related to the idea of holiness, are considered so important that they may not be recited in their complete form without a proper quorum of ten worshippers.

The basic unit of rabbinic prayer is the "blessing" (*berakhah*). This consists of a sentence beginning "blessed are you, Lord our God, king of the universe" and concluding with specific content. Blessings are employed in diverse settings. For example, one may recite one before performing an action as a way of indicating that the action constitutes the performance of a religious precept ("... who has sanctified us with your commandments and commanded us to ..."); or before partaking of food or some other kind of pleasure, as an expression of gratitude.

The norms that were described thus far were for normal weekday worship. Variations exist for Sabbaths, festivals and other special occasions. Biblical festivals include an "additional" (*Musaf*) service.

The standard daily liturgy is composed of two basic elements:

1. The *Shema*, recited every morning and evening.

2. The *Tefillah*, recited every morning, afternoon and evening. The times for the *Tefillah* coincide with those of the morning and afternoon daily sacrifices (*tamid*); and the evening or nighttime service corresponds to the overnight burning of the sacrificial leftovers. In practice, the *Shema* and *Tefillah* are juxtaposed in the morning and evening services, so that on a normal weekday there are actually three prayer services.

The Shema'

The name *Shema'* is taken from the opening Hebrew word of the scriptural passage (Deuteronomy 6:4–9) "Hear, O Israel, the Lord our God is one Lord." Ancient Jewish tradition understood that there exists an obligation to recite this passage, whether as a declaration of "taking on the yoke of heavenly kingship," or as fulfillment of the precept contained in the passage itself: "these words, which I command you this day ... you shall talk of them ... when you lie down, and when you rise up."

In addition to this paragraph, the *Shema'* includes two other short sections from the Torah:

- Deuteronomy 11: 13–21, understood by the Mishnah as "acceptance of the yoke of the commandments." This passage deals largely with the rewards and punishments in store for those who obey or disregard the commandments.
- Numbers 15: 37–41, dealing with the commandment to place fringes or tassels on the corners of garments. The passage concludes with the words "I am the Lord your God who brought you out of the land of Egypt" and its recitation was regarded as the fulfillment of a directive to recall the exodus.

When incorporated into the daily liturgy, the Shema' is surrounded by a sequence of blessings. In a congregational setting, the service is preceded by an invitation to prayer recited by the leader: "Bless the blessed Lord!" to which the worshippers respond "Blessed is the blessed Lord eternally!"

The opening blessing of the *Shema'* service relates to the time of day, and expresses the idea that God is the master of nature who (in the morning service) creates light and (in the evening service) brings nightfall. Immediately preceding the biblical *Shema'* passages is a blessing based on the theme that God expressed his great love for Israel by bestowing the Torah upon them. This accords with the premise that the recitation of the *Shema'* functions as the fulfillment of the duty to study Torah. The mention of the exodus at the end of the third paragraph leads to a blessing on the theme of redemption, as exemplified by the exodus from Egypt, which prefigures the future redemption. The evening service contains an additional blessing asking for divine protection from the dangers of night.

The *Tefillah* ("Eighteen Blessings")

The Tefillah portion of the liturgy is often referred to as the "eighteen blessings" (*Shemoneh Esreh*), though the current weekday version actually consists of nineteen blessings. The name reflects its older structure in the Palestinian rite. In the prevailing Babylonian rite, the original blessing for the house of David and the restoration of Jerusalem is divided into two separate blessings. Although its format and much of its phraseology derives from biblical models, especially from Psalms, the text is a rabbinic creation.

The Talmud observed that the structure of this prayer is modeled on the way that a subject should approach a mortal king with a plea: open with words of praise; then present the petition; and then conclude with an expression of gratitude. Accordingly, the first three blessings consist chiefly of praises of God, the last three of thanksgiving, while the intermediary paragraphs contain an assortment of requests for divine assistance. For the most part, the petitions are for the welfare of the people of Israel, including hopes for national and religious restoration. On Sabbaths and holidays, when the appropriate mood is one of satisfaction and wellbeing, the petitions are omitted and replaced with a blessing related to the themes of the holy day.

The *Tefillah* is recited while standing; hence its alternative name, the *Amidah* (standing). Worshippers are supposed to face and direct their prayers towards the site of the Temple in Jerusalem.

When recited in a congregational setting, the worshippers first recite the *Tefillah* quietly by themselves, after which the prayer leader repeats it—a practice that originated in an era before the introduction of written prayer books.

Philosophical Attitudes to Prayer

The impersonal divinity that was contemplated by the Jewish rationalists was very different from the God of traditional religion. There appears to be no obvious purpose in pouring out one's heart in prayer before such an unchanging deity or in expecting the heavenly father to be overcome with compassion. That God is self-contained and invariably does what is just and rational. It is therefore illogical to imagine that he responds to reminders or persuasions from mortals. Viewed this way, prayer and worship can only affect the worshipper as a form of self-examination or a statement of belief. Because all verbal discourse about God is ultimately inadequate and misleading, Maimonides stated that the highest form of worship is not prayer, but silent contemplation.

Maimonides spoke of "love of God" and "fear of God"; however he interpreted both concepts as purely intellectual categories. Fear refers to the existential feeling of awe that overcomes us when we contemplate how infinitely great God is in comparison with our puny selves. "Love" is the corresponding drive to draw as close as is humanly possible to the experience and understanding of God.

Hasidic Prayer

More than any other Jewish religious movement, Hasidism stresses the importance of sincere prayer as an activity that can elevate the soul of the worshippers towards their creator and invoke divine blessings. The Ba'al Shem Tov's doctrine of prayer imbued it with two essential mystical ideals:

- *Devekut* (literally: "clinging"; constant devotion): the unceasing consciousness of God's presence.
- *Hitlahavut* ("bursting into flame"; ecstatic enthusiasm): the experience of spiritual exultation as the soul is elevated towards God.

Hasidic prayer developed a reputation for disregarding the technical regulations and ritual formalities imposed by Jewish law, especially the fixed times for prayer services. It celebrated the sincere devotion of the unlettered—even by means of simple whistling or recitation of the Hebrew alphabet—rather than the learned and precise recitation of the liturgy. Hasidism also encouraged the participation of all limbs of the body and forms of expression in worship: through gesticulation, dance and acrobatics. This feature was singled out for special condemnation by he movement's early opponents. Some features that were once distinctive to Hasidic prayer, particularly the incorporation of moving and spirited singing, have now achieved widespread acceptance in the broader Jewish community.

DIETARY LAWS

The Significance and Purpose of The Jewish Dietary Laws

The Bible and later Jewish traditions pay careful attention to food in relation to its origin, manner of preparation and the method of its consumption. The familiar English word "kosher" originates in the Yiddish pronunciation of the Hebrew *kasher*, "fit," a term that originally did not relate specifically to the permissibility of food. The full observance of these standards, as customary among Orthodox Jews today, extends to the instruments and equipment with which the food was prepared. In practice, Jews who observe these regulations strictly may only eat any cooked or processed food in other observant Jewish homes, or establishments that are under authorized supervision.

As with many other biblical rituals, the ancient sources do not provide consistent rationales for the existence of dietary regulations, allowing the Jewish commentators to suggest a variety of possible reasons. The Torah subsumes the dietary laws under the ideal of achieving "holiness," a concept that was associated, among other things, with the separation of Israel from the pagan world. Indeed, adherence to dietary restrictions has the effect of minimizing social interaction in venues where food is served, and it therefore diminishes the likelihood of intermarriage with gentiles. Moralistic thinkers have stressed that, by compelling Jews to refrain from eating many foods, the dietary laws strengthen the quality of moral self-discipline. Some authors, notably Maimonides, pointed out that there are health-related advantages to the Jewish diet, in that it excludes foods like pork that often caused trichinosis. Most recent commentators, however, have avoided such explanations, because they might be taken to imply that the rules need not apply where there are no health issues—and in fact, some liberal Jewish movements have invoked such arguments to justify the elimination of dietary observances. It is common to point out the moral symbolism of the fact that predatory birds and beasts are forbidden by Torah law, and that the slaughtering process should minimize the animal's suffering.

There are a number of different criteria that affect the ritual permissibility of food. Chief among them are:

Definitions of Permissible and Forbidden Species

The Torah provides specific definitions for different types of creatures:

1. "Beasts of the earth" (quadrupeds). Permitted animals must have cloven hooves and chew their cuds. According to this criterion, sheep, cattle, goats and deer are allowed; while carnivorous beasts are prohibited.

2. Aquatic creatures must have both fins and scales. Shellfish, shrimps, eels, lobsters, and other such species are forbidden.

3. The Torah provides lists of forbidden birds, but does not specify criteria or rationales for their exclusion; though all of the birds on that list are predators or scavengers. Theoretically, Jewish law understood that any bird not on the forbidden list should be permitted. However, because

we are no longer able to identify the biblical names with certainty, it is generally required that permissibility be supported by a local tradition. Among the permitted fowl are: chicken, geese, ducks and (according to most authorities) turkey.

4. "Winged swarming things" (winged insects). The Torah provides a definition that includes locusts and grasshoppers as permitted. In practice, however, there are currently very few Jewish communities that eat these species.

Ritual Slaughter [Sheḥitah]

The permitted mammals and birds must be slaughtered in accordance with Jewish law. The person who performs the slaughter is called a *shoḥet*. The method of slaughter is a single quick, deep stroke across the throat with a perfectly sharp blade with no nicks or unevenness. Maimonides claimed that this is the most humane, cost-effective method of slaughter.

Examinations are made to establish that the animal or bird was not subject to physical disqualifications. The Torah prohibits animals that died of natural causes, that suffered from fatal illnesses, or that were killed other than by proper slaughter.

Removal of Blood

The Torah prohibits the consumption of blood. Therefore the blood must be left to drain after slaughter. Afterwards, the remaining blood is removed by means of absorption through coarse salt, or by broiling.

Removal of the Sciatic Nerve

The Torah tells an enigmatic tale about the patriarch Jacob's struggle with a supernatural being who injured his thigh. The passage concludes, "Therefore to this day the Israelites do not eat the thigh muscle that is on the hip socket, because he struck Jacob on the hip socket at the thigh muscle." In accordance with that story, the sciatic nerve must be removed from meat before it may be consumed.

Separation of Milk and Meat

Based on threefold repetition of the precept "thou shalt not boil a kid in its mother's milk" in the Torah, the Jewish oral tradition prohibits eating meat and dairy together. The rabbis extended this prohibition to include poultry (which has no mother's milk), though it does not apply to fish, which is not considered meat at all (it is also exempted from the requirement of slaughter). The separation extends to utensils and equipment in which meat and dairy foods are prepared, eaten, and washed. Though some kinds of vessels can be cleansed between dairy and meat use, it is usually more practical for Jewish households to keep separate sets or dishes. It is required that one wait after eating meat before one may eat dairy foods. There are varying local customs with regard to how long the interval must be, ranging from one to six hours; these are based on differing views about the precise purpose of the delay.

Tithing

Whether according to biblical or rabbinic law, portions of food and produce must be set aside for the sake of the priests, Levites or the poor. The food remains forbidden until this is done. Traditional interpretation held that most of these rules apply (at least, by the authority of the Torah) only to produce that was grown in the land of Israel.

Modern Developments in the Jewish Dietary Laws

In keeping with their generally negative attitude towards ritual, the classic Reform movement rejected the principle of dietary restrictions, though the movement later adopted a more sympathetic attitude, recognizing some of the benefits of the practices. Of course, they treat the restrictions as optional customs and traditions, not as obligatory laws. There is a general tendency to stress the ethical rationales for the laws, and some authorities in Conservative Judaism have gone so far as to declare veal forbidden because of the inhumane treatment of the animals.

Box 11.1   Key Points You Need to Know

- In traditional Jewish societies, religion permeated all aspects of daily life, affecting such features as food, dress and family relationships.
- As defined by ancient Jewish sources, women were presumed to be mothers and homemakers, and were therefore exempted from many time-defined or public obligations that would have impeded their domestic functions. These limitations were sometimes augmented or diminished in response to social changes.
- Traditional Judaism sees marriage and children as the preferred state of religious and social fulfillment.
- Some important religious precepts were considered the special province of women.

(Continued)

- Traditional Judaism contains an obligatory daily liturgy that consists of morning, afternoon and evening services.
- The *Shema'* recited in the morning and evening, contains passages from the Torah that speak of God's oneness and sovereignty, the commitment to obey his commandments, and other key religious themes. It is embedded in a framework of blessings.
- The *Tefillah* or "eighteen benedictions" is recited at all three daily services. It consists largely of petitions on behalf of the community, and includes pleas for eschatological redemption.
- The rationalist conception of an omniscient and unalterable God can lead to a discouraging of petitionary prayer and an emphasis on meditation and self-examination.
- Hasidism teaches that prayer should be an emotional and mystical experience of intimate conversation with a compassionate father in heaven.
- Traditional Jewish law contains complex and specific rules governing the acquisition, preparation and eating of food. No single agreed-upon reason is provided for those laws.
- The Torah identifies certain species of animals, fowl, sea creatures and insects as permissible and others as forbidden.
- Meat must be slaughtered in a specified manner, and subjected to inspections and the removal of blood and other forbidden portions.
- The principle of separating meat from milk has far-reaching implications that relate to the structure of a family's kitchen and the possible range of social interaction.
- The industrialization of food preparation has had an impact on the observance and religious significance of the Jewish dietary laws.

While traditional dietary laws presuppose that most food preparation (including the slaughter) took place in the home, modern food production is now done on a mass industrial basis. Technological changes also mean that the food is subjected to assorted chemical and biological additives whose precise contents are known only to experts. The upshot of all this is that many of the detailed regulations described in the preceding paragraphs are no longer observed actively within the household. Instead, Jewish communities and organizations maintain agencies that inspect the manufacturers or caterers, symbols printed on the labels. Under these circumstances, the role of the observant Jewish consumer is relegated largely to checking the labels of the retail products they purchase.

Discussion Questions

1. What are some of the pitfalls involved in reconstructing the religious experiences of common people from official documents?

2. In what ways have Judaism and Jewish law defined the roles assigned to women, and to what extent did they merely accept or regulate the existing social norms?

3. Can Judaism's patriarchal division between public masculine and domestic feminine domains be harmonized with egalitarian principles?

4. Discuss how the experience of prayer might differ for a talmudic scholar, a philosopher and a follower of Hasidism.

5. If the Jewish dietary code is designed to achieve "holiness," how might the nature of holiness be affected by modern developments in food preparation and kosher observance?

Further Reading

Religion and Daily Life

Abrahams, Israel, *Jewish Life in the Middle Ages*. New York: Atheneum, 1969.

Ben-Sasson, Haim Hillel and Samuel Ettinger, *Jewish Society through the Ages*. New York: Schocken Books, 1971.

Ben-Sasson, Menahem and Stefan C. Reif, *The Cairo Genizah: A Mosaic of Life*. Jerusalem: The Israel Museum, 1997.

Fine, Lawrence, ed., *Judaism in Practice: From the Middle Ages through the Early Modern Period*, Princeton Readings in Religions. Princeton, NJ: Princeton University Press, 2001.

Goitein, S. D., "Religion in Everyday Life as Reflected in the Documents of the Cairo Geniza." In *Religion in a Religious Age*. Edited by S. D. Goitein, 1–18. Cambridge, MA: Association for Jewish Studies, 1974.

Goitein, S. D. and Jacob Lassner, *A Mediterranean Society: An Abridgment in One Volume*. Berkeley, CA: University of California Press, 1999.

Heilman, Samuel C., *Synagogue Life: A Study in Symbolic Interaction*. Chicago, IL: University of Chicago Press, 1976.

——— *The People of the Book: Drama, Fellowship, and Religion*. Chicago, IL: University of Chicago Press, 1983.

Metzger, Thérèse and Mendel Metzger, *Jewish Life in the Middle Ages: Illuminated Hebrew Manuscripts of the Thirteenth to the Sixteenth Centuries*. New York: Fine Art Books, 1982.

Pollack, Herman, *Jewish Folkways in Germanic Lands (1648–1806); Studies in Aspects of Daily Life*. Cambridge, MA: MIT Press, 1971.

Trachtenberg, Joshua, *Jewish Magic and Superstition: A Study in Folk Religion*, Temple Books. New York: Atheneum, 1970.

Jewish Women

Baskin, Judith R., "Jewish Women in the Middle Ages." In *Jewish Women in Historical Perspective*. Edited by Judith R. Baskin, 94–114. Detroit, MI: Wayne State University Press, 1991.

_____ "From Separation to Displacement: The Problem of Women in *Sefer Hasidim*." *AJS Review* 19, no. 1 (1994): 1–18.

Baumgarten, Elisheva, *Mothers and Children: Jewish Family Life in Medieval Europe*, Jews, Christians, and Muslims from the Ancient to the Modern World. Princeton, NJ: Princeton University Press, 2004.

Falk, Ze'ev W., *Jewish Matrimonial Law in the Middle Ages*. Edited by A. Altmann and J. G. Weiss, Scripta Judaica. Oxford: Oxford University Press, 1966.

Fram, Edward and Agnes Romer Segal, *My Dear Daughter: Rabbi Benjamin Slonik and the Education of Jewish Women in Sixteenth-Century Poland*. Cincinnati, OH: Hebrew Union College Press, 2007.

Friedman, Mordechai A., "The Ethics of Medieval Jewish Marriage." In *Religion in a Religious Age*. Edited by S. D. Goitein. Cambridge, MA: Association for Jewish Studies, 1974.

Friedman, Mordechai Akiva, *Jewish Marriage in Palestine: A Cairo Genizah Study*. Tel-Aviv and New York: Tel-Aviv University Chaim Rosenberg School of Jewish Studies and the Jewish Theological Seminary of America, 1980.

Greenberg, Simon, ed., *The Ordination of Women as Rabbis: Studies and Responsa*, Moreshet Series. New York: The Jewish Theological Seminary of America, 1998.

Grossman, Avraham, *Pious and Rebellious: Jewish Women in Medieval Europe*, 1st ed., Tauber Institute for the Study of European Jewry Series. Hanover, NH: University Press of New England for Brandeis University Press, 2004.

Grossman, Susan and Rivka Haut, *Daughters of the King: Women and the Synagogue: A Survey of History, Halakah, and Contemporary Realities*, 1st ed. Philadelphia, PA: Jewish Publication Society, 1992.

Romer Segal, Agnes, "Yiddish Works on Women's Commandments in the Sixteenth Century." In *Studies in Yiddish Literature and Folklore*. Jerusalem: Hebrew University, 1986.

Prayer and Liturgy

Benor, Ehud Z., "Petition and Contemplation in Maimonides' Conception of Prayer." *Religion* 24, no. 1 (1994): 59–66.

Buxbaum, Yitzhak, *Jewish Spiritual Practices*. Northvale, NJ: Jason Aronson, 1990.

Carmy, Shalom, ed., *Worship of the Heart: Essays on Jewish Prayer by Rabbi Soloveitchik*. Hoboken, NJ: KTAV for Toras Horav Foundation, 2003.

Dan, Joseph, "The Emergence of Mystical Prayer." In *Studies in Jewish Mysticism*. Edited by Joseph Dan and Frank Talmage, 85–120. New York: KTAV, 1982.

Donin, Hayim, *To Pray as a Jew: A Guide to the Prayer Book and the Synagogue Service*. New York: Basic Books, 1980.

———— *To Be a Jew: A Guide to Jewish Observance in Contemporary Life*. New York: Basic Books, 1991.

Elbogen, Ismar, *Jewish Liturgy: A Comprehensive History*, 1st English ed. Philadelphia, PA and New York: Jewish Publication Society and Jewish Theological Seminary of America, 1993.

Green, Arthur and Barry W. Holtz, *Your Word Is Fire: The Hasidic Masters on Contemplative Prayer*, 1st Schocken pbk. ed. New York: Schocken, 1987.

Hartman, David, "Prayer and Religious Consciousness: An Analysis of Jewish Prayer in the Works of Joseph B Soloveitchik, Yeshayahu Leibowitz, and Abraham Joshua Heschel." *Modern Judaism* 23, no. 2 (2003): 105–25.

Heinemann, Joseph and Jakob Josef Petuchowski, *Literature of the Synagogue*, Library of Jewish Studies. New York: Behrman House, 1975.

Heschel, Abraham Joshua, *Man's Quest for God: Studies in Prayer and Symbolism*. Santa Fe, NM: Aurora Press, 1998.

Hoffman, Lawrence A., *The Canonization of the Synagogue Service*, Studies in Judaism and Christianity in Antiquity. Notre Dame, IN: University of Notre Dame Press, 1979.

Idelsohn, A. Z., *Jewish Liturgy and Its Development*. New York: Schocken Books, 1967.

Jacobs, Louis, *Hasidic Prayer*, pbk. ed. London and Washington, DC: Littman Library of Jewish Civilization, 1993.

Dietary Laws

Berman, Jeremiah Joseph, *Shehitah, a Study in the Cultural and Social Life of the Jewish People*. New York: Bloch, 1941.

Blech, Zushe Yosef. *Kosher Food Production*. Ames, IO: Blackwell, 2004.

Central Council of Jewish Religious Education in the United Kingdom and Eire. *The Book of Kashrut*. [England]: Central Council of Jewish Religious Education in the United Kingdom and Eire, 1948.

Greenspoon, Leonard J., Ronald Simkins and Gerald Shapiro, eds, *Food and Judaism*, Studies in Jewish Civilization. Omaha, NE and Lincoln, NE: Creighton University Press, 2005.

Karo, Joseph ben Ephraim, *The Kosher Code of the Orthodox Jew*. Translated by Solomon Isaac Levin and Edward Allen Boyden. Minneapolis, MN: University of Minnesota Press, 1940.

Kraemer, David Charles, *Jewish Eating and Identity Throughout the Ages*, Routledge Advances in Sociology. New York: Routledge, 2007.

Levinger, I. M., *Shechita in the Light of the Year 2000: Critical Review of the Scientific Aspects of Methods of Slaughter and Shechita*. Jerusalem: Maskil L'David, 1995.

Wagschal, S., *The Practical Guide to Kashrus*, rev. and expanded ed., Practical Halacha Series. Brooklyn, NY: Judaica Press, 2003.

Welfeld, Irving H., *Why Kosher? An Anthology of Answers*. Northvale, NJ: Jason Aronson, 1996.

Reading 12 Christianity

By Christopher D. Martinez

NEW VOCABULARY AND CONCEPTS

- Dual nature of Jesus
- Trinity
- Logos
- Gnosticism
- Marcion
- Arianism
- Transubstantiation
- Bishops
- Priests
- Deacons
- Pentecost
- Resurrection (Easter)
- Ascension
- Filioque clause
- Indulgences
- Sola fide and sola scriptura
- First and Second Vatican Councils
- Ecumenism
- Icons
- World Council of Churches

LEARNING OBJECTIVES

1. Understand the basic theology of the Trinity
2. Know and understand the teachings of Jesus
3. Understand the early hierarchy of the Church
4. Take note of early Christian persecutions
5. Know the Bible's evolution and versions
6. Know the historical leaders of Christianity and their accomplishments
7. Understand the different denominations, their origins, and their beliefs
8. Know the holidays and their meanings
9. Understand modern movements in Christianity

Go, therefore, and make disciples of all nations, baptizing them in the name of the Father, and of the Son, and of the Holy Spirit, teaching them to observe all that I have commanded you. And behold, I am with you always, until the end of the age.

—Matt. 19:29

Christian Statistics

With more than two billion members, Christianity is the largest religion in the world and in the history of the world. It makes up about 31 percent of the world's population. The largest denomination is the Catholic Church, with 1.1 billion, followed by Protestants at 376 million, Orthodox at 220 million, and Anglicans at 80 million (sometimes included with Protestants, sometimes not). Interestingly, Independent Christians not affiliated with any denomination are 427 million.[1]

Christian Myth

Christianity is the only religion in the world that claims God became a human being. There are religions that chronicle humans becoming gods (such as Chango, who was elevated from a king to a god in the Yoruba religion) or part god, part human (such as Hercules in Greek mythology).

The Christian myth shares the Jewish myth, as it addresses the creation of the world and the history of the Jews up until the beginning of the Common Era. Like Islam, Christianity views Adam and Eve, Noah, Abraham, Moses, and the other patriarchs and prophets as recognized messengers of God. Unlike Islam, Christianity sees the patriarchs and prophets as Jewish. Christians see Jesus, the founder of Christianity, as the Christ (Greek for "messiah") for whom the Jews were waiting and who was foreshadowed in Jewish scripture. Isaiah criticized King Ahaz of Judah after he tried to conquer Jerusalem—Jew against Jew. "Listen, O house of David! Is it not enough for you to weary men, must you also weary my God? Therefore the Lord himself will give you this sign: the virgin shall be with child, and bear a son, and he shall name him Immanuel" ("with us is God"; Isa. 7:13–14). Although some writers believed Immanuel referred to the birth of the future king Hezekiah—whose mother, during Isaiah's time, had been a young unmarried woman—consensus among Christians was Isaiah foreshadowed the coming of Jesus. Isaiah goes further: "For a child is born to us, a son is given us; upon his shoulder dominion rests. They name him Wonder-Counselor, God-Hero, Father-Forever, Prince of Peace," and he is from the line of King David (Isa. 9:5).

The location of the messiah's origins are also penned by the prophet Micah:

> But you, Bethlehem-Ephrathah, too small to be among the clans of Judah, from you shall come forth for me one who is to be ruler in Israel; whose origin is from of old, from ancient times. Therefore the Lord will give them up, until the time when she who is to give birth has born, and the rest of his brethren shall return to the children of Israel. (Mic. 5:1–2)

Christians also see Jesus's whipping and nailing to a cross for people's sins foreshadowed in the Jewish scriptures. Isaiah referred to the servant of the Lord as one "spurned and avoided by men" and "pierced for our offenses, crushed for our sins, upon him was the chastisement that makes us whole, by his stripes we were healed" (Isa. 53: 3, 5).

The nature of Jesus is described in the New Testament, which is the second part of the Christian Bible. John refers to Jesus as "*logos*," which means "word." John was drawing upon a Greek myth, which the Hellenized Jews knew, that asserted when the gods of Mount Olympus wanted to do something on earth, they sent their logos, it became flesh, did the job, and returned to Olympus. "In the beginning was the Word, and the Word was with God, and the Word was God" (John 1:1).

This would cause some consternation and arguments among early Christians: Who was Jesus? God? Human? Hybrid? John further states, "And the Word became flesh and made his dwelling among us, and we saw his glory as of the Father's only Son, full of grace and truth" (John 1:14). So Jesus is God become human. So which part was human, and which part was God? The human part apparently came from his mother, Mary, and the God part was from, well, God. But which part was which? The New Testament states that Jesus "emptied himself, taking the form of a slave, coming in human likeness, and found human in appearance" (Phil. 2:7). So when he was born in Bethlehem, he knew pretty much what newborn babies knew: nothing, nada, not much. He knew when he was hungry, cold, or colicky, but that was it. Like all humans, he had a human body and a human soul. Then the Bible says, "... the child grew and became strong, filled with wisdom" (Luke 2:40). Wisdom is a code word for the Holy Spirit. That is

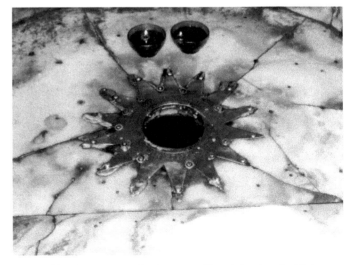

Figure 12.1 This star marks the spot of Jesus's birth in Bethlehem, now inside the Church of the Nativity.

why the former church in Constantinople was named the Hagia Sophia ("holy wisdom"), the Holy Spirit. So the Holy Spirit is Jesus's second soul, telling him who he was and what his mission was going to be. So Jesus grew into knowledge of his Godhood. This is called the duality or dual nature of Jesus—he has two natures: human and divine.

Christian History

The founder of Christianity was Jesus of Nazareth. He was one of the Pharisees, the teaching class of the Jews, but he apparently did not get along with other Pharisees. He was born in Bethlehem during a census called by Caesar Augustus of the Roman Empire. His family was there because, apparently, members of the house of David registered there (Luke 2:1–5). Christians mark this as year one, the beginning of the Christian calendar, but this calendar was not codified until 1,500 years later. So the actual date is in dispute. Luke, the gospel writer, said the census during which Jesus was born was when Quirinius was governor of Syria. That would have put the census between 6–12 CE.[2] The gospel writer Matthew said Jesus was born when Herod was king of Jerusalem, which would have been between 37–4 BCE.[3]

Most of Jesus's life is not known. There are some Gnostic scriptures, such as the First Gospel of the Infancy of Jesus Christ, that were written in the second century ("The Lost Books") and came up with fanciful accounts that were rejected by early Christians. The Bible mentions how Jesus got separated from his family and ended up preaching in the temple as a youth. Then we see him again as an adult being baptized by John the Baptist.

As an adult, Jesus taught for three years and performed miracles. The reason Jesus performed miracles was for street credentials. He wanted people to listen to him. If I said, "Hi, I'm God. Follow me," you'd probably think I was getting paid too little to be God.

Figure 12.2 This icon shows times in Jesus's life and death.

But if I took a stroll on the local lake, cured everyone in town of AIDS, and then raised everyone from the dead at the local cemetery, would you listen to me then? Would you at least give me five minutes of your time? The Bible tells the story of Lazarus, who Jesus raised from the dead, as one of Jesus's miracles. Yet Lazarus eventually would die again, but Jesus's teachings, which are more important, have lasted more than two thousand years.

Jesus's teachings were radical, totally rad. They are more radical than just "being good" or "helping each other" sentiments in a greeting card. They are:

> Blessed are you who are poor, for yours is the kingdom of God. (Luke 6:20)
> [*It is better to be poor than to be rich.*] *Truly I tell you, it is hard for someone who is rich to enter the kingdom of heaven.* (Matt. 19:23)

So the very fact that you are attending college so you can get a high-paying job will probably condemn you to hell. It is a shame the student handbook never mentions this.

- Address God as your father ("Our Father who art in heaven ..."). Treat God as your dad, assuming you have a good relationship with your dad. He is not some distant ogre god but your father. Talk to him as you would your dad. He will give you what you need, not necessarily what you want (you can't afford the insurance on a Ferrari). He forgives, but he will also ground you if you disobey.
- Never fight back. "You have heard that it was said, 'An eye for an eye and a tooth for a tooth.' But I say to you, offer no resistance to one who is evil. When someone strikes you on your right cheek, turn the other one to him as well" (Matt. 5:38–39). So if someone attacks you, your family, your mother, your children, your cat, you are never allowed to fight back. Do you think you could handle that? Rad.
- Love your enemies. "You have heard that it was said, 'You shall love your neighbor and hate your enemies.' But I say to you, love your enemies, and pray for those who persecute you" (Matt. 5:43–44). This includes terrorists, murders, thieves, rapists, and pedophiles. Rad enough?

Jesus taught for three years and then was crucified by the Romans, at the request of the ruling Jews, for treason. Before that, he instituted what is called communion, the Lord's Supper, or the Eucharist, depending on the Christian denomination.

> *While they were eating, Jesus took bread, said the blessing, broke it, and giving it to the disciples, said, 'Take this and eat; this is my body.' Then he took a cup, gave thanks, and gave it to them, saying, 'Drink from it, all of you, for this is my blood of the covenant, which will be shed on behalf of many for the forgiveness of sins.'* (Matt. 26:26–28)

Figure 12.3 These are the original steps Jesus climbed to Herod's Palace for his trial.

Figure 12.4 Pontius Pilate, who sentenced Jesus to death, is credited on this stone for funding an amphitheater on the Sea of Galilee.

Taking his body literally meant taking it and consuming it. This is called transubstantiation, the belief that the bread and wine at communion physically become the body and blood of Jesus. The early Christians practiced this, as verified by Eusebius in his accounting of *The Epistle of the Gallican Churches*).[vii] Most Christians of the world—Catholic and Orthodox—still practice transubstantiation. Protestants do not.

[...] Cults often do not survive the deaths of their founders. Christianity was a cult. To survive, the pattern would be for Christianity to evolve into a sect. But something different occurred: it went from a cult to a cult, because Jesus came back from the dead. This is celebrated as Easter among Christians. Then Jesus hung around with his peeps for 40 days in the flesh and then ascended into heaven, never to be seen again in the flesh. This is called the Ascension.

Figure 12.5 Ile-de-France students mass. Transubstantiation occurs during the mass, when the bread and wine change into the body and blood of Jesus.

Apostolic times. After the death of Jesus, the 12 apostles, Jesus's followers, were scared. The Jews and Romans were looking for them, and if they were crucified, they would stay dead because, unlike Jesus, they were not God. They were hidden in a place called the "upper room" when the Holy Spirit descended upon them. This is called Pentecost because it occurred during the Jewish holiday of Pentecost, but it's also known as the birthday of Christianity because the apostles went out to the known world and began preaching their ministry of the Gospel. (What is not the birthday is Christmas. Christmas is just the mass that celebrates the birth of Christ, and it's probably not even on the date of his birth.) The Holy Spirit gave the apostles and Mary gifts: courage (they would not be fearful anymore); wisdom (because that is what the Holy Spirit is) so they would know what to say or how to act in any given situation; and the gift of tongues so they could preach the Gospel to anyone—no matter what language that person spoke—and be understood. The apostles ruled the young church in Jerusalem with Peter as their leader; Jesus had given him authority over heaven and earth. Jesus had changed Peter's name from Simon and called him "Petra," which means "rock" in Greek:

Figure 12.6 Emblem of Vatican City State; the keys of Peter, gold (for heaven), and silver (for earth) can be seen on the emblem.

> And so I say to you, you are Peter, and upon this rock I will build my church, and the gates of the netherworld shall not prevail against it. I will give you the keys to the kingdom of heaven. Whatever you bind on earth shall be bound in heaven, and whatever you loose on earth shall be loosed in heaven. (Matt. 16:18–19)

The apostles spread across the Roman Empire preaching the gospel. Peter preached throughout Asia Minor (now Turkey) and ended up as the bishop of Rome. There are legends about where the other apostles went, but this is subject to dispute among scholars. James, who was a relative of Jesus, became the first bishop, or episcopus (elder, supervisor), of Jerusalem.

Another important figure in early Christianity was Saul of Tarsus, a Jew. He hated Christians and had his own personal army he used to round Christians up for trial. Christianity was illegal at that time, and Saul considered Christians to be Jewish heretics. He heard there were some Christians hiding in Damascus, so he headed that way. On the way, he literally got "knocked off his high horse" and was blinded. He heard a voice: "Saul, Saul, why are you persecuting me?" Saul replied,

Figure 12.7 St. Paul was known as Saul before his conversion experience.

"Who are you, sir?" The voice said, "I am Jesus, whom you are persecuting" (Acts 9:4–5). So Saul became a changed man. He changed his name to Paul, was baptized, and began preaching to the non-Jewish people of the Roman Empire: the pagans. The common consensus among the apostles was Jesus was the messiah for the Jews. Paul believed Jesus was the messiah for the whole world, Jews and non-Jews alike.

By the way, Paul was a tentmaker, so he had an income to pay his own expenses without being a burden to those to whom he preached. You could say Paul was "in tents."

Paul eventually ended up in Rome and was executed by beheading. Because he was a Roman citizen, he escaped the agony of crucifixion. Peter was crucified upside down: he requested this form of execution because he (having denied Jesus three times) did not feel he had earned the right to be crucified like the Lord. Peter's bones were found under St. Peter's Basilica in Vatican City during World War II.[4] Paul's bones were found under the Basilica of Saint Paul Outside the Walls in Rome and authenticated in 2009.[5]

All the apostles, except for John, were martyred. James was killed when the Romans destroyed Jerusalem. John was exiled to the prison island of Patmos in Greece, where he wrote that strange Book of Revelation. He had scrolls smuggled off the island by visitors and wrote in code in case the Romans intercepted a scroll, so do not take Revelations literally. The number 12 means fulfillment: 12 tribes of Israel, 12 apostles. Seven is perfection. Six is short of perfection, and 666—the number of the beast or antichrist—is the exact opposite of the Trinity, 777. This number also spells a name: Nero. He was the antichrist about whom John was writing. Nero was notorious for having human torches illuminate his evening parties in the Roman circus. He was insane even by Roman emperor standards.

An account by Tacitus from the late first century goes into detail about how Christians were treated by the Roman Empire:

> Besides being put to death, they were made to serve as objects of amusement; they were clad in the hides of beasts and torn to death by dogs; others were crucified, others set on fire to serve to illuminate the night when the daylight failed.[6]

As mentioned, Christianity was illegal, so Christians went into hiding. Initially, they worshipped in synagogues because they saw themselves as Jews who accepted the messiah. But Jews were in danger of losing their dispensation from having to worship the Roman gods for harboring these Nazarenes, so the Christians were kicked out. Instead, Christians began to meet in people's homes. There were two parts of the service: the Liturgy of the Word and the Liturgy of the Eucharist. During the first, they would read a scroll from Paul or John, because the Bible had not yet been created. The second part would be the Liturgy of the Eucharist (thanksgiving) or Agape (unconditional love), when the bread and wine would be presented and transubstantiation would occur.

Post-Apostolic period. By 70 CE, the time of Jerusalem's destruction, the post-Apostolic period begins. Most of the apostles, except for John, were dead. The next generation of administrators come to power: bishops, who were the successors to the apostles; deacons (from *diaconate*, meaning "servant"), who did the grunt work—distributing wealth to widows and orphans and so on; and, when the church membership increased, priests (presbyters), who could do everything a bishop could do except ordain someone.

Figure 12.8 The establishment of a hierarchy in early Christianity is evidenced by this tombstone for a deacon.

By the second century, the church needed to be clear about its beliefs because heresies had been cropping up. One of these heretics was Marcion. He was a presbyter who was very flamboyant: he had two men with trumpets announce his entrance when he came into town. Marcion wrote the first known Bible, consisting of Paul's writings as well as his own. He was kind of vain that way.

Gnosticism was a heresy that taught there were two gods: an evil Yahweh and a good Jesus, who married Sophia (the earth goddess) and beat up Yahweh. Oh, and a blind, insane angel who came down to earth and had sex with women, who then gave birth to giants. The reason you may not have heard of any of this is that gnosticism means esoteric knowledge. These Christians believed they had knowledge no one else had. The most important thing you should know about them was that they did not believe in the dual nature of Jesus: Jesus was God but not human. He only appeared to be human: he was God wearing a human suit. So Jesus did not die on the cross: he just slipped out of his human suit. This belief—Jesus escaping crucifixion—was passed on to Islam through the gnostic Nestorians, who communicated with Muhammad in Arabia.

In the eastern part of the Roman Empire, there was another heresy: Arianism. It was named after a presbyter named Arius who promoted it. Arians believed Jesus was neither God nor human, just a subservient creation.

The new Roman emperor, Constantine—who had legalized Christianity and funded its churches, clergy, and rituals—saw Christianity as a good way to unify his empire. But he heard Christians had different beliefs. So he called the Council of Nicaea (325 CE), told the bishops to decide on Christianity's belief, and said he would enforce it with his army. It was what emperors did. So the council affirmed the dual nature of Jesus, condemning both gnosticism and Arianism, and affirmed the use of the Greek-Roman tradition, or Alexandrine canon, as being the true Bible, therefore condemning Marcion's Bible. The Bible would be codified—what definitely got in and what got left out—during the Council of Hippo in 393 CE. The Nicaean council also created the Nicene Creed, which many churches still use in their services.

An early influential Christian theologian was Bishop Augustine of Hippo, Africa. He affirmed Christians were born with original sin—the sin of Adam and Eve—and needed to be baptized to be saved. He taught that only divine grace can save a person, not do-it-yourself salvation: you had to have faith for God to save you. He also affirmed the sacraments (such as baptism), saying they were outward signs of God's grace. He also affirmed the Trinity—the belief that God was three persons: God the Father, God the Son (Jesus), and God the Holy Spirit (or Ghost). Basically, 3 = 1. But this raised some questions about the dynamics of the Trinity that Augustine attempted to answer. Did God talk to himself? Did the Father die on the cross with the Son (they are one God!)? When Augustine was walking on the beach of Hippo along the Mediterranean Sea mulling this over, he passed a boy who was pouring a bucket of water into a hole he had dug in the sand. He asked the boy what he was doing. The boy, happy that he had been noticed, replied, "I'm putting the Mediterranean Sea into this hole." Augustine responded, "I can see you are trying to do that, but that hole is small, and the sea is big. How are you going to do that?" The boy responded, "I can put the sea into this hole before you ever figure out the Trinity." That is when Augustine realized what God was telling him: the Trinity is the mind of God—what he is apt to do as well as his feelings, dreams, and inner volitions. For one to understand that, one would have to be God. So Christians have accepted the Trinity on faith, not logic. Augustine wrote about his views on Christian theology in *City of God*.

Primacy of Rome and the Great Schism. Starting in the first century, early Christians deferred to the bishop of Rome in matters of morals because that bishop sat on the throne of Peter and was considered the successor to the head of the apostles. He was called by the title "father," "papa," or "pope" (*pappas* in Greek).

A lot occurred between the post-Apostolic period and the Middle Ages: Vikings and barbarians attacked and destroyed the Roman Empire; Christianity was nearly wiped out in Western Europe by the

Norsemen, but the monks from the Monastery of Cluny reintroduced it. Pope Gregory Christianized most of Europe by marrying off orphans raised in convents to the kings of Europe. These pious women converted their husbands and kingdoms. And Gregory created the calendar we now use. But this is not a book on Christianity, so we must move on.

In 1054, Christianity was split in half over three words: "and the Son." This is called the filioque clause. Western Christians, centered around Rome, believed that the Father, the Son, and the Holy Spirit were equal because they were all God. So when the Holy Spirit was sent forth for baptism, for example, both the Father and the Son sent him. It was a collaborative effort. Eastern Christians believed the Father was superior to the Son and the Holy Spirit. So when the Holy Spirit was sent forth, only the Father sent him; he did not discuss the issue with the Son. The Western Church argued that all three were equal. The Eastern Church said the Bible clearly states the Father is superior. The Western Church argued that the clause was in the Nicene Creed: "The Holy Spirit proceeds from *the Father and the Son*." The Eastern Church said the Westerners had snuck that clause in. The Western Church said it did not like baklava. The Eastern Church responded by saying "Your mama." Okay, the last two sentences are fictional, but the argument continued, resulting in the split between the Catholic Church (Western) and the Eastern Orthodox churches.

The Catholic Church became the new temporal power after the fall of the Roman Empire. People flocked to the church, which was the only governing body around for protection from the barbarians ranging across Europe. The pope needed to protect them, so he raised an army. To raise an army, he needed to raise taxes. To raise taxes, he needed to acquire land. So, in a way, the popes became like emperors.

During this period, an influential theologian was Thomas Aquinas (1225–1274). In his book *Summa Theologica,* Aquinas used the methods of the Greek philosopher Aristotle to defend Christian doctrine. Admiring how Aristotle arrived at truths through logic, Aquinas applied that same logic (using the prime mover theory) to prove God exists. To illustrate this theory, consider: When I move an object, such as a chair, what force is acting upon me? Gravity, so I don't fly away when I move the chair. Where does gravity come from? The earth. What gravitational force acts upon the earth? The sun. The sun is affected by the gravitational pull of what? The solar system. The solar system is affected by the gravitational pull of what? The Milky Way Galaxy. The Milky Way Galaxy is affected by the gravitational pull of what? Other galaxies in the universe. So the chain of cause and effect goes on. Now, there are two possibilities in this scenario. One: there is an infinite number of movers. But physics says that is impossible. One cannot have infinite mass or energy. The only other scenario is that there is one prime mover that moves everything but is not moved itself. All emanates from it. And, according to Aquinas, that prime mover is God.

Rise of Protestantism. Martin Luther, a Catholic German Augustinian monk, rebelled against the selling of indulgences. An indulgence replaces penance due for sin. When a Catholic went into the confessional and told his or her sins to the priest, the priest gave the penitent an act of penance to perform to show God true contrition. This could range from saying three Hail Marys or an Our Father to working in a soup kitchen or living with lepers, depending on the severity of the sin. If a person has undone penance at death, he or she gets a second chance: purgatory. There are three levels in the afterlife: heaven, hell, and purgatory. Saints go to heaven. Evil people go to hell. Most people are neither saints nor evil, so they go to purgatory. Anyone with sin cannot enter heaven because God and sin cannot coexist: sin is a rejection of God. Purgatory is a state of existence where souls can work off that penance and sin and then go to heaven. But it is not pleasant. Although it is not hell, one can see hell from the front door. So it is preferable to be sinless and have no penance left in this life.

One of the ways to receive an indulgence was to give to the church. This had always been the case. With St. Peter's Basilica being rebuilt, the popes needed money to pay people such as Michelangelo and Rafael and the laborers. The original basilica had been built by Constantine in the 300s. This was now the 1500s: the building was falling apart. So, if the faithful gave money toward the construction of the church, they received an indulgence. But in the minds of the peasants (and at least one priest), it was salvation at a price. Drop a coin in the tin (box), receive a paper that says you have an indulgence, and then carte blanche. Luther came out of church one day and saw one of his parishioners drunk in an alley. "Why were you not at Mass today?" Luther asked. The man said he had bought an indulgence so he did not have to show up. So Luther became incensed, particularly because his church had a display of saints' relics and asked for an admission fee that would buy an indulgence. So Luther wrote the 95 Theses, which were 95 reasons why the sale of indulgences was wrong, and he nailed them to the door of the Wittenberg Castle church. Unfortunately, he wrote them in Latin, so the general populace could not read them. A copy was sent to the pope, though, who allegedly said, "He's a German. He will change his mind when he sobers up." Luther became angry (he is called the "firebrand of Germany" for good reason), and he added his belief in the doctrines of *sola fide* (by faith alone is one saved; one does not need good works resulting in indulgences) and *sola scriptura* (by scripture alone is one saved; one does not need the church). After a series of confrontations, including a meeting with the Hapsburg emperor at Worms, Luther was excommunicated from the church. The German princes then kidnapped him to protect him from punishment, using his words in their attempt to secede from the Hapsburg Empire.

This was the beginning of the Protestant Reformation. The word "Protestant" comes from the Latin word for protest, because a Protestant protests against the Catholic Church. Other Protestant reformers thought Luther had not gone far enough. John Calvin, also a former Catholic priest, came up with the belief in the depravity of humanity: humans are so depraved they cannot save themselves; only God can save them. Calvin also believed in predestination: some of you are going to heaven and some of you are not going to graduate, and there is nothing you can do about it because God has already decided. Calvin also decided there was no transubstantiation at communion (which is why Protestants do not believe in transubstantiation).

Another break from the Catholic Church came when King Henry VIII of England wanted a male heir after marrying his brother's widow. When he and his wife were unable to produce one, Henry sought a divorce. At that time, only the pope could annul a marriage. Henry sent his request to the pope, who said no. In response, Henry created his own church, the Church of England, and he granted himself a divorce. Some scholars do not consider Anglicans (Church of England) to be Protestant because Henry had no problem with Catholic doctrine; he just had a personal problem.

Protestantism, having no central authority, would fragment into smaller pieces. Breaking off from the Anglicans was John Knox, who formed the Church of Scotland, and from them came the Presbyterians. Also breaking off from the Anglicans was a blue-collar movement, founded by John and Charles Wesley, called the Methodists. Another group that split off from the Anglicans were the Anabaptists, or rebaptizers. They believed their baptisms were the only valid ones, so converts to Anabaptism had to be baptized again. This would give rise to the Baptists, the Amish, and the Mennonites. A final group breaking off from the Anglicans were the Puritans, who wanted to purify Anglicanism of any remaining Catholic elements. They were also known as the Pilgrims. Also breaking off from the Church of England was the Society of Friends (Quakers), pacifists who sat in the Friendship Halls facing each other until someone stood up with a revelation. The Anglicans in the United States were forced to leave the Church of England after 1776 for political reasons: alignment with the enemy during the American Revolution was considered treason. They became the Episcopalians. Breaking off from the Lutherans were the Disciples of Christ and the Reformed Church.

The Great Awakening was a series of revival movements during which itinerant preachers would come to towns and preach in the open or in tents, creating a flurry of emotions. Emotion was seen as the way to truly connect to God. One of these preachers was Jon Edwards, who preached a sermon called "Sinners in the Hands of an Angry God." Out of the Great Awakening movement came the Holiness churches, which handled poisonous snakes because the Bible said one could: "They will pick up serpents (with their hands), and if they drink any deadly thing, it will not harm them" (Mark 16:18). Springing from the Holiness churches were the Pentecostals, who speak in tongues (which are repetitive sounds), employ prophesy, and are "slain in the spirit," falling to the ground like they are dead. A modern-day example of Protestant Pentecostals is the Assemblies of God church. Catholics also have Pentecostals, and they are called charismatics. Also coming out of the Great Awakening was fundamentalism, which is a literal interpretation of the Bible.

Protestant Reformers shortened the Bible by removing the following books—Tobit, Judith, 1st and 2nd Maccabees, Wisdom of Solomon, Ecclesiastics, Baruch, and parts of Esther and Daniel—as not canonical (i.e., the Apocrypha, or "hidden writings"). From his church's Bible, Luther removed the Epistle of James because it states that faith without works "is dead" (James 2:17), which seemed to reject *sola fide*. He called James "so much straw" that should be burned. In addition to James, Luther removed Hebrews, Jude, and the Apocalypse from the New Testament and placed them at the end of his Bible, but later Reformers reinstated them.

The Catholic Reformation was a response to the Protestant Reformation. A major part of it was the Council of Trent (1545–1563), when bishops met to determine what Catholicism believed in light of the Protestants' contentions. Protestants attended, too, but they were not allowed to contribute to the decision-making. In the end, the council rejected most everything Luther said. It reaffirmed that faith and works save (because it says so in Timothy) and that the Church has equal authority with the Bible because it created that scripture, so no *sola scriptura*. And it reaffirmed the books of the Bible that the Protestants had removed.

Another part of the Catholic Reformation was the formation of the Society of Jesus (Jesuits) by Ignatius of Loyola. The former soldier created a military order of priests to counter Protestantism. Candidates are ruddy in appearance, intelligent, and strong. Jesuits convert much of the Americas, Africa, and the Far East to Catholicism.

Modern Christianity

In the 19th century, the Catholic Church's First Vatican Council set the doctrine of papal infallibility. This holds that the pope can never be wrong when he is speaking about Catholic doctrine and morals and that he is speaking *ex cathedra* ("from the chair") of St. Peter. Because the pope is the primary teacher of the Catholic Church, if he is wrong, it would be a monumental catastrophe. The council also set doctrine (this means Catholics have to believe it) on something Catholics have believed for two millennia: the Immaculate Conception. This is the doctrine that Mary was conceived without original sin: Mary could not have been conceived with sin if she were to be the mother of Jesus (God), because sin is the rejection of God. Mary would be rejecting her own son if she had sin.[7]

The Second Vatican Council (early 1960s) changed many important aspects of the Catholic Church. The most notable was allowing the vernacular in worship services. Up until that time, the mass had been said in Latin; after the council, the mass could be said in any language. The council also increased the role of the laity in the parish churches, emphasized ecumenism (unity among Christians) with other denominations, and stated that Jews were not responsible for the death of Jesus. The conference was called by Pope John XXIII ("Johnny Walker," because he liked to take strolls in Rome and surprise people), although it was concluded during the term of the next pontiff, Pope Paul VI.[8]

Pope John Paul II (1978–2005) helped fight European communism, promoted ecumenism (unity) among Christian denominations and other religions, and increased membership to record levels. Particularly successful in increasing membership were his World Youth Days, when he would travel around the world and meet Catholic youth in different cities. He was canonized a saint in 2016 along with John XXIII. Pope Benedict XVI (2005–2013) concentrated on ecumenism with the Eastern Orthodox (working to end the Great Schism) and Protestants. He was the first pope to resign in 596 years and the first pope ever to willingly resign. He was given the never-before-used title of pope emeritus. Pope Francis (2013–present), the first Latin American pope and the first Jesuit pope, brought to Rome his focus on the poor. He told Catholic bishops, priests, and nuns to refrain from having expensive homes and cars. He moved into a dorm for Vatican employees instead of the lavish papal apartments: instead, he allowed two Syrian refugee families to stay in the papal apartments.

Francis also wanted the church to be more open to divorced people and homosexuals, but he made no changes in church doctrine: no homosexual marriages in the church. He has also been a world peace mediator, brokering normalization of relations between the United States and Cuba and serving as a peace ambassador between Israel and the Palestinians.

In the Orthodox churches, leadership is shared among several patriarchs and bishops ("equals" but with autonomous local sees). Unity has been a problem: the Russian Orthodox Church snubbed the Orthodox churches' "Great Council" in 2016, and split from the Patriarch of Constantinople over the latter's decision to remove the Ukrainian Orthodox Church from Russia's control. The Orthodox churches are organized along ethnic or national lines for the most part, and they place emphasis on mysticism: experiencing God instead of analyzing him (unlike Aquinas). For instance, religious icons are holier than statues. Icons are windows through which God's grace flows. If one touches an icon, one will receive God's blessing. By comparison, statues are not holy in the Catholic Church.

In modern Protestantism, an ecumenical movement led by the World Council of Churches brings different denominations together for charitable work projects in Third World countries. There have been some organic unions among denominations: the Methodist Church combined with the Evangelical United Brethren Church in 1969, creating the United Methodist Church. The Lamb of God Church in Fort Myers, Florida, was formed by the union of a Lutheran and an Episcopalian church in 2004. And the Evangelical Church stated in 2016 that there were no doctrinal differences between Lutherans and Catholics.

There are many more divisions in Protestantism than in Catholicism. Protestant churches have split into smaller and smaller groups, with the creation of storefront churches and nondenominational denominations. In 2016, the Episcopal Church USA was suspended from the Anglican communion with Church of England–affiliated churches over the issue of an active homosexual bishop.

The resurgence of Calvinism is occurring among evangelical Protestants. This next generation of Calvinistic churches has become more hard-line, with beliefs in predestination and the depravity of humans as well as no belief in transubstantiation.[9]

There have been some homegrown American Protestant religions. In the 1800s, there was a lot of talk about the impending end of the world. One of those supporting this belief was William Miller, who predicted that the end of the world would be between 1843–1844. After this "great disappointment," other religious groups sprang up. One of these was the Seventh-Day Adventists, an end-of-the-world denomination that meets on Saturdays, the original Jewish Sabbath.[10] They incorporate Miller's beliefs: there will be a rapture, a thousand-year rule of Jesus, and then a final battle with Satan/Antichrist. Many Protestants have adopted these beliefs. Catholics and Orthodox do not believe in a rapture.

Branching off from the Seventh-Day Adventists in 1934 were the Davidians, founded by Victor Houteff. He predicted that the start of the eternal kingdom of David would be soon. His widow, Florence, predicted the date would be in 1959. The Branch Davidians split off in 1955 from the Davidians. Vernon Howell joined the group and became its leader. He renamed himself David Koresh

(Koresh is the Hebrew name of the Persian king Cyrus; David is after King David) and began to "plant the seeds" of the new age by fathering children with congregation women. Koresh believed he was the anointed one to open the Seven Seals described in the Book of Revelation. The way he was going to do that was to write a commentary on it. That was when federal agents attempted a forced entry into his Waco, Texas, compound. Koresh saw this as the end of world, and people on both sides were killed in a shootout before most members of the cult died when their compound went up in flames. The FBI now uses religious scholars in dealing with people like this.

Oh, they're back. Charles Pace has created the New Branch Davidians, which has created dissent among surviving members of the original group who are waiting for Koresh to return from the dead and revive the group.

In 1866, Mary Baker Eddy founded Christian Science after she said she was spiritually healed of a spinal injury after a fall. She wrote about her beliefs in *Science and Health with a Key to the Scriptures*. She concluded that faith, not medicine, should be used to heal because disease and injury are caused by sin. Matter is illusion; only the mind and spirit are real. The Christian Science church has its headquarters in Boston, but it may be declining with the closing of its reading rooms across the country. In 2016, a count of its membership's online directory showed 1,750 members.[11]

Joseph Smith, the son of an evangelical preacher, founded the Church of Jesus Christ of Latter-day Saints (Mormons) in 1822. That year, according to Smith, the Angel Moroni led him to where the golden tablets were buried. Written on the tablets was a history of Christ coming to the Americas and converting the Native Americans descended from the ten lost tribes of Israel who had sailed over to the New World. Not all the Native Americans were converted, and after a big battle, the non-Christian ones (Lamanites) beat the Christian ones (Nephites). Moroni, the last of the Nephites, wrote the story on golden tablets, buried them, and came back several centuries later to tell Smith where they were. Smith dug them up and translated them into the Book of Mormon.

Smith headed west with his followers, but a lynch mob in Illinois killed him in 1844. His widow and his son, Joseph Smith III, formed the Reorganized Church of Jesus Christ of Latter-day Saints (now Community of Christ). Brigham Young led the rest of the church to the Great Salt Lake, Utah, territory in 1847, established the group's headquarters there, declared independence from the United States, refused to pay taxes, and practiced polygamy. When President James Buchanan heard about the Mormon activities, he sent the US Army to regain control of the territory. After initially holding off the army, the Mormons eventually surrendered and conceded on the issues of taxes, government control, and monogamy.

Mormons have different beliefs than other self-professed Christians. They view Jesus Christ as God of this world but also believe humans can be gods (of their own worlds). The latter is not doctrine, but several prophets (heads of the church) have said this. Mormons believe that the Trinity is actually three separate gods; that marriage is eternal; that baptism can occur after death; and that there are three levels after death: the Celestial, Terrestrial, and Telestial Kingdoms. The Celestial is the highest level, where faithful Mormon males can become gods. Again, although this is not official doctrine, several of the church's presidents have stated it. Leadership is through the prophet and a governing body called the Council of the Twelve Apostles.

Sacred scripture for Mormons include the Protestant Bible, the Book of Mormon, the Doctrine and Covenants (teaching of the prophets), and the Pearl of Great Price (Smith's own testimony).

The Jehovah's Witnesses were founded by Charles Taze Russell (1852–1916), son of Pennsylvania Presbyterians. Russell was a haberdasher in his father's men's clothing store. He believed the creeds of other Christian denominations had "elements of truth" but were buried under pagan teachings, like a hierarchy. The Jehovah's Witnesses began as an 1870 Bible study group. Then the group started publishing tracts, such as the *Watch Tower*. They believed that, according to the Bible, only 144,000 people will go to heaven, and then it will be full. The good will rise and live forever on an earthly paradise with Jesus. The evil will stay dead. They also believe Jesus Christ is not God but "a god," and their Bible, the New World Translation, has been rewritten to reflect their beliefs. So Jehovah's Witnesses have a different Bible than those of other Christians.

Also arising during the end of the 20th century was the Black liberation movement. A Baptist minister, Martin Luther King Jr., was a major proponent of this movement. King drew on his religious background to announce that Blacks are equal to Whites because God says so, not because of the government or Constitution. This divine right to equality is also present in liberation theology, which emphasizes power sharing between the rich and the poor. A more radical form of liberation theology in Latin America believes that the rich must share with the poor and that the poor can use violence to take from the rich if the latter are not willing. Pope Benedict XVI condemned this movement before he was elected pope because of the violence involved. Feminist liberation theology, another 20th-century movement, states that women are equal to men because God says so. She does. God is a woman, and men have been hiding that fact for centuries so they could dominate women. Ecofeminism, whose main proponent was Rosemary Radford Reuther, emphasized a love for nature because Gaia, the earth goddess, was a woman, too.

Christian Scripture

Christianity is one of the few religions of the world that has different versions of its scripture. Catholics, Protestants, and Orthodox have different books in their Bibles. Catholics have 72 books, Protestants have 66 books, and Orthodox can have up to 81 books. The reason has to do with history. By the second century, there were several translations of the Bible, the most popular being Old Latin or Itala. The Degree of the Council of Rome in 382 officially approved the books of the Bible. But mistakes were creeping in with each copy made by hand, so the pope commissioned Jerome to revise and correct it: the result was the Latin Vulgate, which would be the official Bible of Christianity for about a thousand years and translated into different languages. Protestants in the 1500s started writing their own, excluding

Figure 12.9 Jerome translated the Bible into Latin, creating the Latin Vulgate, in this cell in Bethlehem.

the Old Testament books mentioned earlier. These included Luther's, William Tyndale's, Miles Coverdale's, and others: Tavernier's Bible, the Great Bible, and the Bishop's Bible. King James I of England had officials rewrite the Bishop's Bible, and this became the King James Bible, which many Protestants use. But because of mistakes, it was revised again in the mid-1800s and is known as the Revised Version. Catholics, in the meantime, created another Bible (called the New American Bible) in 1970 from original Greek, Aramaic, and Hebrew sources. Orthodox churches generally used the Catholic Bible before the Great Schism. But other Orthodox, such as Egyptian Christians, used other books as well, since they were read in their liturgy.[12]

Christian Beliefs

Humans can be separated from God due to sin, which is a rejection of God. The original cause of sin is original sin, the sin of Adam and Eve in the Garden of Eden. All humans inherit this sin, and baptism removes it. So no one is born a Christian; they have to be baptized first.

The ultimate goal is the kingdom of God in heaven as well as on earth. Christians want to go to heaven, not hell. Catholics also have the concept of purgatory as another afterlife option (though temporary), while Protestants generally do not believe in purgatory: the kingdom of God on earth is the mandate to convert the world to Christianity, as mentioned in the passage that opens this [reading]. Some Protestants believe there will be a rapture on earth, with the good being taken up to heaven before the end of the world. Catholics and Protestants do not.

The means to get to heaven is through God's grace, faith that God can save one, and sacraments. Catholics have seven: Baptism, Reconciliation, Eucharist, Confirmation, Marriage, Holy Orders, and the Sacrament of the Sick. Most Protestant churches have two: Baptism and the Lord's Supper (communion).

Christian Branches

Catholicism

Catholicism is the largest branch of Christianity and the oldest, dating back to Peter as the first pope. Other popes followed for two thousand years. The religion has two major "rites." The Latin Rite is the largest and requires its priests to be celibate. The Eastern Rite reflects the local ethnicity of a community, such as the Greek Catholic or Russian Catholic Church. Loyal to the pope, its clergy can marry, though bishops and monks must be celibate. As mentioned before, the Catholic Church has seven sacraments, which are ritual actions through which God's grace is bestowed: Baptism, Eucharist, Confirmation, Reconciliation, Marriage, Holy Orders, and the Sacrament of the Sick (formerly known as Last Rites). Catholics believe in a communion of saints that can intercede for people on earth with God.

Protestantism

Protestantism does not have a common theology or structural organization, so there are literally thousands of Protestant denominations with different interpretations of the Bible. Some common beliefs include Luther's *sola fide* and *sola scriptura*. The supreme authority of the Bible is emphasized. Some denominations believe in the Trinity; some do not. Some denominations have consubstantiation; others believe the Lord's Supper is purely symbolic. Anglicans tend to have a communion of saints, while other denominations do not.

Orthodox

Orthodox Churches tend to reflect the national or ethnic makeup of its members (Russian, Greek, Romanian, Egyptian, etc.). There are 14 autocephalous, or autonomous, Orthodox churches, all of which are titled equal to each other, but the Ecumenical Patriarchate is titled first among equals. They consider themselves to be united in faith, but unity has been a problem with the Russian Orthodox Church, as mentioned earlier in this [reading]. Orthodox have the same seven sacraments as the Catholic Church. They also have the communion of saints.

Christian Holidays

Christian holidays vary depending on the denomination. Some are universal.

>**Advent**: four weeks before Christmas; the beginning of the liturgical (worship) year; observed by Catholics, Orthodox, and some Protestants; preparation spiritually for Christmas (Orthodox fast)

Figure 12.10 An altar was erected in what was once Mary's house.

Immaculate Conception: December 8; commemorates the conception of Mary without sin; celebrated by Catholics

Christmas: December 25 for Catholics and some Protestants; January 7 for Orthodox (based on the Julian and not Gregorian calendar); celebrates the birth of Jesus, if not his actual birthday

Solemnity of Mary, the Mother of God: January 1; celebrates Mary in her title as the mother of Jesus; observed by Catholics

Epiphany: the 12th day of Christmas in January for Catholics; celebrates the arrival of the three wise men to Jesus's home; January 6 for Orthodox, it celebrates the baptism of Jesus by John the Baptist

Ash Wednesday: about six weeks before Easter; the beginning of Lent, a period of fasting and abstinence from meat on certain days, penance, and preparation for Easter; for Catholics, Anglicans (Episcopalians), and Lutherans

Lent: about a six-week long preparation for Easter; for Catholics, Orthodox, and some Protestants

Palm Sunday: Sunday before Easter; commemorates Jesus's entry into Jerusalem and Jesus's passion

Holy or Maundy Thursday: the Thursday before Easter; celebrates the Last Supper by Catholics, Orthodox, and Protestants

Good Friday: the Friday before Easter; observes the crucifixion of Jesus; for Catholics, Orthodox, and Protestants

Easter: celebrates the resurrection of Jesus from the dead; for Catholics, Protestants, and Orthodox (though often on a different day for Orthodox)

Ascension: 40 days after Easter; observes Jesus's ascent into heaven; celebrated by Catholics

Pentecost: 50 days after Easter; observes the descent of the Holy Spirit upon the Apostles; celebrated by Catholics, Orthodox, and Protestants

Nativity of the Virgin Mary: September 8; celebrates the birth of Mary; for Catholics and Orthodox

Elevation of the Life-Giving Cross: September 14; observes the finding of the Cross by the Empress Helen (the mother of Constantine); observed by Orthodox

Presentation of the Virgin Mary in the Temple: November 21; observes Mary's consecration to God by her parents; observed by Orthodox

Presentation of Christ (or Lord) in the Temple: February 2; observes the circumcision of Jesus; celebrated by Catholics and Orthodox

Annunciation: March 25; celebrates Gabriel's announcement to Mary that she will conceive a son; observed by Catholics and Orthodox

Transfiguration: August 6; observes Jesus's appearance to the apostles with Elijah and Moses on the mountain; God the Father tells them to listen to Jesus

Assumption (Catholic), Repose, or Dormition of the Virgin Mary (Orthodox): August 15; observes Mary's resurrection into heaven; Orthodox believe Mary's body was taken to heaven three days after her death; Catholics believe Mary did not die but was assumed into heaven bodily

Figure 12.11 This church marks the spot where Mary was born.

Figure 12.12 Orthodox Christians believe Gabriel visited Mary at this well.

Figure 12.13 Pope Pius XII made the Assumption doctrine for Catholics.

Reformation Day: October 31; Protestants celebrate the Protestant Reformation

All Saints' Day: November 1; celebrates all saints in heaven; observed by Catholics; Orthodox celebration is on the first Sunday after Pentecost

Notes

1. C. Hackett et al., "The Future of World Religions: Population Growth Projections, 2010–2050." Pew Research Center, 2015, http://www.pewforum.org/2015/04/02/religious-projections-2010-2050/.

2. T. Johnson, "World Christian Database: Navigating Statistics on Religion," American Theological Library Association proceedings, 2014, http://ezproxy.lib.usf.edu/login?url=http://search.ebscohost.com/login.aspx?direct=true&db=rfh&AN=ATLA0001456958&site=eds-live.

3. W. Durant, *Caesar and Christ* (New York: Simon and Schuster, 1944).

4. *New American Bible* (Washington, DC: Catholic Biblical Association of America, 1970).

5. John Walsh, *The Bones of St. Peter: The First Full Account of the Search for the Apostle's Body* (Doubleday & Co., 1982).

6. Nick Squires, "Bone Fragments Confirmed to Be Saint Paul," *The Telegraph*, 2009, https://www.telegraph.co.uk/news/worldnews/europe/vaticancityandholysee/5685157/Bone-fragments-confirmed-to-be-Saint-Paul.html.

7. H. Bettenson and C. Maunder, eds., *Documents of the Christian Church,* 3rd ed. (Oxford, UK: Oxford University Press, 1999).

8. "First Vatican Council." *Encyclopaedia Britannica*, https://www.britannica.com/event/First-Vatican-Council.

9. Jordan Teicher, "Why Is Vatican II So Important?" National Public Radio, 2012, https://www.npr.org/2012/10/10/162573716/why-is-vatican-ii-so-important.

10. Lillian Kwon, "Resurgence of Calvinism is Real Despite Survey, Pastors Say," *Christian Post*, 2010, https://www.christianpost.com/news/resurgence-of-calvinism-is-real-despite-survey-pastors-say-47678/.

11. William Miller, *Christianity Today*, https://www.christianitytoday.com/history/people/denomination-alfound-ers/william-miller.html.

12. *Christian Science Journal Directory*, 2016, http://directory.christianscience.com/search?query=&language=all&distance_select=any&manual_location=&location=.

13. M. Bonocore, "Why Does the Orthodox Bible Have More Books Than the Catholic Bible?" Catholic Bridge. com, 2016, http://catholicbridge.com/orthodox/why_orthodox_bible_is_different_from_catholic.php.

Credits

Reading 13 Christian Ethics and Politics

By James R. Adair

> Throughout the Bible God appears as the liberator of the oppressed. He is not neutral. He does not attempt to reconcile Moses and Pharaoh, to reconcile the Hebrew slaves with their Egyptian oppressors or to reconcile the Jewish people with any of their late oppressors. Oppression is sin and it cannot be compromised with, it must be done away with. God takes sides with the oppressed.
>
> (*Kairos Document*, 1985)

In This [Reading]

Christianity involves more than just a system of beliefs. It demands that its adherents live moral lives, bearing witness to the world by lived example and by prophetic proclamation. For most Christians, active involvement in society is a vital part of the Christian life. A wide diversity of opinion exists among Christians concerning the proper application of the gospel to issues such as sexual mores, issues of life and death, and wealth and poverty. Accordingly, Christians support many different political parties in the countries in which they live, determined in part by their interpretation of the implications of Christianity concerning ethical issues.

Main Topics Covered

- Christ and culture
- Sexual mores
- Life and death
- Wealth and poverty
- Christianity and politics

Christ and Culture

Christians have always understood that their commitment to Christ includes a commitment to live moral lives, but they have not always agreed on the precise parameters of the morality required of Christians. Some early Christians believed it was necessary to obey certain aspects of the Jewish law, such as male circumcision and dietary restrictions, while others believed that Christ had set them free from such obligations. Some believed that abstaining from meat that had previously been offered to pagan gods was a vital part of their Christian witness, while others had no problem eating meat sacrificed to idols, since the pagan gods were not real. Some believed that it was important to observe certain days of the week or year as holy, and others believed that every day was a gift from God and thus equal to every other day. Of course, there are many issues on which all Christians would probably agree, in principle: commitment to both one's family and to fellow Christians, love for one's neighbor, forgiving those who have sinned against them. The Golden Rule summarizes for many the essence of Christian ethics, at least on a personal level: "Do unto others as you would have others do unto you" (Matt 7:12).

The question of whether Christian ethics can be transferred from the personal to the national level is debated by Christian ethicists today. In the past, the debate might never have occurred, because when the church and state were closely intertwined, as they were in many places throughout the history of Christianity, Christian rulers could have theoretically led their nations to follow such New Testament imperatives as loving their enemies, though few, if any, ever did so. In a world in which even official state churches hold little sway over modern governments, should the church expect the state to abide by Christian ethical principles? Reinhold Niebuhr, in his book *Moral Man and Immoral Society,* argues that nations can never be held to the same moral standards as individuals, in part because the use of coercive force, which all nations must wield to stay in power, by its very nature tends toward the principle that the end justifies the means, a notion that almost all Christian ethicists would reject if applied to individual Christians. While some Christians agree with Niebuhr's analysis, others assert that while no nation is Christian in the same sense as individuals are, Christian citizens within a nation can still insist that its policies approximate those that Christ demanded of individuals. Some of the ethical debates that exercise Christians today, such as war and peace or the issue of poverty, revolve around the issue of individual versus national ethical obligations.

H. Richard Niebuhr, brother of Reinhold, wrote an influential 1951 book entitled *Christ and Culture*, which examined the various ways in which Christians have historically related to society. The five paradigms he studied are all of interest to Christians today who struggle with the issue of how their faith and their own ethical commitments should be applied to Christian living in the world today, but three seem especially relevant in the modern world. In one option, which Niebuhr calls "Christ Against Culture," Christians see themselves as separate from the world, "in the world but not of it," so they do not even consider trying to change what they see as a hopelessly evil world. The Amish, an Anabaptist group that purposely limits its contacts with the rest of society and rejects most modern conveniences, are a good example of a modern group that follows this paradigm, as are many modern Christian religious who live cloistered lives in monasteries or convents. A second option, "The Christ of Culture," recognizes the importance of communicating the gospel to men and women of today, and it sees the Christian message as compatible with the dominant worldview. What some Christians might call unwarranted compromise with the world, "Christ of Culture" Christians call necessary accommodation of the gospel to the prevailing culture as a means of communicating the message effectively. A third option, "Christ the Transformer of Culture," acknowledges the inherent distance between Christianity and any culture, but it seeks to transform culture nevertheless, not so

---

Box 13.1 Christ and Culture

The five approaches to the question of how the Church should relate to society, as identified by H. Richard Niebuhr, are:

1. Christ Against Culture: Christians are called to be "in the world but not of it," and thus separate themselves from the world as a witness.
2. The Christ of Culture: Christians should accommodate their practices as much as possible to the prevailing culture in order to communicate the gospel message to others from the perspective of one immersed in the culture.
3. Christ Above Culture: Christians live in God's good creation and must participate in it, yet without compromising the essential teachings and example of Christ; the goal is to find a synthesis of Christ with culture.
4. Christ and Culture in Paradox: All human acts and efforts are sinful, unless sanctified by God's grace, so culture itself, whether of a secular or a Christian nature, is opposed to God, and Christians must learn to accept themselves as redeemed sinners who are called to follow the voice of God in a sinful world.
5. Christ the Transformer of Culture: Christians must recognize that the world is corrupt, but through Christ they seek to transform it so that it approximates the highest ideals of Christianity, though it will never reach it.

---

that it becomes Christian, but so that the highest ideals of Christianity are reflected in culture to as great an extent as possible. This approach to the question of the proper relationship between Christ and culture is probably the dominant one among Christians today, though many remain committed to the second, "Christ of Culture," option.

Sexual mores

> If the God you believe in hates all the same people you do, then you know you've
> created God in your own image.

(Anne Lamott)

Almost all religions and cultures have rules and taboos that elucidate proper and improper expressions of sexuality in a culture, and Christianity is no exception. Early Christians adopted many of the Jewish customs regarding marriage and sexuality. For example, Paul rebukes a man in Corinth for cohabiting with his (presumably former) stepmother (1 Cor 5:1; cf. Lev 18:8). He also condemns various forms of "sexual immorality," such as engaging in sex with prostitutes. One way in which Christians differed from both the Jewish and Roman law was in their attitude towards divorce. Jewish law allowed men to divorce their wives, and Roman law also allowed women to divorce their husbands. However, Christians, pointing to Jesus' teaching, strongly discouraged divorce. Elders and deacons, according to 1 Tim 3:2 and 12, must be "husbands of one wife," which probably reflects a prohibition of divorce among church leaders, though some scholars believe it refers to polygamy instead. The question of divorce continues to face Christians today, especially in the West, where divorce, once a cultural taboo, has become widely accepted. Most churches have many members who are divorced, and churches generally do their best to minister to their needs, just as they do other members. However, churches differ over the question of whether divorced people are eligible to serve as deacons, pastors, or other ministers. Some allow divorced people to serve in any capacity, and others do not.

At some point in the first century or so of Christian history, the idea became current among many Christians that celibacy was the path to greater holiness and that remaining single was preferable to being married. In the second century and beyond, this belief was probably based more on the dualistic notion, derived from the surrounding Greek culture, that spirit was good and matter was evil, than on the earlier, first century idea that the Parousia was imminent, which seems to have been Paul's rationale for urging those who were single to remain single (1 Cor 7). Most later Christians rejected extreme dualism, though many returned to the Pauline idea that a life of celibacy was more consistent with a life of complete devotion to God. Symeon the New Theologian, a medieval Eastern Christian, saw the monastic life as ideally suited for the pursuit of the purest form of Christianity. The canon law enacted in the eleventh century that mandated clerical celibacy in the Western Church was formulated both because of the idea that complete commitment to God precluded the entangling commitment to a wife and because of the corruption inherent in the practice of appointing one's children to positions of power within the church. The Reformers explicitly rejected the idea of clerical celibacy, however, as a recent innovation. Today clerical celibacy is the rule for Catholic bishops and priests and for Orthodox bishops. Other Christian denominations do not have any restrictions against married clergy.

One of the most divisive sexual issues facing churches today is the question of the proper Christian approach to homosexuality. Homosexual activity has traditionally been considered a sin in the church, and many Christians point to selected passages from both the Old Testament and New Testament to support the traditional view (e.g. Lev 18:22; Rom 1:26–27). Other Christians believe that the modern understanding of human physiology and psychology, including evidence that supports a genetic component behind homosexuality, suggests that traditional Christian attitudes toward homosexuality need to be reconsidered. Many Christians make a distinction between homosexual tendencies and homosexual activity. Only a few Christian denominations currently allow practicing homosexuals to serve as clergy or to marry in the church, though the number is slowly increasing. The issue has caused heated debate in several individual Protestant denominations, and the worldwide Anglican communion has struggled to deal with the U.S. Episcopal Church's ordination of an openly gay bishop, as some autonomous Anglican bodies have advocated forcing the U.S. Church to

Figure 13.1 Bishop Gene Robinson was the first openly gay bishop to be ordained in the Episcopal Church (USA). His ordination set off strong protests in many other Anglican bodies around the world.

rescind its practice of ordaining homosexuals or face expulsion from the Anglican family. Similarly divisive is the issue of whether Christians should support legalizing gay marriage (already legal in a few jurisdictions worldwide), oppose it, or stay out of the controversy entirely. The controversy over the proper roles that gays, lesbians, bisexuals, and transgender persons can play within the church has spawned at least one entirely new denomination, the Metropolitan Community Churches, which originated in 1968 as a church that openly welcomed GLBT persons into its fellowship. Strident voices exist on both sides of this issue, but many Christians have chosen to sit down with one another and try to achieve mutual understanding with those who have a different point of view. This issue is, at least in part, related to the larger issue of the relationship between the teaching of the Church and the discoveries of science, so future information that scientists discover either supporting or denying the link between genetics and homosexuality will undoubtedly be part of the ongoing discussion.

Life and Death

> *God's haiku on Iraq*
> Some think I condone

the bombing of my children.
They must not know me.
(*Progressive Theology*)

Issues dealing with life and death are some of the most important and difficult that Christians have to face. The main issues may be subdivided into two subsets of issues, those dealing with the beginning of life and those dealing with the end of life. Artificial birth control, artificial insemination, surrogate motherhood, abortion, cloning, and embryonic stem cell research all deal in one way or another with beginning of life issues. Some denominations, notably the Roman Catholic Church, are on record as officially opposing all these procedures or areas of investigation because, the official policy of the Church states, they kill a human being. Many ordinary Catholics apparently disagree, at least in part, since large numbers practice artificial birth control as a means of family planning. Many Evangelical and Pentecostal Churches would similarly disagree with many of the items listed above, with the exception of artificial birth control and perhaps artificial insemination and surrogacy. Again, however, a considerable gap often exists between the stated view of the denomination as a whole and the view of individual Christians who belong to a church affiliated with the denomination.

Proponents of artificial birth control say that opposition is based on the pre-scientific notion that conception occurs when the man "plants his seed" in the soil of the woman's womb, whereas modern biology shows that both the man and the woman contribute 50 percent of the genetic material that their child has. They also say that in a world with more than six billion humans on it, it is the Christian's responsibility not to contribute to overpopulation, which puts an undue burden on the poor, especially in the developing world. Opponents of birth control concede the point that women as well as men contribute genetic material to their offspring, but they counter that birth control takes out of God's hands the question of whether a child will be born from the act of sexual intercourse. They use a similar argument when opposing artificial insemination and surrogacy, except this time the point is that humans, through artificial means, are creating life that God may not have ordained.

Few issues are as controversial as abortion, and though advocates on both sides of the issue often claim that the path to the right decision on this matter is straightforward, many Christians do not believe that it is. First, proponents of abortion rights—that is, the right of a woman to terminate her pregnancy prematurely—must admit that, although it is not mentioned explicitly in the New Testament, early Christians apparently viewed abortion, along with infanticide, also common in the Roman Empire, as wrong. The *Didache* specifically says, "You shall not abort a child nor commit infanticide" (*Did.* 2.2), and other early Christian texts voice similar strictures. On the other hand, opponents of abortion rights must admit that most people in society, perhaps including most Christians, make a distinction between the use of a pill that will prevent a fertilized egg from being implanted in the uterus and ending the life of a six month old fetus. Does life begin at conception? Many Christians say yes, but others point out that many doctors define pregnancy as starting with implantation of the fertilized egg. Others would draw the line at the distinction between embryo and fetus (about eight weeks), or at the point of viability (currently about 24 weeks). Other Christians point out that although abortion is not ideal, in certain circumstances, such as rape, incest, or the immaturity or family situation of the mother, bringing a baby to full term might have dire consequences for the mother's wellbeing. Despite what some say, there is no single, "Christian" position on the topic. Recent attempts by abortion opponents to try to reach a political and/or theological compromise with abortion rights advocates prove that dialog on this issue is possible and perhaps even productive.

Opposition to embryonic stem cell research shares a similar theoretical basis with opposition to abortion. If life begins at conception, as many Christians argue, then a fertilized egg represents human life, even if it is in a Petrie dish. Other Christians argue that since the egg is never allowed to develop beyond the stage where it has eight cells, and since it had no chance of implantation in a uterus, it cannot be classified as human life. Furthermore, proponents of the research say, the potential benefits of stem-cell research are so great that the moral objections of a minority should not be allowed to decide the issue. Some scientists are currently working on ways to derive similar results from stem cells that were not originally derived from an eight-celled embryo, and a breakthrough in this area might turn some Christian opponents of the research into advocates.

Two types of human cloning are contemplated by researchers: reproductive cloning and therapeutic cloning. Almost all Christians agree at this point that reproductive cloning is ethically problematic, but opinion is divided over therapeutic cloning. Therapeutic cloning is an attempt to grow certain types of tissue, for example, a liver or pancreas, from a single cell. In addition to concerns involving the use of embryonic stem cells in therapeutic cloning, some Christians are concerned that developing the techniques necessary to produce a particular organ from a single cell will greatly increase the danger that similar techniques could be used to create an entire cloned human, and based on cloning successes with several mammal species over the past decade, they say, such concern is warranted. Christian proponents of therapeutic cloning reply that the practice represents an important step forward in medical research and treatment, one that is preferable to the practice whereby parents purposely conceive a child so that the new baby's tissues, a kidney, for example, can be used to help a gravely ill sibling (without, of course, killing the baby). Furthermore, they say, the "slippery slope" argument is invalid, and what is needed is strict prohibitions against using cloning techniques to produce a living human. Based on the rapidity with which cloning technology has advanced over the past decade or two, and despite worldwide restrictions on reproductive cloning, it seems likely that soon Christians will have the face the issue of how to deal with babies that were produced by the cloning process.

On end of life issues, such as euthanasia and capital punishment, Christians similarly have differences of opinion, and the opinions of individual Christians do not always match the official position of their denominations. Euthanasia, or mercy killing, as it is sometimes called, is decried by most Christians, and probably by all Christian denominations that have taken an explicit stand on the issue, but the question of when life ends is not an easy one. Many people today spend their last days in a hospital hooked up to machines that supply medicine and food, relieve pain, stabilize the heartbeat, filter the blood, and force air in and out of the lungs. Does turning off one or more of these machines constitute euthanasia, or does doing so simply let nature take its course? Does increasing medication to relieve pain, when doing so might result in a death that could otherwise have been postponed, constitute euthanasia, or is it simply compassionate pain management? These are issues that families, medical staff, and spiritual advisors often have to face, and most clergy who regularly work with families going through these sorts of difficult decisions have come to the conclusion that under such circumstances, no decision should be subject to second-guessing from outsiders who have no involvement with the family. The most difficult situations are those in which family members themselves disagree on the proper course of treatment, and it is the role of spiritual advisors, clergy, or chaplains in such a predicament not to take sides but rather to help the family work through the issues in a way that is faithful to their Christian beliefs and also shows concern for their sick family member.

Many denominations, including the Roman Catholic Church, Anglicans, Eastern Orthodox, Lutherans, Methodists, and others oppose capital punishment under any circumstances, citing Jesus' command to love one's enemies as a reason for their opposition. Other denominations, including many that fall under the Evangelical or Pentecostal banners, support the judicious use of capital punishment for perpetrators of certain serious crimes, pointing to the Old Testament *lex talionis*, calling for "an eye for an eye, and a tooth for a tooth." This issue is one that affects the U.S. Church more than any other, since few countries in the world that are either predominantly Christian or that are industrially developed employ the death penalty. Capital punishment is another example of an ethical issue in which the official positions of the Church do not always comport with the opinions of believers in the pews. Christian critics of capital punishment point to many of the same arguments that secular opponents use—the lack of a deterrent effect, the racially biased way in which it is implemented, the futility of using violence to combat violence—but they also add arguments from a specifically Christian perspective. For example, they argue that Jesus' command to love one's enemies is not consistent with executing someone. Some, particularly in the Evangelical community, argue that executing someone who has not yet accepted Jesus as Savior will condemn that person to hell. Still others argue that since it is inconceivable that Jesus himself would have taken part in the execution of another person, Christians should not do so, either. For their part, supporters of the death penalty say that Jesus' command to love one's enemies does not preclude the possibility of capital punishment, and at any rate the command was meant for the individual, not the state. Support for capital punishment among citizens in the U.S., as well as among Christians specifically, is greater than 50 percent, though the percentage has been slipping somewhat in recent years. Still, it is clear that for American Christians, in any case, the proper Christian position on the death penalty is debatable.

The Roman Catholic Church, Orthodox Churches, the Anglican Church, and most Protestant Churches have either officially or unofficially adopted the Just War theory as their approach to evaluating the validity of a nation going to war. Using the Augustinian model, they look at such issues as the justice of the cause, the imminence of the threat, and the likelihood of success. They may disagree with other Christians on the conclusions drawn from a Just War analysis of a particular situation, but they go through many of the same steps to make their determination as their opponents do. The Historic Peace Churches—including the Mennonites and other Anabaptists, the Moravian Brethren, and the Quakers—have a different attitude toward war. They are pacifists, opposing any war, no matter the circumstances. Some in the Just War camp criticize the pacifism of the Peace Churches as idealistic, unsuited to the realities of the modern world, where the use of lethal force in war is sometimes necessary. On the other hand, many denominations in the Just War camp have slid toward the pacifist stance in recent decades, as many Christians in those traditions point out that *every* war is a just war in the mind of the country going to war. For this reason, many Christians from a variety of denominations that support both the Just War tradition and Pacifism have proposed a third solution, Peacemaking. Unlike Pacifism, which critics charge is entirely passive, the Peacemaking approach advocates extensive efforts to avert wars that appear ready to start by working in troubled areas to teach people how to resolve conflicts peacefully. Some peacemakers also support sending unarmed Christian civilians into potential war zones to discourage nations from dropping bombs on the citizens, knowing that they would be killing Christian peacemakers as well. Efforts in the direction of Peacemaking are still relatively recent, and critics sometimes dismiss the approach as naïve. Whether it develops into a third major tradition, alongside Just War and Pacifist approaches, remains to be seen.

Wealth and Poverty

Most of Jesus' followers during his public ministry were from the peasant class, and most early Christians were poor as well. Paul speaks of his concern for the poor in several of his letters, and he encourages his readers to contribute financially to the relief fund he is collecting for the poor in Jerusalem. Throughout most of Christian history, in fact, the poor have made up the bulk of the Christian Church. Those who were not poor were always encouraged by the Church to contribute to the needs of the poor as part of their Christian duty. At some point in the twentieth century a different attitude towards the issue of wealth and poverty arose in some quarters of the Church. Some preachers, including some well-known televangelists, began to teach that wealth and good health were blessings from God and that those who were faithful to God would be blessed both physically and financially. The implication of this prosperity, or "health and wealth," gospel was that those who were poor, both individuals and countries, were poor because they had been unfaithful to God. The health and wealth message was widely condemned by most denominations, but it tapped into deep-seated resentment that many Christians felt about spending their "hard-earned" money, either through taxes or through offerings to the church, on the needs of poor people. This attitude was found among wealthy and middle class Christians from a variety of different denominations, but it was especially identified—fairly or unfairly—with Evangelicals, Pentecostals, and other theologically conservative Protestants.

In 1977 Ronald J. Sider, an Evangelical Christian and the founder of Evangelicals for Social Action, published a book that became very influential, especially among other Evangelicals: *Rich Christians in an Age of Hunger*. Sider examined both the biblical text and statistics regarding poverty to present his case that rich Christians (including especially the middle class) should take action to serve the poor in a variety of ways, including giving directly to Christian relief organizations, as a matter of sacred duty. The Roman Catholic Church, which had sometimes been criticized in the past for seeming to side with the rich and powerful (e.g. in colonial Latin America), issued a number of papal encyclicals and other documents calling on Christians around the world to support the poor, beginning with Pope Leo XIII's 1891 encyclical *Rerum Novarum* (On Capital and Labor), and continuing with Pope John XXIII's *Pacem in Terris* (Peace on Earth, 1963), Pope Paul VI's *Populorum Progressio* (On the Development of Peoples, 1967), and Pope John Paul II's *Sollicitudo Rei Socialis* (The Social Concern of the Church, 1988). Roman Catholic bishops from Latin America also pushed the Church in the direction of paying more attention to ministry to the poor, particularly in their conferences at Medellín (1968) and Puebla (1979). Some Catholics have criticized portions of these documents for not going far enough in their condemnation of oppressive structures that adversely affect the poor (e.g. Leo XIII was criticized for condemning the potential evils of socialism without addressing the potential evils of capitalism), but taken as a whole, they do push Catholic Christians, and all Christians who read and agree with them, toward a concern for the poor that is in accord with consistently enunciated historic Christian values.

Christianity and Politics

The issues revolving around the relationship between church and state have already been discussed, so this section will concentrate on the church's attitude toward specific political systems (monarchies vs. republics) and politico-economic theories (communism vs. capitalism).

Ever since the days of Constantine, the church had supported the Christian state and the Christian emperor, king, or ruler. When the barbarians destroyed the Western Roman Empire, Germanic Christian kings replaced Roman emperors, but the Church's support for Christian rulers continued. When Constantinople fell to the Turks, many in the Eastern Church had no new Christian emperor to support, although the Russian Orthodox Church transferred its loyalty to the czar. In the West, the idea of the "divine right of kings" developed, an idea that claimed that those who were on the throne were put there by God and were specially chosen, as were their families. The Roman Catholic Church supported the Christian kings, as did the leading Protestant Churches at first. However, the French Revolution and the rise to power of Napoleon divided the Protestant churches. On the one hand, many were aghast at the French Republic's attempt to reduce the influence of Christianity in society, not mention the excesses of the Reign of Terror. On the other hand, Napoleon presented himself at first as one who could bring order to the chaos and who was more favorably disposed to the church. Napoleon's expansionistic moves, however, cost him the support of both the Catholic Church (Napoleon captured the Papal States) and the Protestant churches outside France, in the countries that Napoleon's troops invaded. The Year of Revolution, 1848, led to the adoption of representative forms of government in many European nations, and the Protestant churches for the most part accepted them, even though the new republics no longer recognized any particular state church, or, if they did, the state church had little political influence. The Roman Catholic Church, on the other hand, remained adamantly opposed to the very idea of representative government, which was contrary to the organization of the Church and, the popes argued, contrary to the desire of God. Particularly galling to the Church was the capture of the Rome by King Victor Emmanuel II in 1870. Pope Pius IX refused to acknowledge the Church's loss of sovereignty over Rome, as did his successors, until in 1929 Pope Pius XI finally signed the Lateran Treaty that restored the pope's temporal powers by creating the Vatican City. The overthrow of the ruling families of Europe was finally more or less completed at the end of World War I, when the Habsburgs of Austria and the Hohenzollerns of Germany were removed from power. Those monarchs that remained in Europe reigned over constitutional monarchies in which their powers were greatly restricted.

The long association of the Roman Catholic Church with European monarchs helps explain, in part, their opposition to the politico-economic systems called socialism and communism. In the mid-nineteenth century, Karl Marx advocated a new form of government in which the means of production (capital) would be taken from the owners of the factories (capitalists) and given to the workers (the proletariat). The middle classes (the bourgeoisie), which tended to support the upper classes and the capitalists against the proletariat, would lose their influence as well. All these changes would require revolution, Marx said, but eventually a classless society would result. Marx, an avowed atheist, also advocated the removal of all religious institutions from positions of authority. Both the call for revolution, with its ensuing disorder, and the attack on Christianity, which was after all the dominant religious tradition in Europe, alarmed Catholics, Orthodox, and Protestants alike. The Russian Revolution of 1917, which again destroyed a Christian empire affiliated with the Orthodox Church, was alarming to the Catholic Church and to most Protestants as well. However, some Protestants argued that Marx's critiques of the capitalist system were accurate, and even his attacks on Christianity had their merits, because the church had all too often sided with the rich against the poor. Some Protestants, then, became supporters of Christian socialism, which rejected both atheism and, in most cases, the need for revolution, but adopted many of Marx's concerns about capitalism. The Roman Catholic Church, still wary of the new republics in Europe, was strongly opposed to all aspects of communism. Pope Leo XIII, in his 1891 encyclical *Rerum Novarum* (On Capital and Labor), harshly criticized communist/socialist proposals as harmful to the poor, but did not direct a similarly harsh critique against capitalists who, their critics claimed, were making their fortunes on the backs of the poor. As World War II approached, Pope Pius XI was an early supporter

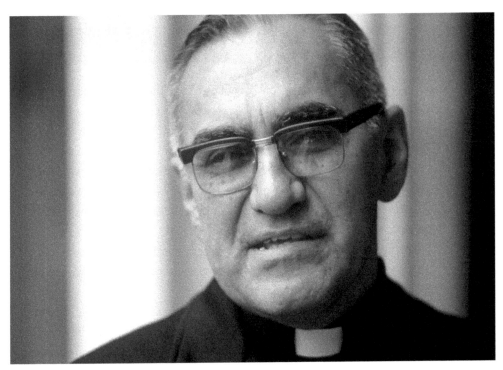

Figure 13.2 Oscar Romero, the Roman Catholic archbishop of El Salvador, paid for his outspoken support of the poor with his life. He was assassinated in 1980 while celebrating mass.

of fascism in Italy, chiefly because of Mussolini's opposition to communism. He eventually turned against both Mussolini and Hitler, but he continued to support Franco's fascist regime in Spain, for the same reason that he had originally supported Mussolini: Franco's opposition to communism.

Pope John Paul II was a fierce opponent of communism, and many historians credit his papacy with being one of the important factors in the downfall of communism in Europe. Although he was deeply concerned for the poor, his innate anti-communist tendencies led him to crack down hard on liberation theologians within his own church who used certain aspects of Marxist theory in their theological and historical analyses. Ironically, liberation theology received greater acceptance in many Protestant churches, which were not as ideologically opposed to all aspects of communism as many popes were. John Paul was also a harsh critic of unbridled capitalism as well as communism, however, so his attitude toward both communism and capitalism may be described as critical. In conservative Protestant churches, especially associated with the Evangelical and Pentecostal/ Neocharismatic branches of the church, many church leaders spoke out strongly against "godless communism." They promoted capitalism, free trade, and democracy, believing them to be the key components of the politico-economic system that was ordained by God to bring people political freedom and personal wellbeing, and to allow the gospel to spread further throughout the world.

- Reinhold Niebuhr argued that nations cannot be held to the same moral standards as individual Christians, even if the nation is predominantly Christian. Though Niebuhr won some support, many Christian scholars and ethicists disagreed with his analysis.

- While most Christian groups believe that engaging culture is a duty demanded by their faith, a few advocate remaining outside the dominant culture. Some who engage culture generally see the Christian message as compatible with the dominant worldview, while others believe that the two are radically different but that it is their obligation to work to transform their culture.

- Christians disagree over the proper stance regarding such issues as divorce, clerical celibacy, and homosexuality. Debates over homosexuality in particular have divided, or are threatening to divide, some denominations.

- Although almost all Christians proclaim their belief in the sanctity of life, significant differences of opinion concerning issues such as artificial birth control, abortion, embryonic stem cell research, therapeutic cloning, capital punishment, and euthanasia exist. Most Christians are wary of, or reject outright, the idea of reproductive cloning of human beings.

- Although the Just War theory is widely accepted among most Christian groups, an increasing number of contemporary Christians are questioning either the validity or the practicality of that approach to war, advocating instead the alternative of Peacemaking. The Historic Peace Churches advocate a stance of pacifism.

- Christianity has traditionally advocated care for the poor in society, but during some historical periods the Church has been derelict in its duties to the poor. Although some Christians have understood the gospel message as promising prosperity to the faithful, most reject that analysis.

- Christians support many different political parties—left, right, and center—as their views of the needs of the world, the demands of the gospel, and the efficacy of the politicians varies.

Christian critics of this approach, Catholic and Protestant alike, pointed out that "godless capitalism" was just as big a problem as "godless communism," and in fact it was capitalist democracies in the industrialized West that were responsible for much of the suffering around the world. The debate over the relative merits of socialism and capitalism continues unabated today, as does the issue of whether democracy can or should be imposed on countries that now have other forms of government, such as dictatorships.

Discussion Questions

1. What are the relative merits and weaknesses of the "Christ Against Culture," "Christ Of Culture," and "Christ the Transformer of Culture" positions?

2. Why do debates among Christians over sexual mores often seem to drown out other issues?

3. How do opinions regarding beginning of life issues relate to opinions regarding end of life issues?

4. Has the Church been committed to care for the poor throughout its history, or was such concern merely lip service? How committed is the Church today to care for the poor?

5. Is socialism, capitalism, or some other option more consistent with the teaching and example of Jesus Christ?

Further Reading

The Didache

Kairos Theologians 1986. *The Kairos Document: Challenge to the Church*. 2nd edn. Braamfontein, South Africa: Skotaville.

King, Martin Luther, Jr. 1963. *Strength to Love*. Philadelphia, PA: Fortress.

Marx, Karl and Friedrich Engels 1990. *Capital* and *Manifesto of the Communist Party*. 2nd edn. Chicago, IL: Encyclopaedia Britannica.

Niebuhr, H. Richard 1951. *Christ and Culture*. New York: Harper & Row.

Niebuhr, Reinhold 1932. *Moral Man and Immoral Society*. New York: Scribner.

Papal Encyclicals Online. http://www.papalencyclicals.net.

Rauschenbusch, Walter 1997. *A Theology for the Social Gospel*. Louisville, KY: Westminster John Knox.

Sider, Ronald J. 1977. *Rich Christians in an Age of Hunger*. Downer's Grove, IL: Inter-Varsity Press.

Villa-Vicencio, Charles, ed. 1987. *Theology and Violence: The South African Debate*. Johannesburg: Skotaville.

Reading 14   The Qur'an

God Speaks

By William E. Shepard

We have revealed it as an Arabic Qur'an so that you may understand.

(Qur'an 12:2)

The Qur'an is the Muslim scripture and the primary authority for Muslim life. It is comparable in some respects to the Christian and Jewish scriptures. An English-speaking non-Muslim who first approaches it will probably find some of the content familiar, but the form and the style will often seem strange. This [reading] will focus on how Muslims understand their scripture and the influence it has on their life and culture.

In This [Reading]

- What is the Qur'an?
- The Qur'an in Muslim culture
- The main teachings of the Qur'an on God, faith, prophecy, other spiritual beings, the Last Day, social teachings
- Interpretation of the Qur'an
- Modern critical approaches to the Qur'an

What is the Qur'an?

For Muslims the Qur'an consists of the verbatim words of God, conveyed in the Arabic language to the Prophet **Muhammad** by the Angel Gabriel, and not modified by Muhammad's personality. The Qur'an commands Muhammad to say, "It is not for me to change it of my own accord. I follow only what is revealed to me" (10:16). The messages were conveyed in relatively short

William E. Shepard, "The Qur'an: God Speaks," *Introducing Islam*, pp. 65-83, 407-410. Copyright © 2014 by Taylor & Francis Group. Reprinted with permission.

sections over the twenty-three years of his prophetic mission in response to his needs and those of the *umma*. Muhammad's own words and deeds are also important for Muslims [...] but the distinction between his words and God's words is kept clear. This view is held by virtually all Muslims today although a few modernists have sought ways to say that the Qur'an is human as well as divine [...]. Non-Muslims usually treat the Qur'an as Muhammad's words, but this can be offensive to Muslims. When quoting the Qur'an, it is best to say, "The Qur'an says ... " rather than "Muhammad said ... ".

As passages of the Qur'an were revealed to Muhammad, whom most Muslims believe to have been illiterate, he recited and memorized them and others wrote them down on materials that were available. It is claimed that from time to time Muhammad reviewed with Gabriel the content of what had been revealed, but at the end of his life it was still scattered on "pieces of papyrus, flat stones, palm-leaves, shoulder-blades and ribs of animals, pieces of leather and wooden boards, as well as [in] the hearts of men" (Watt, 1970, 40), as one source puts it. The "hearts of men" refers to the fact that many had memorized part or all of it. From the beginning the Qur'an was transmitted both in written form and in memorized form. The memorized form was the more important since the society of the time was one in which literacy was limited and which therefore relied mainly on memory. The heritage of pre-Islamic poetry was also memorized and was only written down much later. Moreover, the Arabic script of the time was very primitive and did not distinguish all of the letters (e.g. *b*, *t*, *th*, and sometimes *y* and *n* were written the same way), so that it was mainly useful as an aid to memory. It would take two centuries before it was to be fully adequate to record the Qur'an.

The best known account of the compilation of the Qur'an is as follows. In a battle the year after Muhammad's death a number of those who had memorized the Qur'an were killed and **Abu Bakr**, the first caliph, decided that the whole should be collated and recorded. This was done by Zayd ibn Thabit, who had been one of Muhammad's secretaries, and the text was eventually passed to Hafsa, the daughter of '**Umar** and widow of Muhammad. Under the third caliph, '**Uthman**, as the *umma* spread geographically, it became evident that different people were writing and reciting the Qur'an in slightly variant ways. This he considered a threat to the unity of the *umma* and so he had Zayd and others produce a definitive edition and sent copies of it to the main centers, ordering all others to be destroyed. In this edition there are 114 chapters, or *suras*, of quite unequal length, the shortest having three and the longest 286 verses, or *āyas*. Except for the short first *sūra* (quoted below), the *suras* are placed roughly in order of length, from the longest to the shortest, not in the order in which they were revealed nor in any clear thematic arrangement. Many Muslims believe that at least two of these copies still exist, one in Tashkent and one at the Topkapi museum in Istanbul. Most critical scholars, however, doubt the authenticity of these. In spite of 'Uthman's effort, there came to be some seven to ten different "readings" of the Qur'an that vary in details but are all judged to be acceptable. Some hold that all of these were revealed to Muhammad, possibly to accommodate different dialects of Arabic. Muslims do not consider that these variations compromise the integrity of the text, which they believe has been protected by God from distortion. In recent years most printed editions of the Qur'an follow the edition authorized by the Egyptian government in 1925.

If the Qur'an is the verbatim speech of God, it can only be so in the Arabic language, in which it was revealed. A "translation" into any other language is merely an imperfect effort to convey some of its meanings. Therefore, the Qur'an is always recited in Arabic and serious study of it is done in Arabic. Even apart from this "theological" point, it is a fact that Arabic generally is difficult to translate into English and the Qur'an, with its particular style, is even more so. It is usually not possible to render all of the ideas, allusions and emotions present in a Qur'anic passage adequately into English.

In fact, Muslims insist that the Qur'an is a literary miracle that cannot be equalled as literature. The Qur'an, indeed, makes this claim for itself (2:23–24) and Muslims have devoted a considerable literature to elaborating this claim. It is said that 'Umar, who was to be the second caliph, had been a bitter opponent of Muhammad but was converted after reading a page of the Qur'an. It is believed that every prophet's mission was confirmed by a miracle from God and Muhammad's main miracle, according to many his only miracle, was the Qur'an. The miraculous aspect is heightened by the fact that he is believed to have been illiterate.

This literary claim is not easy for the outsider to appreciate. The parts of the Bible Westerners most often read have a fairly straightforward narrative, poetic or doctrinal line and the whole has a fairly clear organization. The Qur'an by contrast often jumps unexpectedly from one topic to another, tells only part of a story and elliptically omits words and phrases. (It should be noted, though, that some of the prophetic books of the Bible are closer to the Qur'an in this respect.) Apart from the decreasing length of the *suras* it is hard to discern any overall principle of organization. Thomas Carlyle, who was one of the first writers in English to write favorably of Muhammad, spoke for many who approach the Qur'an for the first time when he described it as "a wearisome confused jumble, crude, ... endless iterations, long-windedness, entanglement ... ", though he also went on to say that in it "there is a merit quite other than the literary one. If a book come from the heart, it will contrive to reach other hearts; all art and authorcraft are of small amount to that" (Carlyle, 1910, 86–87). One problem, of course, was that he had to read the Qur'an in English, and in a poorer translation than those available today. Even in Arabic, though, the Qur'an's style and organization often appear fragmented. It is important, however, to bear in mind that the Qur'an is more recited and listened to than read and is mostly recited in relatively short sections, so that the power of the words and the immediate content is more important than the logical coherence of the larger context in which it is set. Muslim scholars have devoted considerable attention to the rhetorical features of the Qur'an. Many have also claimed to discern coherent organization in the text though this may be a different sort of coherence from what Westerners look for. In any case, incoherence can be only apparent, for God has undoubtedly given the Qur'an the form it has for a good reason.

Since Muslims view the Qur'an as the actual speech of God, it is for them the point where God is most fully present in the mundane world. The significance of this can be underlined by a comparison with Christianity. It would seem obvious to compare the Qur'an with the Bible, but on closer reflection we may conclude that the person of Christ provides a closer parallel. For orthodox Christians it is not the Bible but the person of Jesus Christ, the incarnation of God (God "in the flesh"), who is the point where God is most fully present in the world. There is a confirmation of this point in the history of Muslim theology, where the debates over whether the Qur'an was created or uncreated [...] resemble the Christian debates over the nature of Christ [...]. Orthodox Jews, on the other hand, will find that the Muslim view of the Qur'an is fairly close to their own of the written Torah (first five books of the Bible) given to Moses on Mount Sinai.

Being the speech of God, the Qur'an has *baraka*, a spiritual or almost magical power (we shall see this term again later). This is illustrated at the popular level by such practices as putting a passage of the Qur'an into a small container and hanging it around one's neck as an amulet to ward off bad luck or evil forces or writing a passage on paper and dissolving the ink in water to drink as a medicine. There are stories such as one that the horse of a Companion of the Prophet bolted when someone recited the Qur'an. One should be ritually pure before touching a copy of the Qur'an or reciting it. Arabic copies of the Qur'an usually have on the title page the following, which comes from the Qur'an: "a well guarded book which none may touch except the purified" (56:78–80). It is also worth noting that the word *āya*, used for a verse of the Qur'an, also means sign or even miracle. It is used in the Qur'an for God's activity in creation, e.g. the rain, the winds, the alteration of day and night (2:164), for a victory in battle such as Badr (3:13) and for "miracles" such as Moses' rod turning into a serpent (7:106, cf. Exodus 4:3 and 7:10 in the Bible). All of these are signs of God and so is, pre-eminently, each *āya* of the Qur'an.

The Qur'an in Muslim Culture

The Qur'an penetrates Muslim cultures to a degree even greater than that to which the Bible used to penetrate Western, especially Protestant, cultures. Muslim names are commonly drawn from the Qur'an, as we shall see later. Phrases such as *al-ḥamdu li-llāh* (praise be to God), *inshā'allāh* (if God wills) and *Allāhu a'lam* (God knows best) are constantly on people's lips. Muslims recite a portion of the Qur'an in their regular prayers (*salah*) and on many other occasions during the day. The *Fātiḥa*, the opening chapter of the Qur'an, is recited on many occasions, such as the closing of marriage contracts. The Qur'an also generates what Westerners would call "art forms". One of these is calligraphy. The Arabic script, which has been developed in several styles, lends itself particularly well to graceful presentation. One finds Qur'anic calligraphy often on the walls of mosques and other public buildings, as well as on posters and in pictures in people's homes and elsewhere [...].

Since the Qur'an is primarily a book to be recited and listened to, recitation also gives rise to something like an art form. Until modern times recitation of the Qur'an, along with its use in learning to read and write, was the mainstay of Muslim primary education. Many people memorize and recite the Qur'an even though they don't know Arabic and cannot understand the words; they and their listeners still benefit from the *baraka*. Those who memorize the whole of the Qur'an are called *ḥāfiz* and have

Figure 14.1 Boy reading the Qur'an. Courtesy of iStockphoto

considerable prestige. For some, recitation becomes a profession. They will be called on to recite at weddings, funerals, and various other religious, civic and family occasions. (See *Online Resources for Qur'an Recitation* under Further Reading at the end of this [reading] and also on the website.) For purposes of recitation and also learning, the Qur'an is divided into thirty "parts" of equal length and each of these into two *ḥizb*; this is separate from the division into *suras* and *ayas*. There are two styles of recitation, *tartīl*, which is fairly plain, and *tajwīd*, which is more ornamental and "musical" (Qur'anic recitation is in fact not considered "music" by Muslims) and more difficult to master. It may be said that a leading Qur'an reciter has a status comparable to a leading opera singer in the West and evokes an intensity comparable perhaps to a rock star. Kristina Nelson describes a dramatic moment in the public recitation of the Qur'an in Cairo in terms that suggest both art and *baraka*:

> Suddenly the power of the phrase seizes the scattered sensibility of the crowd, focusing it, and carrying it forward like a great wave, setting the listeners down gently after one phrase and lifting them up in the rising of the next. The recitation

proceeds, the intensity grows. A man hides his face in his hands, another weeps quietly. Some listeners tense themselves as if in pain, while, in the pauses between phrases, others shout appreciative responses to the reciter. Time passes unnoticed.

(Nelson, 1985, xiii)

The Main Teachings of the Qur'an

God

The main teachings of the Qur'an relate, of course, to God, **Allah**. The Qur'an does not introduce Allah, since the Arabs already knew of Him, but it has much to say about Him. First and foremost, He is One and has no partner. "Say: He is Allah, One, Allah, the Eternal; He has not begotten nor has he been begotten, and none is equal to Him." (Qur'an 112). The recognition that Allah is one is called *tawhīd* (literally, considering [Allah] to be one), a very important term in the Muslim lexicon. Moreover, Allah is the creator and sustainer of everything. He created the universe in six days and "settled on the throne" (32:4 and elsewhere). He did not rest on the seventh day, as the Bible claims, but immediately took charge of His universe. He created humans to praise and obey Him and He guides them. On the Last Day He will dramatically bring the universe to an end and judge humankind.

Most of these themes are captured in the *Fātiḥa,* the opening *sura,* and the one most often recited by Muslims.

> In the name of Allah, the Merciful, the Compassionate.
> Praise be to Allah, Lord of the worlds
> The Merciful, the Compassionate
> Master of the Day of Judgment
> You only do we serve; to You only do we turn for help
> Guide us in the straight path,
> The path of those whom You have blessed,
> Not of those with whom You are angry,
> Nor of those who are astray.

The Qur'an has a number of epithets or names for Allah, and from these Muslims have compiled lists of ninety-nine names (they vary slightly), of which the first two are the Merciful (*Raḥmān*) and the Compassionate (*Raḥīm*), mentioned in the *Fatiha*. These names are often recited and appear in calligraphy in pictures and posters. They also appear in Muslim names, such as 'Abd al-Rahman, servant

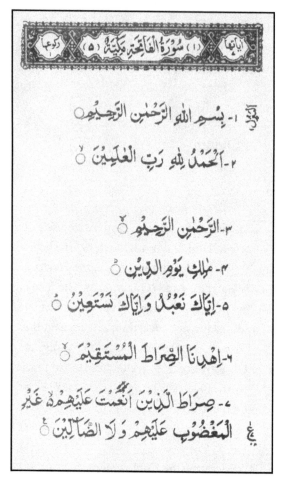

Figure 14.2 Calligraphy of the opening *sura* of the Qur'an, the *Fatiha*.

of Merciful One, 'Abd al-Nāṣir, servant of the Helper (name of the former president of Egypt, usually known in the West as Nasser), and of course, 'Abd Allah (usually transliterated Abdullah), servant of God.

The opposite of *tawhid* and the most serious sin humans can commit is *shirk* (commonly and slightly inaccurately translated "polytheism"), meaning to ascribe partners or associates to Allah, something the Meccans did with three of their pagan goddesses, whom they considered to be daughters of Allah, as the following passage indicates:

> Have you considered al-Lat and al-'Uzza,
> and that other, Manat, the third?
> Are you to have sons, and He only daughters?
> That would be a most unfair division!

They are naught but names you have named,

you and your fathers.

Allah has sent no warrant for them.

They follow only their own ideas and desires,

Even though sound guidance

has come to them from their Lord.

(53:19–23)

It is interesting to note that this is the site of the so-called "Satanic verses", made famous by Salman Rushdie's novel. According to some reports Muhammad was overly anxious to convince the **Meccans** to accept his message and Satan took advantage of this to suggest the following verses as a compromise: "They are the exalted swans whose intercession is to be desired" (after the second line, above). The Meccans were so happy they joined him in prayer, but soon Gabriel appeared and told him these were not from God and replaced them with the present text. The Meccans turned away. Gabriel guaranteed that nothing inspired by Satan would be allowed to stand. Most Muslims today deny the historicity of this account. While *shirk* in its most obvious form involves the worship of other gods, most Muslims would say that it also includes giving anything, whether pleasure, wealth, career, family, or nation, equal place in one's life with God.

Faith

The most important requirement for humans is faith, *īmān*. In fact, the word *mu'min* (believer) is the most common word used in the Qur'an to denote Muhammad's followers, the word *muslim* being comparatively rare. Even today, *mu'min* is preferred by many. The term *iman* became the subject of considerable theological discussion [...]. The opposite of *iman* is *kufr*, unbelief or, more precisely, the refusal to recognize and act on the blessings of Allah. It carries the strong connotation of ingratitude and is perhaps the most forceful negative term in the Islamic vocabulary.

Prophecy

Allah's power and mercy can be perceived in the universe by those with eyes to see but He conveys his commands and moral standards to humans primarily by way of prophets (*nabī*) and messengers (*rasūl*) (the relation between these terms is too complex to enter into here). The Qur'an names some twenty-five of these and makes it clear that there are many it does not mention. Muslim traditions suggest that there have been as many as 124,000 prophets over the whole course of history. Most but not all of those named correspond to Biblical figures. In most cases the accounts of each prophet are scattered through the Qur'an with each account giving part of the story from a particular perspective. We will consider a few here.

Although Adam, the first man, is not specifically called a prophet or messenger in the Qur'an, Muslims have generally taken him to be such. Adam was created to be God's *khalīfa*, or deputy, on earth (2:30–39 and elsewhere). This is the same term that is used in a different context for the later leaders of the *umma*, in their case commonly transliterated "caliph". Adam and his wife, not named in the Qur'an, are placed in paradise (called "the garden", *janna*) and told not to eat of a certain tree, but they disobey and are therefore expelled to the earth. There is no indication that Eve first disobeyed and then tempted Adam; they appear to have disobeyed together. Adam then repented and was forgiven and received "words of guidance". While they are put on earth where they will face temptation and difficulty, sin consists of specific acts of disobedience to God, not the corruption of their moral nature (as in the Christian doctrine of original sin). They have the ability to obey.

Nuh (Noah) and several other prophets, including Arabian prophets such as Hud and Salih, who are not in the Bible, convey a warning from Allah to their communities (*ummas*), most of whose members reject the message and are destroyed by Allah, while only the prophet and a few followers escape. The story of Nuh's ark is presented in the Qur'an and fits this pattern (11:25–48 and elsewhere).

Ibrahim (Abraham) is particularly important. The Qur'anic Ibrahim was raised in an idolatrous family, discovered the truth of *tawhid* while observing the heavens (6:75–80), destroyed his father's idols (21:51–67), was thrown into a fire from which Allah saved him and migrated to Palestine (29:24–26 and elsewhere, the term **Hijra** is used here). After this, among other things, he was commanded by God to sacrifice his son, who was ransomed at the last minute (37:102–11). The Qur'an does not say which of his sons this was but Muslims believe it was Isma'il (Ishmael), not Ishaq (Isaac). He also traveled with Isma'il to Mecca where they built, or rebuilt, the **Ka'ba** (2:125–28) (some think it was built originally in Adam's time). Ibrahim's descendants, Ishaq, Isma'il, Ya'qub (Jacob) and Yusuf (Joseph), were all prophets. The people of Israel (Banu Isra'il) were descended from Ishaq, Ya'qub and Yusuf, and the Arabs from Isma'il, though the Qur'an is not explicit on the latter point.

The story of Musa (Moses) has much in common with the Biblical account. He is saved from death as a baby (28:4–13 and elsewhere), flees after killing a man (28:15–21), is called to by God from a burning bush (20:9–24 and elsewhere), and sent to confront Pharaoh, who is more consistently evil than in the Biblical account, and who is drowned as Musa's people escape (2:50 and elsewhere). Musa receives the Torah from God, but the people worship the calf and prove disobedient in other ways (2:51–54 and elsewhere).

'Isa (Jesus) is understood to be a messenger sent to the people of Israel and is explicitly stated not to be Son of Allah or part of a Trinity (19:35; 5:73–78). He is born of a virgin and there are accounts of the annunciation and the birth that differ considerably from the Biblical ones (3:42–47; 19:16–34). He receives a scripture, the *Injīl* (Gospel), preaches, performs miracles, and raises the dead. His enemies try to crucify him but fail as Allah raises him to Himself (4:157–58 but see 19:33).

The Qur'an calls Jews and Christians "People of the Book" (*ahl al-kitāb*) and in some places seems to put their faith on the same level as that preached by Muhammad, whose message is said to be the same as theirs and as all the other prophets (2:136; 42:13 and elsewhere). Elsewhere they are criticized for disobedience, for changing their scriptures (4:46 and elsewhere) and for rejecting Muhammad. Though critical of both, the Qur'an is more consistently critical of Jews while having some favorable things to say about Christians (5:82). The Qur'an says, "No compulsion in religion" (2:256), but it also calls on Muslims to fight the People of the Book until they are humbled and pay *jizya*, a special tax (9:29).

Many of the elements in the accounts of the prophets that are not found in the Bible are found in other Jewish and Christian sources, one example being Ibrahim breaking the idols. This has led many Western scholars to speak of Jewish and Christian influence on Muhammad and even to speculate whether Muhammad was more influenced by Judaism or Christianity. For Muslims all these stories come from Allah. They and others were undoubtedly circulating in the environment; otherwise the Qur'anic versions, which are usually highly elliptical, would not have been understood. God in the revelation confirmed what was true in the material being circulated and discarded what was false, as well as adding new material.

These stories are still very much alive in Muslim societies, just as Old Testament stories are alive in Christian circles. "Stories of the prophets" is and always has been a very popular literary genre. These works collate the Qur'anic accounts of each prophet and fill in the gaps. In the process, a considerable amount of Biblical and other Jewish and Christian material is often included. For example, in these works, contrary to the Qur'an, usually Eve's name is given (Ḥawā' in Arabic) and she is first tempted and then tempts Adam, as in the Bible. Many Muslims are named after these prophets and allusions are often made to events in their lives. Khomeini, the leader of the Islamic revolution in Iran, was given the epithet "idol breaker", alluding to Ibrahim's action. Several rulers, including the Shah of Iran and President Sadat of Egypt, have been labeled "Pharaoh" by their enemies [...].

Other Spiritual Beings

In addition to Allah, the Qur'an speaks of other spiritual beings. Angels are servants and messengers of Allah who praise Him and do His bidding. *Jinn* (singular: *jinnī*) are beings made of invisible fire who may harm or help humans and may be believers or unbelievers. The Qur'an gives an account of a group of *jinn* who were converted by hearing it recited (46:29–31). *Jinn* are, of course, the "genies" who supposedly are let out of bottles and grant three wishes. Among the *jinn* is Iblis (devil) or Shaytan (satan), who was commanded along with the angels to bow down to Adam, after he was created, but refused. For this he was thrown out of heaven, but has been allowed to tempt human beings (17:61–65).

The Last Day

Some of the most dramatic passages of the Qur'an deal with the Last Day. For example:

When the heaven is split open,
When the stars are scattered,
When the seas are poured forth,
When the tombs are overturned,
Then a soul shall know what it has done,
And what it has left undone.

(82:1–5)

Descriptions of Paradise and the Fire (hell) are likewise vivid, including the heavenly maidens (*houris*) who will attend those in Paradise (no number is given in the Qur'an). Feminists complain that the description of Paradise is very male oriented. Interestingly, it is reported that some of the women of the time thought so, too, and complained to Muhammad. Following this he received the following verses: "Muslim men and women, believing men and women, obedient men and women ... for them God has prepared forgiveness and a mighty wage" (33:35). In this worldly life social rights and duties differ but in the final accounting gender, like other social distinctions, falls away.

Social Teachings

Many of the Qur'an's social and moral teachings will be dealt with in later [readings], but it is worth mentioning three that underline the contrast between the Qur'anic ethos and the *jahili* ethos of the pre-Islamic Arabs.

[...] The highest loyalty of the pre-Islamic Arabs was given to the tribe. The *jahili* poet Durayd ibn Simma sang:

I am of Ghaziyyah: if she be in error, then I will err;
And if Ghaziyyah be guided right, I go right with her.

(Nicholson, 1969, 83)

By contrast, the Qur'an says:

O, humankind,
Surely, We have created you from a male and a female,
and made you into nations and tribes
so you may know each other.
Surely, the most noble of you in God's sight
Is the most pious.

(49:13)

That the *jahili* attitude of Durayd lives on is suggested by the following statement of the American Stephen Decatur in 1816: "Our country! In her intercourse with foreign nations may she always be in the right; but our country, right or wrong!" This supports the view of many Muslims today that modern nationalism is the moral equivalent of *jahili* tribalism and is *shirk*. The same Qur'anic passage also signals a shift in what it means to be noble (*karīm*). For the *jahili* Arabs nobility meant having noble ancestry and demonstrating this by noble deeds such as bravery in battle and generosity. For the Qur'an nobility is piety, which requires no ancestry.

[...] *Jahiliyya* meant not so much ignorance as a glorying in extreme behavior, as illustrated by the accounts of Imru al-Qays, with his drinking, womanizing and then persistent quest for vengeance and Hatim al-Tayyi giving away all of his father's camels as an act of hospitality. The Qur'an, by contrast forbids fornication, gambling and wine drinking, and calls for the limitation of vengeance or, preferably, forgiveness (5:45). As for generosity, "be neither miserly nor prodigal" (17:29).

For the *jahili* Arabs the motive of ethical action was essentially honor, especially the honor of the tribe. Hatim says to his father,

> Oh my father, by means of [the camels] I have conferred on you everlasting fame and honor that will cleave to you like the ring of the ringdove and men will always bear in mind some verse of poetry in which we are praised. This is your recompense for the camels.
>
> (Nicholson, 1969, 86)

As for a future life, the Qur'an quotes them as saying, "There is this life and no other. We live and die; nothing but Time destroys us!" (45:24). For the Qur'an, on the other hand, the primary motive is precisely the "mighty wage" of the future life:

> Say: "It is God who gives you life and later causes you to die. It is He who will gather you all on the Day of Resurrection. Of this there is no doubt. ... As for those who have faith and do good works, their lord will admit them to His mercy. Theirs shall be a glorious triumph. To the unbelievers. ... The evil of their deeds will manifest itself to them and the scourge at which they scoffed will encompass them. ..."
>
> (45:27–33)

Out of fear for honor or fear of poverty *jahili* Arabs would sometimes bury their girl babies (16:58–60). The Qur'an forbids this, "Do not kill your children, fearing poverty. We shall provide for them and for you. Killing them is a great sin" (17:31).

Interpretation of the Qur'an

Like all scriptures, the Qur'an needs interpretation. Indeed, some interpretation is involved in the material presented above. A basic level of interpretation has been the effort to determine the temporal order of the Qur'anic material. Muslim scholars have distinguished between *suras* revealed in Mecca and those revealed in Medina. In general the first group are shorter and more poetic while the latter are longer, more prosaic and more likely to deal with legal material. Beyond this there has been an effort to determine the order of the *suras* within each group and this appears in the chapter headings of the Egyptian edition. It is recognized, though, that in some cases a *sura* includes material from different periods. One reason the temporal order is important is the idea that sometimes a later passage abrogates an earlier one. This is one explanation of apparent contradictions and is also important for applying the Qur'an in practice. In such cases it is important to know which is the later passage. For example, Qur'an 2:219 says that wine is of some value but greater evil but Qur'an 5:90, which is later, unreservedly forbids it.

An important part of interpretation is the effort to determine the "occasions of revelation" (*asbāb al-nuzūl*), that is the specific circumstances under which a passage was revealed and the issues that were being addressed. Much of the Qur'an cannot be understood without this information, since the Qur'an usually does not provide the context of its statements or at most alludes to it without giving the details. The case of the women questioning about paradise is an example of this.

The commentaries to the Qur'an that follow the order of the text are called *tafṣīrs* and a considerable number have been written. These are sometimes divided into those based on transmission (especially of *hadiths*, statements of the Prophet [...]) and those that make greater use of rational opinion. The most famous of the first group is that of Ibn Jarir al-Tabari (d. 922) and of the second that of al-Zamakhshari (d. 1144), condensed and edited by al-Baydawi (d. c. 1286). These and other traditional *tafsirs* usually contain a considerable amount of linguistic analysis and other technical material, as well as discussion of "occasions of revelation" and stories of the prophets, and much else. *Tafsirs* continue to be produced in modern times, some of them ideological in character, such as those of Mawdudi and Sayyid Qutb [...] and some especially concerned to relate the Qur'an to modern science, such as that of Tantawi Jawhari (1940). These are generally less technical and more accessible to the general reader. A distinction is also often made between *tafṣīr* and *ta'wīl*. The former is a straightforward, exoteric interpretation, while the latter seeks hidden, esoteric meanings. An example of *tafsir* is the interpretation of "Lord" in the *Fatiha* as meaning not only master but also nurturer, based on the root of the Arabic word. An example of *ta'wil* would be the interpretation of the first letter of the same *sura* as symbolizing the beginning of creation and also ʿAli, the first Shiʿi *Imam*.

One can see that the scholarly interpreter of the Qur'an faces a considerable task. He or she must master the various approaches just described as well as the fine points of the Arabic language and sciences related to the *Hadith* [...].

Modern Critical Approaches to the Qur'an

Most Western scholars accept that the present text of the Qur'an is essentially what Muhammad presented as divine revelation, though they raise some questions at particular points and question the traditional accounts of its compilation. The German scholar Nöldeke (1836–1930) developed an analysis of the *suras* that divided them into three Meccan stages and one Medinan. This analysis has been extremely influential though more recent scholarship questions whether the *sura* can be the unit of analysis, since many *suras* contain material from different periods. Indeed, many doubt whether the temporal sequence of the Qur'anic material can in fact be determined. In a refined form, though, Nöldeke's approach is still used by most Western scholars and many Muslims. A Muslim scholar has recently developed a highly sophisticated analysis of stylistic elements, discerning seven chronologically ordered groups of material.

Western scholars have also come up with different interpretations from traditional Muslims on specific points. For example, traditionally the word *ummī* when applied to Muhammad is taken to mean "illiterate". Westerners, by contrast, generally take it to mean something like "gentile", i.e. belonging to a community that has not received a scripture.

Since the 1970s the "revisionists" [...] have developed a much more radical criticism. John Wansbrough and others have applied to the Qur'an methods of literary criticism that have long been applied to the Bible. Denying any historical value to the traditional accounts of the compilation of the Qur'an and stressing the piecemeal and, in their view, contradictory nature of its contents, they conclude that the Qur'an was authored and edited over a period of some two centuries before it reached its present form and does not all come from Muhammad. Less radically, others note that the earliest surviving written passages of the Qur'an date from the late seventh century and often have wordings that are not standard (e.g. in the Dome of the Rock and a large number of ancient Qur'an fragments discovered in Yemen in 1972). Even though these variations are minor they are significant in a text whose wording is supposed to be sacrosanct and they suggest that the text was still developing long after the Prophet's death. If, as is commonly held, the orally transmitted version was (and is) the most authoritative minor written discrepancies would not prove much. These critics, however, claim a greater role for the written text even in the early period and argue that the existence of the discrepancies makes the existence of an authoritative oral version unlikely. Some critics argue that much of the Qur'an is in, or closely related to, the Aramaic language. One, going under the pseudonym of C. Luxenberg, has gained considerable media attention by claiming on this basis that the *houris* are not heavenly virgins but really white grapes, a view hardly accepted by other scholars. Other scholars, however, have argued on critical grounds that the Qur'an as we have it substantially goes back to Muhammad and question the idea of 'Uthman's compilation.

These various revisionist views are not accepted by most Western scholars, much less by Muslims, but they have had some influence and have to be taken seriously. For the purposes of this book, however, it will usually be appropriate to assume that the Qur'an is at least from Muhammad.

Box 14.1   Key Points

- The Qur'an is central for Muslims; it is the verbatim word of God and the point where the divine comes most in contact with earth.
- For Muslims the recited form of the Qur'an is of particular importance and Qur'an reciters are highly respected.
- Muslims consider the Qur'an to be a literary miracle.
- The Qur'an insists on the unity and centrality of Allah.
- The Qur'an tells the stories of a number of prophets, including Ibrahim (Abraham) and 'Isa (Jesus).
- The Qur'an rejects tribal honor as the central goal of life.
- Critical Western scholars have questioned the traditional understanding of the Qur'an in diverse ways.

Discussion Questions

1. A comparison between the Qur'an and Jesus has been suggested. How convincing is this? What are its implications?

2. What difference would it make if the Qur'an were read and studied in its written form rather than mainly memorized and recited?

3. What might a Muslim say in response to Carlyle's statement, "If a book come from the heart, it will contrive to reach other hearts; all art and authorcraft are of small amount to that."

4. What are some of the points on which the Qur'an differs from the Biblical tradition on God and prophets? What is the significance of these?

5. Why do most Muslims hold that the Qur'an cannot be adequately translated into another language?

Box 14.2   Critical Thinking

Discuss the quotations from Durayd and Stephen Decatur from a historical, social and ethnical point of view. Are they tribal/nationalistic chauvinists? (There are some helpful references on the website.)

Box 14.3   Critical Thinking

Examine the passages dealing with the prophet Ibrahim (Abraham) in the Qur'an. How is he presented? What is his story? Does this story develop from earlier to later *suras* in the Qur'an? How does this story differ from that found in the Bible? How does he illustrate the general message of the Qur'an? (A list of the passages is on the website. You may also consider the accounts of Ibrahim in the "Stories of the Prophets" literature. See the website for some examples.)

Box 14.4   Critical Thinking

"To historicize the Koran would in effect delegitimize the whole historical experience of the Muslim community," says R. Stephen Humphreys, a professor of Islamic Studies at the University of California at Santa Barbara.

> The Koran is the charter for the community, the document that called it into existence. And ideally—though obviously not always in reality—Islamic history has been the effort to pursue and work out the commandments of the Koran in human life. If the Koran is a historical document [i.e. at least to some extent a product of human history], then the whole Islamic struggle of fourteen centuries is effectively meaningless.
>
> (Lester, Toby, **"What Is the Koran?"** *The Atlantic Monthly*,
> January 1999, 283(1): 43(1). Online:
> http://www.theatlantic.com/magazine/archive/1999/01/
> what-is-the-koran/304024 (accessed 17 August 2013)

To what extent do you agree? (The article from which the quote is taken will be of help on this.)

Companion Website

Features considerable additional information and reading lists relating to the Qur'an, including additional translations, and websites for the names of God and other items.

Further Reading

Translations of the Qur'an; Concordance

The Koran Interpreted (1980) trans. A.J. Arberry, reprint. London: Allen and Unwin. (The translation most used by Western scholars, at least until recently, seeks particularly to convey the literary quality of the original, both in wording and formatting but has some odd usages at points.)

The Qur'an: A New Translation (2008) trans. M.A.S. Abdel Haleem. Oxford: Oxford University Press. (Straightforward attractive prose translation, easy to understand. Emphasizes comprehension over literal fidelity to text. Paragraph format aids understanding, hinders emotional appreciation. Good for the beginner.)

The Meaning of the Glorious Koran (1953), trans. M.M. Pickthall, reprint. New York: New American Library. (Long and popular translation in which it is easy to find chapter and verse; King James style English impedes appreciation; has some notes based on traditional Muslim scholarly interpretation.)

Holy Qur'an (1975) trans. A. Yusuf Ali, reprint. Lahore: Sh. Muhammad Ashraf. (Used a lot by Muslims; English is somewhat stilted and there are a lot of interpretive interpellations; has a modernist commentary that is omitted in some editions. My edition has the Arabic text in parallel column.)

The Qur'an With a Phrase-by-Phrase English (2004) trans. 'Ali Quli Qara'i. London: Islamic College for Advanced Studies Press. (Phrase-by-phrase translation with Arabic text beside; translation is quite precise but also reads well and captures some of the literary quality. Chapters, verses and parts are clearly marked. Author is Shi'i.)

Approaching the Qur'an: The Early Revelations (1999), trans. Michael Sells. Ashland, OR: White Cloud Press (accompanied by an audio CD). (Includes *suras* 1, 53 (part), 81–114. Translation with a scholarly commentary that seeks to convey the Qur'an's distinctive "combination of majesty and intimacy".)

Kassis, Hanna (1983) *A Concordance of the Qur'an*. Berkeley: University of California Press. (Concordance to Arberry's translation.)

"The Qur'anic Arabic Corpus" http://corpus.quran.com. (Accessed 5 September 2013; if you click on "Translation" on the sidebar you will come to a page from which you can get seven different English translations of each verse of the Qur'an, including Pickthall, Yusuf Ali, Shakir and Arberry, as well as a recitation.)

About the Qur'an

Denffer, Ahmad von (1983) *Ulum al-Qur'an: An Introduction to the Sciences of the Qur'an*. Leicester: Islamic Foundation. (A fairly standard Muslim discussion of issues relating to the Qur'an and its use.)

Watt, W.M. (1970) *Bell's Introduction to the Qur'an*. Edinburgh: Edinburgh University Press. (This is a considerable revision of an earlier work and for many years the "standard" study in English of matters related to the Qur'an; still very useful.)

Esack, Farid (2002) *The Qur'an: A Short Introduction*. Oxford: Oneworld. (Covers much the same ground as this chapter though in greater detail and from a Muslim modernist perspective that critically engages in a positive way with Western scholarship while remaining definitely Muslim.)

Cook, Michael (2000) *The Qur'an: A Very Short Introduction*. Oxford: Oxford University Press. (Begins with modern use and interpretation of the Qur'an and works more or less back to a mildly revisionist understanding of its origins, discussing various important issues along the way.)

Gätje, H. (1976) *The Qur'an and its Exegesis*. London: Routledge & Kegan Paul. (A wide sampling of Qur'an commentaries from various times and perspectives with a brief introduction to the history of Qur'an commentaries.)

Rahman, Fazlur (1980) *Major Themes of the Qur'an*. Minneapolis, MN: Bibliotheca Islamica. (A high-level discussion of topics such as God, man, nature, prophethood, etc. from a Muslim modernist perspective that largely accepts the presuppositions of modern Western scholarship. See page 336 for his view of revelation.)

McAuliffe, Jane Dammen (ed.) (2006) *The Cambridge Companion to the Qur'an*. Cambridge, UK and New York: Cambridge University Press. (Articles by various scholars on topics related to the Qur'an, including its history, literary characteristics and interpretation. Chapters 1–3 provide basic accounts of traditional and critical views of the compilation and development of the Qur'an, with chapter 3 having a particularly concise and clear summary of the main revisionists. Chapter 11 provides a basic survey of Western scholarship from the Middle Ages to the revisionists.)

See also: Renard, *Seven Doors to Islam* and *Windows on the House of Islam* (Ch. 1) [F]; Knysh, *Islam in Historical Perspective* (Ch. 5) [F].

Online Resources for Qur'an Recitation (Accessed 2 September 2013)

http://www.youtube.com/watch?v=B74JX-kcGKo&feature=related. (By the well-known Qur'an reciter Abd al-Basit; there are several others linked to the same page including a very nice one by a young woman, another by a child and a recitation of the names of God.)

http://www.mp3quran.net/ajm.html. (Has the whole Qur'an recited by Ahmad al-Ajami; each section has one *sura*, click on the left-hand column. Unfortunately for some the labeling is in Arabic, but the *suras* are in order, so the first one is the *Fatiha*.)

References

Carlyle, Thomas (1910) *On Heroes and Hero Worship*, London: Ward, Lock & Co. First published 1841 under the title *Heroes, Hero Worship and the Heroic in History*.

Lester, Toby (1999) "What Is the Koran?" *The Atlantic Monthly* 283/1 (January 1999): 43 (passim). Also online: http://www.theatlantic.com/doc/199901/koran (accessed 17 August 2013).

Nelson, Kristina (1985) *The Art of Reciting the Qur'an*, Austin, TX: University of Texas Press.

Nicholson, R.A. (ed.)

———— (1969) *A Literary History of the Arabs*, Cambridge: Cambridge University Press, first edition, 1907.

Watt, W. Montgomery (1970) *Bell's Introduction to the Qur'an*, Edinburgh: Edinburgh University Press.

END OF UNIT QUESTIONS

Directions: Use what you have learned in Unit IV to respond to the questions below.

1. Describe why Abraham is important to Judaism, Christianity, and Islam.

2. What is the important text in Judaism, and how does it inform the practices of the religion?

3. Describe the importance of Jesus Christ in Christianity. Why are his life and teachings still important?

4. Who is the founder of Islam? Describe the growth of this religious tradition.

FOR FURTHER READING

Judaism

Cohn-Sherbok, Dan. *Judaism: History, Belief and Practice.* London: Routledge, 2003.

De Lange, Nicholas. Introduction to Judaism. Cambridge: Cambridge University Press, 2000.

Christianity

Bowden, John. *Christianity: The Complete Guide.* London: Continuum, 2013.

McGrath, Alister. *Christianity: An Introduction.* 3rd ed. Oxford: Blackwell, 2015.

Powell, Mark Allan. *Jesus as a Figure in History: How Modern Historians View the Man from Galilee.* Louisville, KY: Westminster John Knox Press, 1998.

Islam

Pratt, Douglas. *The Challenge of Islam: Encounters in Interfaith Dialogue.* Aldershot, UK: Ashgate, 2005.

Brown, Daniel. *A New Introduction to Islam.* Oxford: Blackwell, 2009.

Hillenbrand, Carole. *Introduction to Islam: Beliefs and Practices in Historical Perspective.* London: Thames & Hudson, 2015.

The Abrahamic Religions

Corrigan, John et al. *Jews, Christians, Muslims: A Comparative Introduction to Monotheistic Religions.* Upper Saddle River, NJ: Prentice Hall, 1997.

Hauer, Christian E., and William A. Young. *An Introduction to the Bible: A Journey into Three Worlds,* 8th ed. Upper Saddle River, NJ: Prentice Hall, 2011.